Eating behaviour

Eating behaviour

Terence M. Dovey

Open University Press

Open University Press
McGraw-Hill Education
McGraw-Hill House
Shoppenhangers Road
Maidenhead
Berkshire
England
SL6 2QL

email: enquiries@openup.co.uk
world wide web: www.openup.co.uk

and Two Penn Plaza, New York, NY 10121-2289, USA

First edition published 2010

A catalogue record of this book is available from the British Library

ISBN-13: 978-0-33-523583-4 (pb) 978-0-33-523584-1 (hb)
ISBN-10: 0335235832 (pb) 0335235840 (hb)

Library of Congress Cataloging-in-Publication Data
CIP data applied for

Typeset by RefineCatch Limited, Bungay, Suffolk
Printed in the UK by Bell and Bain Ltd, Glasgow

Fictitious names of companies, products, people, characters and/or data that may
be used herein (in case studies or in examples) are not intended to represent any
real individual, company, product or event.

Mixed Sources
Product group from well-managed
forests and other controlled sources
www.fsc.org   Cert no. TT-COC-002769
© 1996 Forest Stewardship Council

The McGraw·Hill Companies

This book is dedicated to Chin Won Khoo

Contents

List of figures and tables

Figures

Tables

Acknowledgements

It is with a great sigh of relief that I write these acknowledgements. For you, the reader, they are one of the first things you read, while for me they denote the end of a long journey. It is at this point I have time to reflect on the process of writing this book and have a chance to thank all those that have helped me along the way. Credit must go to those that shaped my professional mind – Dr Josie Odber, Dr Patrick Brady, Dr Jolanta Opacka-Juffry and Dr Jason C.G. Halford. This book would have not come to fruition without them. Equally, those that provide me with motivation and support to continue to strive towards my goals should also take some of the credit. These are principally my family Dr Chin Won Khoo, Sheila M.P. Howard, Colin Howard and Terence G.R. Dovey. As a minimum, they have at least allowed me to practise what I have learned over my professional training. My colleagues have also provided me with advice and knowledge that has found its way into the pages of this book. My colleagues are the eating disorders research team (LUCRED) – Dr Caroline Meyer, Dr Debbie Wallis, Dr Emma Haycraft, Dr Claire Farrow and Dr Jon Arcelus. Above all, one individual provided me with the inspiration and confidence to write this book – Dr Mark Foreshaw. He encouraged me to march to my own drumbeat. I am confident in saying that without him this book would never even have made it past the proposal stage. Finally, I would like to extend my gratitude to Dr Monika Lee who has worked constantly behind the scenes to get this book reviewed and edited.

In writing these acknowledgements I realize that I hang out with a lot of doctors; I really need to get out more . . . I guess now I can!

1 Introduction
Widely held assumptions and methods

We all share the same obsession, an obsession that is not a sign of a psychological disorder. Well, it is not disordered for the vast majority of people and, statistically speaking, the odds are in your favour that you are one of them. People obsess about food all day long and never get bored doing so. Eating is an essential need, and without food we would die within a matter of weeks. No persuasive argument or manipulation can stop one thinking about eating, and this socially ingrained, biologically predetermined obsessive tendency around food is as it should be. It is right that all humans are 'hardwired' to obsess about gathering, preparing and consuming food. If we were not so obsessed with eating, we would not have made it this far on our evolutionary journey. In short, it is acceptable, appropriate and altogether normal to think about eating . . . a lot!

In this book, we explore what it is that controls, manipulates and elicits eating behaviour. We will cover the way that the brain and body control eating, the environmental factors that infiltrate the consciousness to make us think it is time to eat, and childhood, to unravel how eating behaviour develops within the individual – which provides the cornerstones to each individual's eating behaviour. I do not attempt to sensationalize the subject by looking only at the rare or pathological; rather, the reader will be offered an explanation from the perspective of the average person. The book is punctuated with side-shoots and offers some insights into eating behaviour that has gone wrong, but on the whole it will provide an explanation of the mundane. So mundane in fact that everyone, 'normal' or otherwise, experiences these concepts and phenomena many times every single day. However, even the mundane can be fascinating and complex.

The aim of this book is to provide the reader with the ability to find out anything he or she wants to know about eating behaviour. Although the book is an introduction to the field of study, it is hoped that interested readers will come to understand the technicalities behind the psychology of eating from all the different perspectives and sub-fields of the discipline. For someone truly obsessed with the subject, it would be quite easy to spend at least three years of their life researching into just one tiny aspect of eating behaviour – most aspects are simply that rich and full of information. And it is not the intention of the book to replace the lecturer or course of study; rather, the book is designed so that the course can quickly progress to the more advanced debates, ensuring that the student has the basic knowledge.

Before we delve into the fascinating area of human behaviour, it is important that some socially held assumptions about food and eating behaviour are not embraced. To get as much as possible from this book, it is important that the reader 'opens up' to a potentially new perspective. Knowledge that circulates within the general population is a mix of the information that individuals have gathered, personal experiences and popular [mis]conceptions. Unfortunately, there is much folklore about eating that circulates through popular consciousness. This comes about through a mix of poor explanations by scientists, media representations or interpretations, and general misunderstandings.

Widely held assumptions about food and eating

There are so many myths about food that it would be possible to fill the pages of this book many times over if we were to describe them all. Therefore, the aim of this section is for you to question what you currently believe to be true. Unfortunately, within science we can never totally disprove a concept. Science, as a doctrine, can only provide evidence; there is no such thing as 'facts' or 'right and wrong', only that one idea has a lot of supporting evidence and another has little or none. Thus scientists cannot be dogmatic in their explanations and have to weigh up the evidence from two or more perspectives. There are many examples throughout history of the proponents of new – or even old – theoretical perspectives offering better explanations of the available evidence only to be mocked by the 'establishment' for tens or even hundreds of years before theirs becomes the predominant view. In short, when a scientist says something, what they are really saying is that 'it is accurate, to the best of my knowledge, at this moment in time, based on the reading and experiments I have done, but it could change in the future'. However, this cannot explain all current misunderstandings and misinterpretations.

One of the most common misunderstandings around food and eating is the belief that it is possible to 'self-medicate' through nutrition (Lockwood, 2007). A statement that begins 'eat this, it will make you . . .' is an example of such an assumption. Classic examples include 'eating oranges will help you recover from a cold' and 'eating fish will make you intelligent'. Nutrients are not pharmacological agents in the same way as drugs. To obtain the positive benefits associated with a specific food, it has to be eaten as part of a habitual diet (for intelligence, see Benton, 2001; for illness, see Shenkin, 2006): it has to be eaten on a weekly or daily basis. Thus if we believe that eating fish will make us more intelligent, we need to eat fish every week or every other week for most of our lives. We do not see the immediate effects from food that we do from pharmaceuticals. The particular assumption about fish is that some oily fish are higher in essential fatty acids. Essential fatty acids are chemicals that our bodies cannot create on their own and so we must introduce them into our bodies through our diet. It is believed that essential fatty acids found in oily fish aid brain function and thus concentration and memory retrieval (Gadoth, 2008). Eating any type of fish the day before an exam will thus not offer the same benefits as consuming a specific type of oily fish will when it is eaten as part of a habitual diet. As for oranges, they contain vitamin C, which is required for the creation of immune cells (Hemilä, 2003), cells that attack bacterial or viral infections. However, once you have contracted an illness and are showing the symptoms, you are already using the immune cells in your system. It takes time to create an immune cell, and thus unless you have an illness that lasts for more than several days the benefits from eating oranges once you have contracted the illness will be minimal, although the vitamin C found in oranges will help replenish the lost cells during your recovery. This makes eating oranges a preventative measure rather than a remedial one.

Other popular assumptions are perpetuated by parents. Many parents believe that their children are fussy eaters to the point of dysfunction. If you believe some sources, this could be as many as half of all parents (Coulthard & Harris, 2003). The reality of course is very different. To be considered to be particularly fussy, a child must be significantly different from the norm. Most children require at least eight to fifteen separate exposures to a specific food before they accept it as such and are willing to try it (Birch et al., 1987). But if the same set of parents are asked whether they have offered a particular food to their child eight to fifteen times, they usually reply: 'no, who has the time to do that?' Simply telling a child that something is a food is not enough for them to accept it. This is a complex subject and the interested reader will find that Chapter 4 is devoted to it.

A common belief about eating is related to weight status – specifically, the 'speed' of metabolism and whether one is underweight or overweight. Individuals who are underweight are often heard to say, 'I can't help it, I eat and eat but just do not put on weight, I am just naturally thin'; whereas those who are overweight often state, 'I eat nothing at all but I still put on weight . . . I just have a slow metabolism'. These perspectives are covered in detail in Chapters 8 and 9. In reality, excess food consumed will be stored as fat and thus lead to weight gain unless that energy is used immediately. Individuals who do not put on weight do not consume as much, in terms of calories, as those who do; or, alternatively, they expend more energy during the day. Importantly, the heavier a person is the faster their metabolism (Garrow, 1987). Any given individual's resting metabolic rate is directly proportional to their lean muscle mass and thus the heavier a person is, the more muscle mass they need simply to move around. Therefore, the heavier a person is, the more muscle mass they have and the faster their metabolism. Being dismissive of the metabolic explanation for weight status often outrages members of the general public, with some people zealously defending the slow metabolism belief. However, such views have all but disappeared from credible scientific explanations of weight status.

A recent assumption is that food is 'addictive'. This is simply untrue – eating is essential for survival. Not to eat would result in death and you cannot be addicted to anything that you need to keep you alive. If eating or food is addictive, so must be breathing or going to the toilet. Since no one has ever suggested that going to the toilet is addictive, how can eating be? This view may stem from the advertising strategies of companies (Page & Brewster, 2009), whereby it is more likely that proponents of the belief that food is addictive have an officially diagnosed eating disorder (Baicy, 2005), which is not the case for most members of society. Proponents of this view who do not have eating disorders, are likely to be emotional eaters (see Chapter 7). Such people turn to food in times of emotional stress: it is important to understand that they are not addicts and do not have a psychological morbidity around food; rather, they use food as a form of coping with emotion. This is not wrong or abnormal, but simply what some individuals do to cope. To believe that this behaviour is pathological would suggest that all other avoidance-based coping responses are too. Although this form of coping is not beneficial in the long term, it can be so in the short term, offering release from the problem that is provoking anxiety. The only drawback to it as a coping response is that individuals may put on weight.

Caveats to the addiction hypothesis include cravings for food and whether the food contains a psychoactive chemical. A craving is the sudden desire to eat a specific food at that moment in time (Baker et al., 1986), which, importantly, does not have to derive from an addiction. Cravings for foods hold additional emotional value for us beyond their energy content (Tiggemann & Kemps, 2005). We have memories of and emotional associations with them and we crave them as much for their emotional value as for any other. This can be especially pronounced during pregnancy, which is usually indicative of low concentrations of iron in the blood (anaemia) (López et al., 2007). Foods that contain psychoactive chemicals may be considered addictive; however, very few foods contain these ingredients. Common foodstuffs believed to be addictive are coffee and chocolate. Although chocolate does contain some natural psychoactive chemicals derived from the coca plant, the tiny amounts in which those chemicals are found would require the consumption of such a large quantity of chocolate that the sugar content or the basic quantity of chocolate itself would cause problems long before the psychoactive ingredients had an effect. Similarly, coffee contains caffeine, which is very mildly addictive. Caffeine competes with adenosine within the adenosine pathways of the brain (Bertorelli et al., 1996). Adenosine is a naturally occurring neurotransmitter (see Chapter 2) in our brain that controls the transition between wakefulness and sleep. The effects of caffeine on this pathway are very short-lived. Therefore, to become effectively addicted to caffeine would require the continuous consumption of a very high amount of it. As soon as caffeine is not consumed, adenosine quickly reasserts itself. Although there are geographical variations in the consumption of caffeine, very few individuals consume enough caffeine to be addicted to it and those that do quickly become habituated (tolerant) to the high consumption so that its effects are minimal. Moreover, in large doses, caffeine is a fairly potent diuretic: that is, the consumption of large quantities of coffee results in excessive urination. In short, caffeine does not create a strong or long-lasting biological dependence and recovery from even heavy consumption is very quick – measured in hours rather than days or months (Nehlig, 1999).

Hopefully, you are now starting to think that a little of what you know is bound up in some assumptions that do not hold up to scientific rigour. Scientists have used various methods to investigate these assumptions and have found some to be wanting. It is important to understand both the strengths and weaknesses of these methods to fully comprehend the evidence offered in the following chapters.

Scientific methods of eating behaviour research

The methodological approaches employed in eating behaviour research vary depending on the research question. Some researchers favour less intrusive self-report measures such as questionnaires and food diaries, while others adopt observational methods by measuring and recording a person's eating behaviour during a meal. In the remainder of this chapter, the strengths and weaknesses of these methods are discussed. Understanding the relative strengths and weaknesses of the methodological approaches highlights the basic criticisms of this field of research beyond those specific to the sub-field in question. It is critical that these field-specific methodological approaches are understood before the presentation of the evidence derived from a specific piece of research. This is to ensure that there is empathy with the restrictions incurred by adopting the field-specific methodological approaches in this type of investigation.

Qualitative approaches and case studies

Qualitative investigative approaches pertain to a variety of different techniques related to collecting rich detailed data from a small number of participants. Qualitative research techniques have been used recently in work on healthy eating (e.g. Gough & Conner, 2006), eating disorders (e.g. Winzelberg, 1997) and understanding the context of meals (e.g. Blake et al., 2008). The general remit of the various qualitative approaches is difficult to surmise due to the wide range of perspectives that are attributed to this umbrella term (Symon & Cassell, 1998). However, it might be argued that the objective in this type of research is to uncover the widely held suppositions around eating that constitute the basic knowledge that most individuals adhere to. Although qualitative research methods are varied, they can be differentiated based on how the participants are questioned (i.e. in groups or individually) and how the subsequent data are analysed. Techniques of collecting qualitative research data include focus groups (Kubik et al., 2005) and structured and semi-structured interviews (Krall & Lohse, 2009). The data are analysed using a variety of techniques, including conversational analysis (Mondada, 2009), discourse analysis (Bouwman et al., 2009) and observation analysis (Orrell-Valente et al., 2007). It is from this form of more open-ended participant-led research that new avenues of research and holistic theoretical explanations of eating behaviour often develop.

The criticism often railed against this form of research is whether results can be generalized from the study participants to the population as a whole. Adherents to this criticism have become less vocal in mainstream psychology now that there is a general acceptance of the qualitative school and equal emphasis on the qualitative and quantitative approaches in many undergraduate programmes. A field of research without detailed examination of its epistemological basis will ultimately lead to studies based on supposition. The quantitative approach, and the hypothesis in particular, derives from the beliefs of the researcher (Smith, 2009), which purport to be based solely on previous 'findings'. It cannot be denied that testing variables in this manner (i.e. in isolation of their environmental context and usual 'background noise') disregards the complexity of human eating behaviour and presupposes that the variables in question are important to each participant tested. Qualitative approaches actively test this assumption, whereas quantitative ones avoid it. Appropriately, qualitative investigative techniques have moved away from the fringe of eating behaviour research and into the more mainstream publications. This is especially the case for research into healthy eating and, to a lesser extent, eating disorders.

Another technique frequently reported in published research is the case study. Although this is not strictly either a qualitative or quantitative research technique, it does share some similarities with qualitative methods, such as its dependence on a small number of people and describing their experience. Case studies are often used in the medical profession and are limited to simply describing a particular individual's experience of their illness. In eating behaviour research, case study descriptions have been widely used, especially towards the pathological end of the spectrum (Vansteelandt et al., 2004; Baer et al., 2005). Case studies involve the description and outcome of a successful therapeutic intervention resulting in the recovery from or improvement in eating pathology. This type of evidence is often used preferentially by clinicians and by individuals whose primary interest is practical interventions. Academic pursuits in psychology do not tend to rely on this research technique. The main strength of this research is it provides guidance for successful management strategies for specific psychopathologies. Beyond this information, the case study approach has numerous shortcomings that primarily involve its specificity to the individual case and therefore is often only applied to the rare or unique individual.

In the following, we consider the more quantitative research techniques.

Psychometrics

Psychometrics is the creation of questionnaires based on scientific principles of validity and reliability. The perfect questionnaire should be clear, unambiguous, workable and well designed. It is generally asserted that the time spent on design and repeated refinement (through piloting the questionnaire on large groups of people) will be reflected in the overall usefulness of the end product (Murray, 1999). Within the initial design of a questionnaire, factors such as question wording, question type, question presentation order, scales, method of response and response rates need to be considered. For more information about preliminary questionnaire design, see Murray (1999).

Within eating behaviour research, several psychometric questionnaires are used to measure different aspects of eating behaviour. These are used to gauge the level of a behavioural trait in a participant. For example, if emotional eating is an important aspect of an investigation, the researchers may require their participants to complete the emotional subscale of the Dutch Eating Behaviour Questionnaire (DEBQ). High scorers on this subscale would be considered susceptible to eating during emotional distress. Table 1.1 lists psychometric questionnaires used in eating behaviour research and which constructs they are used to measure.

Even well-constructed psychometric questionnaires have weaknesses. Although usually more accurate than simply asking a single question such as 'are you a binge eater?', they do not always offer accurate insights into an individual's eating behaviour. Such questionnaires are often confounded by

Table 1.1 The most common psychometric questionnaires on eating behaviour

Original paper	Name of questionnaire	What does it measure?
Gormally et al. (1982)	Binge Eating Scale (BES)	Assesses severity of binge eating
Henderson & Freeman (1987)	Bulimic Inventory Test, Edinburgh (BITE)	Measures both symptoms and severity
Thelen et al. (1991)	Bulimia Test-Revised (BULIT-R)	Measures symptoms of bulimia
Whitehouse & Harris (1998)	Child Feeding Assessment Form (CFAF)	Assesses mealtime negativity, food refusal, food fussiness
Birch et al. (2001)	Child Feeding Questionnaire (CFQ)	Assesses parental beliefs, attitudes and practices regarding child feeding
Van Strien et al. (1986)	Dutch Eating Behaviour Questionnaire (DEBQ)	Assesses restrained, emotional and external eating behaviour
Garner et al. (1983)	Eating Disorders Inventory (EDI-1)	Measures severity of anorexia nervosa and bulimia nervosa
Pliner & Hobden (1992)	Food Neophobia Scale (FNS)	Measures levels of food neophobia in adults
Herman & Polivy (1980)	Restraint Scales (RS)	Identifies dieters – shows disinhibited food intake
Stunkard & Messick (1985)	Three-Factor Eating Questionnaire (TFEQ)	Assesses restrained, disinhibited and trait hunger eating behaviour

Note: Some of these questionnaires have been revised following the original publication; however, these revisions are generally minor in nature with the alteration or addition of one or a few questions.

the fact that participants get bored of answering repetitive questions on a similar topic, leading them to pay little attention to their responses or not read the questions properly. Furthermore, depending on what the questions ask, they can breed suspicion among participants. For example, asking questions about parental mealtime techniques or what parents feed their children can be an emotive subject. Even with completely honourable intentions, a non-judgemental attitude, total participant anonymity and careful explanation of the aims of the research, parents still often try to please the researcher by offering socially acceptable responses. It is inappropriate to simply administer eating-related questionnaires to participants without offering an explanation alongside them; otherwise, the participants are unlikely to reveal anything meaningful. Furthermore, eating behaviour is bound up within the social psychological factor of impression management (see Chapter 6), thus revealing the aims of the research or asking questions about socially unacceptable food choices can seriously undermine the findings of the research. For best practice, it is believed that either administering questionnaires after any observational data have been gathered or hiding the questions within a set of dummy questions[1] will achieve the best results.

How participants are asked to complete psychometric questionnaires varies considerably. It is generally accepted in eating behaviour research that the best quantitative data are derived from visual analogue scales. However, a second method is to use a Likert scale. Which method is employed will have a bearing on the strength of the data obtained.

Visual analogue scales and Likert scales

Three types of scale are often employed alongside single-item questions in psychometric questionnaires: Likert-type fixed-point scale, unipolar visual analogue scale and bipolar visual analogue scale (also called 'absolute' and 'comparative' visual analogue scale respectively; Joyce et al., 1975). Figure 1.1 provides an example of each of these three types of scale. The reliability and validity of these scales was researched extensively during the late 1980s and early 1990s, with unipolar visual analogue scales generally found to be more reliable than their bipolar equivalents (Carlsson, 1983). However, it was also reported that both Likert and visual analogue scales were less reliable than verbally reporting a score (Papas & Schultz, 1997). Visual analogue scales suffer slightly more than Likert scales from limitations in repeatability, specifically test–retest reliability, and when measuring naturally fluctuating phenomena (e.g. hunger, fullness and mood; McCormack et al., 1988). Therefore, it is essential that the construction of a visual analogue scale is not haphazard; rather, researchers must consider the length (Seymour et al., 1985), orientation and anchors (Scott & Huskisson, 1976) in this form of scale. In eating behaviour research, it is widely accepted that carefully constructed unipolar visual analogue scales should be used when asking single-item questions (Blundell & Hill, 1988).

Likert scales are categorical in nature and offer the participant up to seven potential responses to choose from. For example, these categories can range from 'none' to 'sometimes' through to 'all of the time' (Guyatt et al., 1987). The participant is presented with a question and must choose the category that best defines their current answer to the question from the category list. Having a categorical list to choose from makes completing a Likert scale comparatively easy compared with a visual analogue scale, as the participant does

---

[1] Dummy questions are not related to the topic under investigation but provide a means of 'hiding' the experimentally relevant questions. They are designed to obscure the reason for the research, making it harder to predict what the researcher is looking for so that the participant cannot offer a good impression through social stereotypical behaviour.

Likert

Tick the box that most suits you when asked how hungry do you feel right now?

Not at all	A little bit	Neither	Moderately so	Extremely

Bipolar

Bisect the line where you think you are when asked how hungry do you feel right now?

Hungry   Full

Unipolar

Bisect the line where you think you are when asked how hungry do you feel right now?

Not Very   Very

Figure 1.1 Examples of typical Likert, bipolar visual analogue and unipolar visual analogue scales.

not have to translate an abstract answer onto the visual analogue scale. Moreover, the ability to select the answer to the question from a list of possible answers allows the researcher to infer how the participant was feeling with relative certainty. This makes Likert scales much easier to interpret (Guyatt et al., 1987). Due to this ease of interpretation, it has been argued that Likert scales are more appropriate for inferring clinical significance (Brunier & Graydon, 1996). However, this possible inference is undermined by the fact that the participant might not think that any of the possible categories on offer accurately portrays their perceptions. To overcome this problem in eating behaviour research, a Likert scale is often used in a questionnaire that asks multiple questions on the same or similar topic and then an aggregated response is recorded.

To complete a unipolar visual analogue scale, participants place a bisecting mark on a line 100 mm long anchored, for example, at one end by 'very' and at the other end by 'not very'. By allowing answers to be recorded in this way, the participant can offer a gradation of responses that other answering techniques do not allow. Moreover, this technique of answering allows for a more sophisticated mathematical modelling approach to be applied to the data obtained. Thus, although visual analogue scales are less reliable than Likert scales, they are more sensitive (Joyce et al., 1975; Brunier & Graydon, 1996). This distinction between reliability and sensitivity is a longstanding issue in all forms of scientific measurement. The more the experimenter offers the participant choice in their response, the less generalizable the response will be, as the answer will inherently contain a significant amount of individuality (Carlsson, 1983).

Measuring food intake

At some point within the research paradigm, the eating behaviourist will have to acquire information about the quantity and type of food their participants have consumed. Unfortunately, asking a person what they ate in the previous 24 hours is riddled with problems (Hébert et al., 2001). People often find it hard to remember what they recently ate and how much of something they ate (Blake et al., 1989; Black et al., 1997). Moreover, research participants are often reluctant to mention or find it particularly hard to remember consuming snacks. This means that, when asked, a participant may not provide an accurate representation of what they have eaten, making research findings reliant on data collected in this manner particularly fallible. Two ways have traditionally been used to overcome this memory problem: food diaries and actually feeding participants.

Food diaries

The use of food diaries (see Figure 1.2 for an example) is a way of noting down what and how much has been consumed, preferably as it was being eaten. The amount of information required within a food diary is often a lot more than participants would habitually provide. It is not enough to say that 'I ate one cheese and tomato pizza'. Researchers need to know the type of pizza, brand, manufacturer, size, weight, time of day eaten, and so on. Therefore, in-depth training of participants is often required to obtain valid measures of food intake throughout a day, a week or longer. Common food items such as pizza have so many different recipes that it is hard to gauge the energy, macronutrient (carbohydrate, fat and protein) and micronutrient (vitamins and minerals) contents from the generic name alone.

Despite an extensive training regime and a participant who is highly motivated to complete it, a food diary is often inaccurate or missing a significant amount of information (Zegman, 1984). Moreover, carrying a food diary around and completing it when eating with friends or family can be very intrusive to the normal eating process. Also, by completing a food diary, an individual will be artificially aware of their food choices, which may lead to deviation from their habitual choices. Food diaries are also particularly onerous to complete and may only include what the participant wants to portray.

FOOD DIARY

PARTICIPANT ID:
STUDY:
DATE:
INSTRUCTIONS:

- We would like to know exactly what foods and drinks you have consumed.
- We would like you to record **all** the foods **and** drinks you have consumed, including the quantities and brands where possible. It is important that you record all these items as you consume them. Please do not report them from memory at the end of the day.
- It would be helpful to us if you were to save the nutritional information from the foods you have eaten. Please collect the packets/wrappers where possible.

Example.

TIME	FOOD		BRAND NAME	QUANTITY, SIZE, WEIGHT	DESCRIPTION AND PREPARATION
	MEAL	SNACK			

Figure 1.2   An example of a food diary.

Often, participants may simply forget to complete the diary until the end of the day, and thus fallibility of memory recall will be brought back into the equation, or they simply omit certain eating episodes from their diary to portray a socially acceptable image to the researchers. The perceived failures of food diaries have led some researchers to question the consistency and reliability of the data derived from this approach. For those against this form of data collection, or where the use of a diary would not be appropriate, there is only one other approach – to feed the participants.

Feeding participants

The general approach to feeding people within eating behaviour research is to bring them into a designated research facility and feed them following or during some form of experimental manipulation. In many ways, an eating behaviour laboratory resembles a mixture between a scientific laboratory and a restaurant. The typical eating behaviour laboratory will include a designated kitchen for the preparation of food, which should be bound by the laws associated with selling food to the general public, and a selection of other rooms for eating meals in different contexts. Usually, a room is provided for eating alone and another for eating together in groups. In addition, rooms will be set aside for specialist equipment related to eating or energy balance, including an indirect calorimeter[2], Universal Eating Monitors[3], exercise facilities[4], living facilities[5], and so on.

The facilities available and the importance of this type of research to the institution of which the eating behaviour laboratory is a part will have a bearing on the different types of foods that can be offered to research participants. In most eating behaviour research, participants are fed snacks or easily prepared cold foods such as sandwiches. This is a drawback if we consider that most of an average person's daily calorie intake is from hot food items. Several of the larger eating behaviour laboratories are attempting to rectify this bias. Offering participants hot food, however, brings with it a range of additional problems of experimental control. For example, if the food is too hot the participants will have to wait for it to cool down, or if it is too cold they may stop eating it. It is also easier for participants to eat to fullness and select what they want to eat from a cold buffet arrangement than it is to offer a selection of hot foods. Furthermore, eating within a laboratory environment is not representative of a natural eating episode. Often, eating experiments require the participant to eat alone within a cubicle without any other form of distraction. This simply does not reflect the habitual eating patterns of the modern person. Rarely do people eat without some form of additional distraction, such as watching television, reading or conversing with other people. Therefore, the results gained in this way could be considered to be too 'sterile' and may not reflect normal eating behaviour.

Despite the above criticisms, feeding participants guarantees that what they eat within the laboratory is everything that they eat and thus eating behaviour can be measured. How this is measured will vary depending on whether the researcher is interested in food choice or the amount of food eaten. Food choice is generally straightforward, with researchers assessing how much of a particular item is eaten versus another one. In terms of measuring how much is eaten, scientists have two options: they can either weigh the food before and after the meal or they can continuously measure the amount consumed during it.

---

[2] This is a piece of equipment designed to measure resting metabolic rates.

[3] The Universal Eating Monitor is discussed in detail later in the chapter.

[4] This includes everything you would find in your local gym set out in a similar arrangement.

[5] A space that contains a room or a few rooms that allow a person to spend 24 hours or more in the laboratory so that they can participate in more long-term studies. It will include a sleeping area, a living area, a washing area, and so on.

Measuring total food intake

The most common way to measure food intake is to weigh food before a meal and then let the participant eat and weigh the remainder after they have finished. This then gives the researcher an idea of how much was consumed, usually expressed in grams or calories. This method is often accompanied by additional visual analogue scale subjective measures such as hunger and fullness. Here the investigator will be trying to determine whether the experimental hypothesis affects the subjective feelings and emotions associated with eating, the actual amount of food consumed or both. It is commonly assumed that the amount of food consumed and feelings of hunger and fullness are proportionally related to each other. Unfortunately, the research evidence does not support this assumption (Kral, 2006).

Measuring the amount of food consumed before and after eating may inform the researcher about how much was eaten but not how the food was eaten. This method cannot derive information about bite size, speed of eating or changes in subjective feelings/emotions of the participant while eating. To address this, specialist equipment in the shape of a Universal Eating Monitor is required.

Within-meal measurements

The microstructure of feeding behaviour considers how a person is feeling while eating a meal and not just the measurements before and after consumption. In animal experiments, microstructure refers to licking bouts or chewing rate. Human equivalents of eating microstructure are a little more complex, but work on similar principles to the animal model. Early studies on human microstructure of feeding assessed bite size and eating rate over time. Analysing meal microstructure in this way has led to the development of novel theories, including sensory-specific satiety (see Chapter 2) and the divergent behaviours of people with an eating disorder, specifically bulimia nervosa (see Chapter 9).

Specialist equipment has been developed to test microstructural changes during food intake. Early attempts employed automated dispensers, which offered the first theoretical interpretations on human microstructure. Meyer and Pudel (1972) suggested that normal eating behaviour fits into a quadratic equation (see Figure 1.3), with rates of consumption slowing as a meal progresses. This was termed the 'biological satiation curve'. Unfortunately, these early studies could only use liquid foods, which generated different intake curves from those for solid foods, probably due to the absence of chewing. Modern accounts of the biological satiation curve suggest that one of three possible 'eating curves' exists (Dovey et al., 2009a), with a linear, quadratic or cubic relationship. Cubic relationships (also termed S-shaped curves) usually portray a slower initial build-up to the meal (e.g. a slower rate at the beginning and end of the meal rather than just at the end as observed in the original quadratic curve). The inability to apply the 'biological satiation curve' to 'real' meals led to the development of the Universal Eating Monitor (UEM). This equipment has the ability to analyse the consumption of more solid foodstuffs such as pasta dishes and casseroles. In recent years, this paradigm has increased in complexity, with the addition of appetite ratings (fullness, hunger and hedonic value; Yeomans, 2000). These additional data in the UEM paradigm can be programmed into the computer so that they interrupt the participants after a preset specific amount of food has been consumed. This allows scientists to evaluate the transition of subjective feelings within a meal and allows evaluation of how the food was consumed (Robinson et al., 2005).

As with all other research strategies in eating behaviour research, there are several problems within the UEM paradigm that limit its applicability. The foods offered to the participant have to be homogenous from one fork to the next (Dovey et al., 2009a). This means that only dishes such as pasta dishes can be offered. Foods that are mixed, such as traditional meat and two vegetable options cannot be tested, as they have differing weights and effects on fullness. Any subjective choice within the meal will distort subjective feelings.

Armed with the knowledge of the methodological techniques for collecting data in eating behaviour research and their limitations, as well as the notion that most of what is publicly 'known' is usually half true at best, it should be possible to empathize with and visualize the various concepts that are discussed in the remainder of this book. As we also consider biological aspects to eating behaviour, additional biological methods within endocrinology, neurology

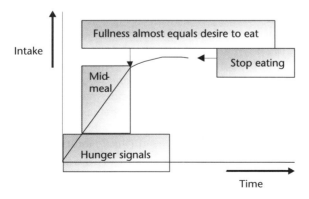

Figure 1.3   Graphical representation of an intake curve.

and genetics will be used to explain the biological underpinnings of eating behaviour. However, understanding these methodological approaches is not as important as understanding eating behaviour.

The scope of this book

Chapters 2 and 3 explore the biological aspects of eating behaviour from the perspective of the brain and the rest of the body. The reader is exposed to the minimum required rather than a total assessment of the biological process. The text is tailored to those with a predominant interest in the behaviour rather than the biology and so the material covered will reflect this. Moreover, no assumptions will be made regarding the underlying principles of biology and therefore these will be briefly explained within the context of eating behaviour.

Following the 'biological' chapters, the more traditional aspects of eating behaviour will be covered within chapters on developmental, cognitive, social, individual and abnormal psychology. Chapter 4 explores psychological concepts observed during childhood that affect our eating behaviour. Cornerstones to developmental influences on eating behaviour are learning to like new foods, being able to categorize foods into a sensible habitual diet and the role of significant others in the learning process. 'Significant others' usually refers to a child's parents but it can also extend to other individuals who are important to them. Chapter 5 explores the cognitive aspects of eating behaviour. The focus within cognition is primarily the role of decision-making. In Chapter 5, we will explore the factors that make us choose one food over another. Then, Chapter 6 explores the social aspects to eating behaviour: How does our eating behaviour alter when we are in a group setting? What are the social pressures that force us to choose different foods in the social domain compared with at home? Answers to these questions will be considered.

Following the discussion of the more traditional aspects of psychology and their influence on eating behaviour, the book moves to a different focus. Chapters 7, 8 and 9 delve into the individual, both the 'normal' and 'abnormal'. Chapter 7 addresses what is going on within people's heads when faced with food and what makes them start and stop eating beyond the typical biological explanation of the process. Factors such as cognitive restraint around food (the propensity to terminate meals early or to psychologically control meal size rather than allow natural feelings of fullness to stop us eating), emotional eating and disinhibition (the inability to self-monitor food intake when distracted by something else) are considered. Chapter 8 considers the modern pandemic of obesity. How we define obesity, the cause and consequences of having excess weight and potential treatment strategies for weight loss will be considered within the pages of this chapter. Chapter 9 considers the fascinating world of disordered eating. The eating disorders of anorexia nervosa and bulimia nervosa are addressed, together with other less well-known disorders. Furthermore, Chapter 9 offers an up-to-date examin-ation of the field of eating disorders and considers the different sub-types of anorexia nervosa and bulimia nervosa. Although sufferers of these disorders share similar characteristics, they have additional and unique aspects to their disorder making it harder for us to treat them effectively.

The final chapter draws all of these disparate strands together into a com-bined model of eating behaviour from all of the perspectives discussed in the book.

2 The energy demands of the brain
Central mechanisms of eating

Introduction to appetite regulation

This and the next chapter focus entirely on the biological process of eating behaviour usually referred to as 'appetite regulation'. In a rather crude way, the process can be separated into neurochemical responses and reactions that happen within the brain (known as central control) and those that happen outside of it (peripheral control). To aid understanding, these two 'types' of control will be taken independently. This chapter explores the brain's role while Chapter 3 addresses the biological changes that occur as a consequence of food. The purpose of these chapters is to offer an overview of appetite regulation, to arm the reader with the basics. Appetite regulation contains a lot of field-specific terminology, which must be understood; however, by the end of these chapters it should be possible to understand and navigate the scientific literature on appetite regulation.

Human appetite regulation, determined by the biological control of energy, must be understood and incorporated into any theory about eating behaviour. This biological framework provides not only the mechanistic control of the feeding process but also the physical domain to which all psychological theories must adhere. Essentially, appetite regulation is the 'hardware' of eating behaviour.

Appetite regulation begins with a single meal; however, the conscientious reader must not accidentally discard biological terms and processes that may appear unrelated. The cornerstones of appetite regulation terminology can be summed up in four theoretically distinct processes that compartmentalize a meal into different 'periods' or 'phases'. These provide the context to a meal and the biological consequences of it. Understanding these concepts is important, as they allow us to categorize the process of eating and break it down into its constituent parts. The four processes are as follows:

1 *Hunger and fullness*. Fullness within appetite regulation is referred to by two separate terms: 'satiation' and 'satiety'. Satiation is the fullness that exists within a meal (i.e. the fullness that stops us from actually eating any more), while satiety comprises all the factors that stop someone from starting their next meal.

2 *Episodic and tonic signalling*. This refers to the neurotransmitter and hormonal control of hunger, satiation and satiety within one meal (episodic) or over a longer period of time (tonic). Episodic control of eating is the tri-daily cycle of biochemicals that make you eat and feel full, while tonic signals attenuate the strength of the episodic ones by letting the brain know how much energy it has stored at any one time.

3 This biological signalling is often referred to as *pre- and post-absorptive signalling*. These concepts are roughly differentiated by the biochemicals that are responsible for hunger, taste perception and digestion (pre-absorption), and those released after a food item has been broken down and are available in the blood (post-absorption).

4 The final process is associated with the *phases* of a meal and is separated into three distinct stages: cephalic, gastrointestinal and nutrient (or sometimes called substrate). The *cephalic* phase encompasses the drivers to eat, taste perception and culminates in swallowing. The *gastrointestinal* phase considers the stomach and intestinal transit of food, including both the mechanical movement of food through the digestive system and the hormonal correlates of this movement. Finally, the *nutrient* phase explores the absorption of the nutrients into the blood stream and what happens to these products within the body in terms of their storage, utilization and effects.

Figure 2.1 shows how these various terms interact during a meal. Armed with this knowledge, it should be easier to understand biological papers on appetite regulation, as they must use one or more of these 'anchors' in the explanation of their findings.

Historical development

Early theories of appetite regulation progressed from direct stomach control of feeding (Cannon & Washburn, 1912) to a more nutrient-dependent approach. This meant that early researchers believed that changes in the sensations and perceptions associated with the stomach provided the motivation to eat – something like your stomach growls, you are hungry, and so you eat. This idea did have several critical and obvious flaws. For example, how does this type of control motivate us to eat specific foods? Or how does it control how much we consume? Therefore, it was quickly postulated that perhaps certain qualities of

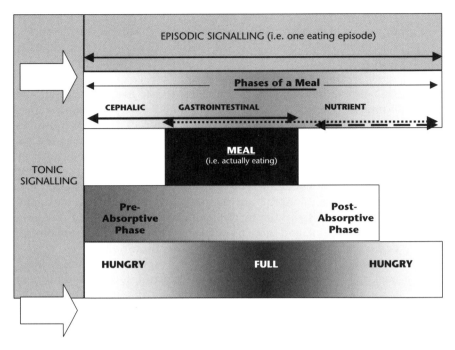

Figure 2.1 Diagrammatic representation of the terminology specific to appetite regulation.

a specific food were responsible for the motivation to consume it. Initial investigations were characterized by the nutrient content of food. The nutrient hypothesis has stayed with us ever since and is represented as the third 'phase' of a meal (see Figure 2.1). This 'nutrient approach' concerns the macronutrient content of a particular food item – fat (lipids), carbohydrate (glucose) and protein (amino acids), represented by the lipostatic (Kennedy, 1953), glucostatic (Mayer, 1953) and aminostatic (Mellinkoff et al., 1956) control of eating respectively. These three theories suggest that the body (periphery) and not the brain (central) controls eating behaviour, in that the concentration of macronutrients in the blood controls directly whether or not we start a meal. Although insightful for their time, these postulations do not reflect entirely what we now understand constitutes and controls appetite regulation.

At the same time as the scientists were considering macronutrient models of eating, other researchers were suggesting that the brain, and specifically the hypothalamus, was integral to appetite regulation (Brobeck et al., 1943; Anand & Brobeck, 1951). Ultimately, Stellar (1954) combined these central and peripheral theories, showing that the brain can monitor nutrients in the circulatory system through a complex mixture of neurotransmitter and hormone concentrations that change in response to food. Neurotransmitters are small chemical 'messages' released by specialist cells in the brain, called neurons. The function of a neurotransmitter is to cause a reaction in another neuronal cell. Neuronal cells are separated by tiny enclosed gaps between them, called synapses. Any chemical released into a synapse is defined as a neurotransmitter. If the target neuron releases a neurotransmitter in response to communication from the previous cell, it is deemed to be part of the same neurotransmitter pathway. Activation of these neurotransmitter pathways is the biological underpinning of behaviour in the brain. Hormones are slightly different from neurotransmitters. Although hormones and neurotransmitters can be similar in their structure and function, they differ in terms of how they are released in the body. Whereas neurotransmitters are released into synapses, hormones are released into the blood or a duct. Consequently, hormones tend to be active for longer and communicate with biological targets situated anatomically further away.

There is a fundamental difference between how the brain communicates with target structures and how the body does so. While the brain is a more controlled environment releasing neurotransmitters into synapses, with one or a few target cells to interact with, the organs in the periphery have to rely on a much cruder form of communication. Organs involved in the digestion of food release hormones into the blood stream in order to have an effect on a distant target structure. Therefore, peripheral sites communicate by increasing concentrations of specific appetite-related hormones in the blood to ensure that the signal is received. Identifying biochemicals as neurotransmitters or as hormones is determined by whether they are found predominantly in the central nervous system or in the periphery.

Over the past fifty years, the field of appetite regulation has expanded and new information has been acquired on a regular basis. Scientists have discovered many neurotransmitters and hormones that control food intake, which at various times over the last century has caused a shift towards and away from dominance of the body or the brain in eating behaviour. We now have a good understanding of the biological system controlling appetite regulation and, arguably, we can conclude that both the brain and the body control specific components of our energy intake. All the factors that affect eating behaviour underpinned by appetite regulation have been combined into an elegant and yet simple theory known as the 'satiety cascade' (Blundell & Rodgers, 1991).

The satiety cascade

The satiety cascade is a means of conceptualizing the experience of hunger, satiation and satiety, which, in turn, determine the beginning, middle and end of a meal. It details the operations of four domains that underpin the transition from hunger, through satiation, ending with satiety before cycling back to hunger again (Blundell & Rodgers, 1991). These four biopsychological domains consist of contributions from four distinct groups of factors: cognitive, sensory, post-ingestive (pre-absorptive) and post-absorptive. Cognitions and learned associations about food, such as memory for the last meal, precede our desire to eat. Sensory factors such as the sight and smell of food can also lead to eating, as these factors stimulate gastric secretion (Reid, 1992). Post-ingestive (pre-absorptive) factors arise from the presence of food in the gastro-intestinal tract. Finally, the post-absorptive stage refers to the presence of metabolites in the blood. The impact of these signals can occur instant-aneously to a number of hours post-ingestion (i.e. the nutrient approach). To provide adequate communication between the body and brain, signals from each of the domains have differing time frames, some disappearing in a matter of minutes, while others last hours. The remainder of this chapter will consider how the brain controls energy levels and eating behaviour.

The central control of eating behaviour

Central control of appetite regulation appears to change little throughout the animal kingdom. All animals, from fish to humans, appear to share similar biological pathways and neurotransmitters responsible for controlling feeding behaviour. This suggests that the system arose early in our evolutionary past and has changed little over time. Although the pathways are similar, this fact does not undermine the complexity of the process. Most organs and systems are employed in the storage or mobilization of energy and all contain bio-logical processes that have a direct influence on feeding behaviour. Although complex, there is a definite hierarchy within the system.

Within the brain, three specific regions are heavily involved in eating behaviour. These are the hypothalamus, the cortex and the brainstem, which together constitute the central control of appetite regulation. The hypo-thalamus is a region in the brain that contains many tiny nuclei responsible for controlling hunger, fullness and the search for food. Regions in the brainstem, along with the cortex, are responsible for the more sensory and motivational components to eating (e.g. taste). Understanding the central control of eating is essential to understanding the structures and functions of these central regions, as well as the neurotransmitters they employ to communicate with each other.

Hypothalamic control of eating

The episodic control of eating behaviour is managed directly by a region in the brain called the hypothalamus, which cycles through three stages during each meal: hunger (time to start eating), motivation (go search for food) and stop eating. These three stages are controlled by different nuclei[1] in the hypothalamus and have different neurotransmitters that signal for the message. The nuclei responsible within this circuit are the arcuate nucleus, the lateral hypothalamic area and the paraventricular nucleus. It is important to understand that this system does not operate outside of the other organs and sites within the body; rather, it has communication pathways with all structures and organs associated with appetite regulation, changing the process from the top down accordingly.

The position of the arcuate nucleus is of great importance to the overall communication between the peripheral and central appetite-related structures. It is located at the bottom of the hypothalamus near the median eminence. The median eminence is where the blood–brain barrier[2] is weak, giving the arcuate nucleus direct contact with the blood. Its position means that the arcuate nucleus is able to directly monitor nutrient concentrations in the blood and can initiate eating accordingly. The arcuate nucleus is responsible for feelings of hunger and initiation of eating.

The lateral hypothalamic area has long been associated with the initiation of eating (Cupples, 2002). It is an area of the hypothalamus that contains no distinct nuclei but does contain neurons that have a potent stimulation effect on eating. This region in the hypothalamus is responsible for making the individual search for food. Damage to either the arcuate nucleus or the lateral hypothalamic area results in withdrawal from normal eating behaviours and loss of body weight (Hetherington & Ranson, 1940). Moreover, the location and severity of the damage is directly correlated with the duration of suffering and chances of recovery from this form of anorexia[3]. In all, this suggests that few, albeit important, neurons in this region are responsible for releasing neurotransmitters that make one eat (Cupples, 2002).

The paraventricular nucleus is the junction between neurotransmitters that make you eat (Xu et al., 1995) and those that stop you eating (Huang et al., 1998; Currie et al., 2001). This implies that both types of neurotransmitter are present in the paraventricular nucleus. It is therefore possible that the paraventricular nucleus is an important site for initiation and inhibition of feeding. Damage to this area may result in defective communication between the competing feeding signals responsible for eating behaviour. Specifically, the paraventricular nucleus is the site that contains the neurotransmitters that stop us eating after a meal has started.

---

[1] Small sub-regions in the hypothalamus – not to be confused with the nuclei of an individual cell.

[2] This structure separates and protects the brain from the rest of the body.

[3] Anorexia can be used in many contexts within eating behaviour and appetite regulation. Basically, it means a very low weight status through a loss of appetite and should not be confused with anorexia nervosa, which is an eating disorder.

The anatomical control by the hypothalamus suggests that eating behaviour is cyclical. Each neurotransmitter found in each area signals the next region until one cycle is complete. This is not entirely accurate, as the neurochemistry is a little more complex with multiple neurotransmitter pathways at each stage, although it may help to conceptualize the process in this manner. It is here, in the neurochemistry, that the complexity of appetite regulation is found. Essentially, not just one neurotransmitter is responsible for each process; rather there are several at each stage that excite or inhibit the next anatomical area responsible for eating. These competing neurotransmitters are separated into two groups based on the effect they have on eating behaviour. If they act to promote eating they are called orexigenic, while those that stop eating are known as anorexigenic (see Table 2.1). Both types of chemicals can be found in the arcuate nucleus, the lateral hypothalamic area and the paraventricular nucleus. This competing mechanism allows for a more sophisticated communication and thus more finite control of eating behaviour.

There are four neurotransmitters within the arcuate nucleus that battle constantly for supremacy. Two are responsible for initiating a meal, while the other two have the opposite effect. They inhibit each other and compete directly in the lateral hypothalamic area to stop us searching for food. The two neurotransmitters responsible for making us eat are neuropeptide Y (NPY) and

Table 2.1 Pre-absorptive and post-absorptive neurotransmitters involved in the control of eating behaviour

Inhibits feeding behaviour	Induces feeding behaviour
Arcuate nucleus	**Arcuate nucleus**
Cocaine and amphetamine regulated transcript (CART)	Neuropeptide Y (NPY)
Alpha melanocyte-stimulating hormone (αMSH)	Agouti-related protein (AGRP)
Paraventricular nucleus	**Lateral hypothalamic area**
Corticotropin releasing factor (CRF)	Melanin-concentrating hormone (MCH)
	Orexin A
Monoamines	Orexin B
Serotonin	
Dopamine	**Nucleus of the solitary tract (brainstem)**
	Endogenous opioid peptides (EOP)
	Nucleus accumbens
	Gamma-aminobutyric acid (GABA)
	Monoamines
	Noradrenaline

agouti-related protein (AGRP). Their competitors are cocaine and amphetamine regulated transcript (CART) and pro-opiomelanocortin (POMC) respectively. Throughout the day, CART and POMC inhibit the release of NPY and AGRP. At mealtimes, NPY and AGRP turn the tables on CART and POMC and initiate one episodic eating cycle. Peaks in the release of NPY and AGRP happen three times a day and are set early in life. Therefore, early life experience (or early parental influence) set the strength and number of cycles the individual goes through in a day. In the West, this is set at three times (e.g. breakfast, lunch and dinner); however, there are some inter-individual differences in the amount and strength of each cycle.

Each neuron, through the neurotransmitter it releases, passes on its signal through the use of chemical receptors. Receptors are small protrusions on the surface of the cell[4] that are made from proteins and bind specifically with a single neurotransmitter. Therefore, each type of neurotransmitter (e.g. NPY) has a unique receptor, or 'family' of receptors, that it binds with and can only cause a specific reaction within the target cell through these receptors. This reaction usually causes a release of the target neuron's neurotransmitters, which leads to a cascade effect within a neurotransmitter pathway (e.g. NPY binds to orexin neurons causing the release of its neurotransmitter). In this case, the neurotransmitter pathway would be the communication between the ARC, the lateral hypothalamic area and the paraventricular nucleus. Each neurotransmitter may have more than one receptor, depending on its function and pathway. Basically, the brain will use the same biochemical to perform several related, and sometimes unrelated, tasks. It can do this through the use of different sub-types, or 'families', of receptors. For example, NPY has six known receptors (Y_1 to Y_6) that are involved in its multiple functions, one of which includes eating (Blomqvist and Herzog, 1997). Receptors Y_1 and Y_5 are related to eating, while the others seem to have different functions related to other behaviours. Why this is needed goes beyond the scope of this book and indeed the differing activation effects of one receptor type over another, as well as the constant discovery of new subtypes of receptors, is very much the frontier of appetite regulation. Additional information about the significant neurotransmitters involved in controlling eating behaviour can be found in Appendix 1.

If you understand the interaction between these four neurotransmitters, you will have a handle on the current theory of the central control of episodic initiation of a meal. Essentially, it could be said that when we ask ourselves 'are we hungry?' the answer comes from the current interactive state of these four neurotransmitters. Once the NPY/AGRP combination overcomes the CART/POMC signal, a cascade effect occurs that initiates the search for, and consumption of, food. This searching behaviour is controlled by neurotransmitters

---

[4] This 'surface' is known as the cell membrane.

situated in the lateral hypothalamic area and specifically the family of neuro-transmitters known as hypocretins (also known as orexins). In addition to the hypocretins, the lateral hypothalamic area also contains another important 'linking' neurotransmitter, melanin-concentrating hormone (MCH), which aids communications between the various regions of appetite regulation.

The arcuate nucleus and lateral hypothalamic area together initiate hunger and provide the individual with the impetus to find food. Once the individual has found food and NPY/AGRP is in control of the system, they will start to eat. It is at this point that the anorexigenic neurotransmitters start to function in order to inhibit the NPY/AGRP and stop eating behaviour. The central control of satiation takes place within the paraventricular nucleus. Within this nucleus, interactions between NPY/AGRP, CART/POMC and hypocretins occur to ensure that the meal lasts long enough to meet energy needs but not so long as to overload the digestive system. The main biochemical signal responsible for terminating eating behaviour in the paraventricular nucleus is corticotropin releasing factor (CRF). Corticotropin releasing factor alone does not operate to terminate food intake; other neurotransmitters, including serotonin, dopamine and noradrenaline (collectively known as amines), all feed into the CRF circuit within the paraventricular nucleus.

The hypothalamic control of eating behaviour may appear at first glance to be a relatively simplistic mechanism. Indeed, the structural control is relatively straightforward, with the arcuate nucleus, lateral hypothalamic area and paraventricular nucleus being responsible for different 'phases' within a single meal. The complexity of the process lies in the biochemical control and communication within the system. Although it could be considered an evolutionary relic bound by many pathways that in the modern world are redundant, this complexity reflects the plethora of circumstances that our ancestors had to face during their lives. The hunting and gathering of food to provide adequately for our omnivorous diet means that when opportunities for collecting food arise, we must still be motivated to gather it despite not wanting to eat it at that moment. The final principle that is not necessarily explicit in this explanation of appetite regulation is that the orexigenic signals must be stronger than the anorexigenic ones. All animals, including humans, are biologically 'wired' to over-consume and not under-consume. It is for this reason that obesity is not inherently pathological but anorexia nervosa is. Therefore, the evolutionary argument dictates that it is necessary to have a system that allows for minor to moderate over-consumption during a meal in times of plenty so that we can create fat stores to provide energy for leaner times.

The complex interaction of the hypothalamic control of food intake can be better understood by viewing Figure 2.2. This figure shows the different structures and neurotransmitters that are involved within the main circuit concerned with appetite regulation. It is important to understand that the explanation of the hypothalamic control of eating behaviour is not comprehensive. Other neurotransmitters and other hypothalamic structures are involved to a lesser extent in the process of eating. The various roles and effects these other biological and biochemical factors have are beyond the scope of this book; however, the current explanation of the system should be adequate for any psychologist or interested party who does not have a specific desire to research this topic. Armed with the knowledge of the biological control of hunger and satiation, it is equally important to be aware of the other roles the brain has in eating behaviour. These include taste perception and motivations to eat particular food items. Essentially, this is the process of liking and wanting foods.

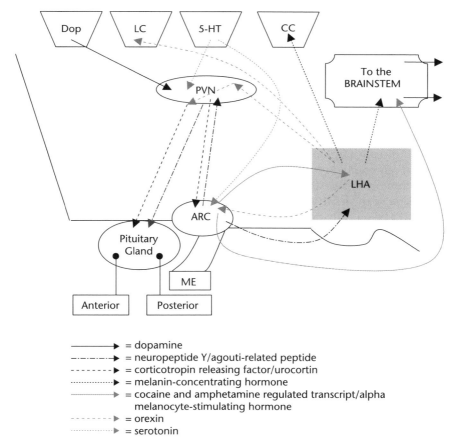

Figure 2.2 The hypothalamic control of eating. ARC = arcuate nucleus; PVN = paraventricular nucleus; LHA = lateral hypothalamic area; ME = median eminence; CC = cerebral cortex; 5-HT = serotonin; LC = locus coeruleus (noradrenaline); Dop = dopamine.

Brainstem and cortical control of eating

Structures outside the hypothalamus are comparatively under-researched even though some important functions have been attributed to them. These functions include the perception of taste. Each taste receptor on the tongue is specialized to detect sweet, salt, sour, bitter or umami content in the food item when it is placed in the mouth. Sweet, salt, sour and bitter taste perception requires little explanation, as these are used accurately in everyday language. Umami taste perception, in contrast, is a relatively recent addition to our understanding of taste perception and responds to 'meaty' foods.

Taste perception has been argued to be a multisensory experience whereby animals and humans gain knowledge about the potential acceptability of a food item from all of their senses (Auvray & Spence, 2008). Such a multisensory experience does have merit, as it has been shown that humans use vision (Marshall et al., 2006), olfaction (Rozin, 1982), touch (Smith et al., 2005) and taste when making decisions about whether or not to eat a particular food. For example, one need only observe a person in a supermarket when they are deciding to buy a particular fruit. They are initially attracted to the visual characteristics of a particular product. Usually this visual assessment is based on colour and shape. They then smell or touch the fruit to determine if it is ripe and, finally, buy it if it matches specifically set individual schemata/criteria (mental representations) about that particular food's value and acceptability. Consumption of the selected product usually occurs later. A more in-depth discussion of the multisensory approach can be found in Chapter 4. Here, the focus will be on taste processing within the domain of tongue and not other sensory processes.

The central biological pathway responsible for controlling taste perception extends from the nucleus of the solitary tract (NTS) in the brainstem to the somatosensory cortex (true taste perception brought about by the 'flavour' of the food) and frontal lobe (reward mechanisms, which is whether the individual likes the food). Information about the taste of a food item is passed from the specialized taste receptors on the tongue and processed by the nucleus of the solitary tract and the lateral parabrachial nucleus in the brainstem. These regions send neurotransmitter signals to several areas. Most importantly for feeding behaviour these signals terminate in: the somatosensory cortex in the parietal lobe; the nucleus accumbens in the ventral tegmental area; and the cortex in the frontal lobe. Figure 2.3 shows how these three regions are connected within the brain. The first pathway from the lateral parabrachial nucleus to the somatosensory cortex concerns the assessment of the taste to gain information about the qualities of the food item currently in the mouth. The connection between the nucleus of the solitary tract and the nucleus accumbens (pathway 2) concerns taste or the acquisition of a particular food and, together with the third pathway from the nucleus of the solitary tract to the cortex in the frontal lobe, controls reward mechanisms associated with taste. Reward mechanisms in feeding can be defined by liking and wanting to eat a specific food item. Liking and wanting are separate constructs that operate independently of one another but are highly interconnected and interdependent (Berridge, 2004). Therefore, food liking and food wanting are controlled by three different pathways that originate in the brainstem but terminate in different regions of the brain. Many people find it hard to conceptualize the difference between liking and wanting. To do this, it is best to think of it as: 'I like a particular food item but I do not want to eat it right now'.

To have a robust functioning appetite system, an animal must have more than just the ability to tell if they like a food item or not from sensory processing in the mouth. They must also have a reward pathway that can differentiate liking of a food item from wanting it. Liking is a relatively simple process controlled by the brainstem. Wanting a food item is a more complex process and can exist outside of liking. It is important to have separate wanting and liking pathways because the system must be able to override an animal's food preferences in times of need. For example, if there is a choice between only consuming a food that is not liked and consuming no food, hunger drives and the wanting pathway will eventually overcome the liking pathway, allowing an individual to eat despite finding the food item aversive. Moreover, this system must incorporate memory systems, as we have to recollect what we like from sensory interactions (e.g. remember what it tastes like from how it looks).

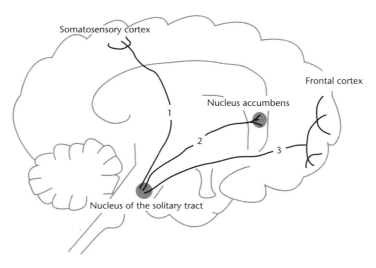

Figure 2.3   The three eating-related pathways from the brainstem to the rest of the brain.

Such a system would be better at recognizing food items in the environment and would provide a rough effort–reward ratio for gathering it. This would then make the animal more efficient at gathering food without going into energy debt. Next, these concepts will be considered and their involvement within eating behaviour evaluated.

Liking

Liking is the hedonic impact or pleasure brought about by the taste experience. In eating behaviour research, liking is often referred to as the palatability of a food. We all have innate preferences to consume foods with high levels of sweet, and arguably, salt tastants. This is known as unconditioned liking, as the human brain is 'hardwired' to like these tastes from birth. Throughout life we are exposed to numerous potential foods that have different tastes outside of sweet and salt perception. Foods that are predominantly bitter or sour can only be liked through a process of learning. Liking based on this learning process is known as 'conditioned liking' and is highly dependent on individual differences. Examples of conditioned liking would be spicy foods, which activate pain receptors in the mouth, and alcohol, which is predominantly bitter tasting. Conditioned liking is very dependent on number and length of exposures to it. The consumption of liked foods, either unconditioned or conditioned, novel or familiar, activates the reward system that enhances mood and reinforces the desire to eat it again. Figure 2.4 provides a diagrammatic overview of the liking process.

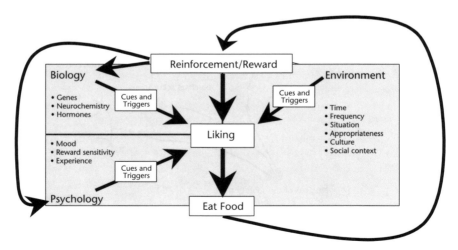

Figure 2.4 A model for liking based on Mela (2001).

The neurobiological pathway responsible for liking lies between the nucleus of the solitary tract and nucleus accumbens. This pathway is controlled by both endogenous opioid peptides (EOP) and gamma-aminobutyric acid (GABA) neurotransmitters. Endogenous opioid peptides (including β-endorphins, dynorphin A and enkephalins) are found in the nucleus of the solitary tract and have been shown to increase food intake. The orexigenic effect of centrally infused EOP lasts for only a short period of time (Yeomans & Gray, 1997) and only slightly increases food intake. This suggests that EOP are downstream of other stronger appetite-enhancing neurotransmitters and are related to factors associated with eating (e.g. palatability) rather than hunger or fullness. The EOP signals terminate in the nucleus accumbens and stimulate the release of GABA. Little is known about the GABA-releasing neurons in the nucleus accumbens beyond their role in liking or disliking specific foods based on taste. It appears that an interplay between the GABA-producing neurons results in a highly individualistic pattern of firing that is interpreted by the individual's brain as liked or not liked. More research is required before a definitive answer can be offered about how the brain processes liking.

The nucleus of the solitary tract also receives signals from the hypothalamus that may suggest that liking for food can be attenuated depending on the magnitude of a person's hunger (Cabanac, 1992). The fact that liking can be altered by other factors like hunger, which are beyond the sensory evaluation of food itself, suggests that hedonic value is not a simple stimulus–response process. This phenomenon of changing hedonic value of food is known as allesthesia. Our liking for a food item can change depending on the time of day, appropriateness of the current situation to eat it, and so on. This context of the meal is believed to attenuate the EOP response to a food item when it is in the mouth. An example of this would be most people's response to eating chocolate bars for breakfast. A chocolate bar when eaten at breakfast will taste and be rated as sweeter than when it is eaten later in the day and therefore may be too sweet to be palatable. Allesthesia is an important component of food selection, as it has the potential to moderate liking and, therefore, has implications for eating behaviour.

The most important area of the brain that controls palatability and liking is the pathway between the nucleus of the solitary tract and nucleus accumbens; however, other areas are also intricately involved in the system. For example, the amygdala has a role in taste preference (Nishijo et al., 1998) and maintains links between the nucleus of the solitary tract and the hypothalamus (Eghbal-Ahmadi et al., 1999). Preferred tastes are important determinants of food selection and palatability, as these tastes will often define the content of an individual's diet and what foods are acceptable to eat. Interestingly, not all of us have the same sensory experience when tasting foods. Some people are more sensitive to different tastes than others. This is known as taste sensitivity and is controlled by the pathway between the lateral parabrachial nucleus, situated close to the nucleus of the solitary tract in the brainstem, and the thalamocortical structures in the parietal lobe (pathway 1 in Figure 2.3). Furthermore, other neurons of the lateral parabrachial nucleus terminate in the frontal cortex and hypothalamus, which are responsible for taste aversion (pathway 3 in Figure 2.3) (Ahima & Osei, 2001). Like the nucleus of the solitary tract, the lateral parabrachial nucleus also employs EOP as its chief neurotransmitters, therefore suggesting a role in endogenous reward for eating 'tasty' foods.

People considered to have high taste sensitivity are known as 'super' tasters and are sought after by the food and perfume industry. To discern the difference between people with high, medium and low taste sensitivity, a liquid solution containing 6-*n*-propylthiouracil (PROP) is generally used. This is a bitter tasting compound that high taste-sensitive people find aversive. The ability to taste PROP is inherited from our parents and about 70 per cent of the population can taste it to some degree – although not everyone has a strong reaction to it. People with high aversions to PROP tend to have a better taste perception for bitter, sweet and spicy tastes, as well as a better sense of smell. People who can taste PROP also have the ability to differentiate tastes within the same food item (Tepper, 1999). The 30 per cent of people who cannot taste PROP do not have as good taste perception. As compensation, non-PROP tasters tend to have the ability to tolerate much stronger tastes; indeed, they often need them to be stronger to 'like' the food item.

Wanting

Liking food is not enough to make us consume it. We must also have the drive to acquire it. This drive comes from our 'want' to consume a specific food item. Wanting is controlled by a single neurotransmitter pathway that extends from the brainstem to the forebrain (see Figure 2.5). This pathway starts in the ventral tegmentum and extends into the mesolimbic forebrain, employing dopamine as its signal. In fact, it follows similar neurobiological controls and it is very hard to differentiate, anatomically, wanting from liking. They exist together and, as such, are controlled by circuits that follow parallel pathways. The difference between liking and wanting is essentially the neurotransmitter that they use. There are other dopamine pathways, but these are not so important for wanting and reward.

Selectively removing dopamine from the brain through pharmacological treatments leaves an animal without the motivation to consume a particular food but still preserves signs of liking it if the food is placed on its tongue. Although taste sensitivity is associated with liking and endogenous opioid peptides, reward sensitivity is associated with dopamine. Reward sensitivity is controlled by the concentrations of dopamine in the brain. People with higher

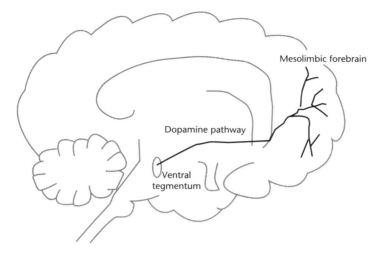

Figure 2.5   Representation of the dopamine pathway in the brain involved in wanting.

concentrations of dopamine tend to be more responsive to food cues – especially if the food offered is liked (Volkow et al., 2002). Essentially, this system controls the wanting of an item irrespective of whether it has been previously tried and liked. Manipulation of dopamine pathways could therefore be said to make humans 'want' everything more. Individuals with higher reward sensitivity will be more responsive to food cues in their environment and are more likely to want foods in the absence of trying and therefore liking them. Reward sensitivity has also been linked with other personality characteristics. High levels of impulsivity[5] have in particular been related to increased reward sensitivity. Although some researchers have used the two terms interchangeably (Wonderlich et al., 2004), it has been shown that they are different constructs (Miller et al., 2004) and can both affect eating behaviour. It has also been shown that people with higher reward sensitivity tend to have higher body mass indexes and food cravings (Franken & Muris, 2005). Furthermore, sensitivity to reward incorporates the hedonic value of food, as it has been associated with the preference for sweet and fatty foods (Davis et al., 2007). This is probably due to the multi-functional role of dopamine and its involvement in the control of movement and sensory processing. Figure 2.6 provides an overview of brainstem control of eating.

[5] This is a psychological construct that is defined by an individual's propensity to engage in an action immediately it is thought of, without thinking about the consequences of doing it.

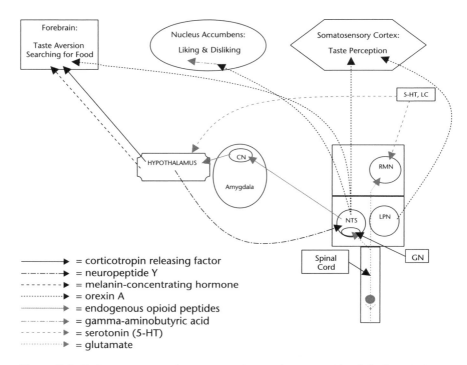

Figure 2.6 Brain structures and neurotransmitter pathways outside of the hypothalamus that have direct control of feeding. CN = central nuclei; RMN = raphe magis nuclei; NTS = nucleus of the solitary tract; 5-HT = serotonin; LC = noradrenaline; GN = gustatory nucleus; LPN = lateral parabrachial nucleus.

Sensory-specific satiety: how 'liking' and 'wanting' stop us eating

Liking and wanting play an important role in food selection; however, when combined they have an additional role in satiation (Rolls et al., 1988). On a behavioural level, the removal of the hedonic and motivational components of eating has a greater impact on behavioural expression than any of the other anorexigenic neurotransmitter signals yet identified. The episodic loss of the motivation to continue to eat within a meal is controlled by both endogenous opioid peptides and dopamine pathways and is termed sensory-specific satiety. Sensory-specific satiety is the gradual loss of the palatability of a particular food during consumption, while the pleasantness of other food items remains intact. As omnivores, humans need to consume a wide variety of food items to meet their nutritional needs and to stave off boredom. This boredom component is important, as the loss of the hedonic quality of the food means that a person has no reward (opioid release) to want (dopamine release) to continue to eat. When we are eating something that is palatable to us, every mouthful results in the release of opioids from the brainstem that provide us with an endogenous neurochemical reward for consuming it. This opioid release gradually decreases during a meal and is more pronounced if consuming only one food item. This removes the hedonic impact of eating and will eventually lead to the termination of the meal. If towards the end of the meal another food item is offered that is sufficiently different in terms of texture, taste and macronutrient properties, opioid release begins again and the person will continue to eat the new food item. A real-world example of this biological process would be an individual's ability to continue eating a dessert (usually sweet) after reaching satiation following the 'main' (usually savoury) part of the meal.

It is important not to confuse food aversion with sensory-specific satiety. Food aversion is caused by negative feedback when, or because of, consuming a particular food item. For example, if a person became ill following consumption of a particular food, they might associate the illness with it and not want to eat it again. Basically, they will inappropriately have associated the food item with the symptoms of the illness. Therefore, when offered the food item, the individual associates the negative feelings related to the illness with the taste of the specific food. Sensory-specific satiety, in contrast, lasts for one meal only and has no real 'conscious' learning to it. It is more of a habituation process whereby the individual becomes less responsive to the food through their endogenous opioid peptides not responding or being released in the same concentrations when the food is repeatedly placed on the tongue mouthful after mouthful. Therefore, sensory-specific satiety is the change of pleasantness during a single meal only.

Eating behaviourists are still unsure how long sensory-specific satiety (SSS) lasts (Sørensen et al., 2003). Some researchers have suggested that it can last for more than an hour following a meal (Hetherington et al., 1989). It is at this point that a theoretical distinction has to be made. This distinction is based on the concepts of satiation and satiety. Sensory-specific satiety can be said to last during within-meal satiation and between-meal duration of satiety. However, sensory-specific satiety cannot transcend into the next meal. If SSS-like behaviours are still present in the following meal, this is termed monotony and not sensory-specific satiety (Hetherington et al., 2000). Monotony is the repeated consumption of meals that are similar in taste, texture and visual cues. It is important that we do not confuse these two concepts, as monotony has more of a tonic effect on eating behaviour by suppressing hunger and desire for specific foods, while sensory-specific satiety has an episodic effect within a meal through earlier onset of satiation.

Summary

The central control of eating is both simple and elegant. NPY/AGRP and CART/POMC are in a constant battle with each other for supremacy over whether we should start a meal. If NPY/AGRP gain the initiative, they will activate the lateral hypothalamic area and the search for food through the release of hypocretins. This search will be heightened by dopamine and motivate the individual to want foods. Wanted items are attenuated over time by food preferences based on what the individual likes. What is liked is based on taste reactivity/sensitivity and is controlled by the release of endogenous opioid peptides. These peptides will start to be released once the food item is placed on the tongue and has caused a reaction in the taste buds. The food is then assessed for content within the somatosensory cortex and a decision is made about whether or not to swallow it. Once a meal has started, cortico-tropin releasing factor and sensory-specific satiety will start to interfere with hunger and motivation signals to stop us eating and allow CART/POMC to regain control of the appetite circuit. Additional neurotransmitters are involved in the process, but appetite regulation is controlled in the main by the pathways between the hypothalamus, brainstem and frontal lobe (see Table 2.1).

Appetite regulatory control within the brain has considerable control over whether or not we eat. Both the brainstem and the hypothalamus receive signals from the periphery (the body) and are attenuated by long-term energy storage biochemicals. The arcuate nucleus in the hypothalamus has direct contact with the blood and is responsive to hormones released from other organs that communicate both episodic and tonic messages from the periphery to the appetite system. Furthermore, the brainstem is essentially a relay station for messages from the body through the spinal cord and the cranial nerves. Rudimentary analysis of signals sent up the spinal column are undertaken in the brainstem before being diverted to higher cognitive functions in the fore-brain and, specifically, the cortex. Although it may appear that the brain is in control of eating, the peripheral organs also have an integral role in initiating feeding behaviour. The brain must be aware of, and at times be subservient to, the digestive and storage systems to maintain a healthy balance in long-term energy intake. In the next chapter, these factors will be explored and a commentary on the body's involvement with appetite regulation will be offered.

3 Storage and digestion
Peripheral mechanisms of eating

Specific regions within the brain, such as the hypothalamus and brainstem, are undeniably important in controlling eating behaviour. There is a large body of evidence that suggests the neurotransmitters found within these regions control appetite regulation and, in particular, when to start eating (episodic control). In addition, the system is geared towards starting eating rather than stopping or not eating. This is based on evidence which suggests that neurotransmitters that inhibit food intake, with the exception of cocaine and amphetamine regulated transcript (CART), appear to be much weaker than those that start it. Although the brain is a highly complex organ, it does have one specific weakness – it cannot store energy. How much energy is currently stored in the body is an important determinant of how strong the biological desire to eat is. This is different from how 'hungry' someone is at any given time, as this is determined by many things, including temporal, psychological and biological factors. This will be discussed in later chapters. Within the biological domain, the desire to eat is related to concentrations of neuropeptide Y and dopamine in specific regions of the brain. Based on this premise, both neuropeptide Y and dopamine concentrations must vary depending on the amount of fat tissue currently stored in the body. Furthermore, key neurotransmitters that initiate a meal react to how much food is currently being processed. This means that biological signals from the stomach and the intestines also need to signal the brain. Thus although the brain may be important in eating behaviour, it is not more important than the peripheral organs and their hormonal indicators.

Hormones of the periphery have two main functions: they inhibit the hypothalamic and brainstem neurocircuits depending on what and how much is in the stomach and intestines; and they modify the release of specific neurotransmitters within the circuit depending on the amount of fat tissue in the periphery. These two roles can be separated out into episodic and tonic influences. Anything involved with the stomach and intestines is episodic and anything released from the adipose tissue (fat storage) is considered tonic. In

Chapter 3, only organs that have an integral role with energy storage or diges-tion will be considered. Nearly every biological structure in the body is involved in energy acquisition in some form, as it is the only factor that keeps them alive and functioning. Here, however, we consider only the stomach, liver, pancreas, intestines and adipose tissue. Although the organs themselves are important, it is the hormones they release that are integral to appetite regulation and eating behaviour, as these alter perception (see Table 3.1). This chapter outlines the most important components of appetite regulation. The brain may be in control of the episodic initiation of a meal, but the periphery can alter the amount consumed or aid CART release to ensure that neuropep-tide Y does not initiate a meal. Therefore, the traditional view that the brain is in control of everything should not be held for eating behaviour. In essence, the body can control the brain – our stomachs can quite literally rule our heads.

To understand how the periphery is involved in appetite regulation, it is essential to understand how the body processes food in the digestive system (see Figure 3.1). Every time a meal is eaten, the digestive system needs to manage the food in a set order. First, the food needs to be broken down to get at the important micro- and macronutrients. The acidic digestive juices of the stomach undertake the initial process of digestion. The stomach is a specialized muscular sack that is able to distend to hold large amounts of food. Its purpose is to make the food into a more liquid state, called chyme,

Table 3.1   Peripheral hormones involved in eating behaviour

Inhibits eating behaviour	Induces eating behaviour
Intestines	**Stomach**
Cholecystokinin	Ghrelin
Glucagon-like peptide 1	
Glucagon-like peptide 2	
Peptide YY	
Apoliproprotein A-IV	
Enterostatin	
Pancreas	
Insulin	
Glucagon	
Amylin	
Adipose tissue	
Leptin	
Adiponectin	
Interleukin-1	
Interleukin-6	
Tumour necrosis factor	

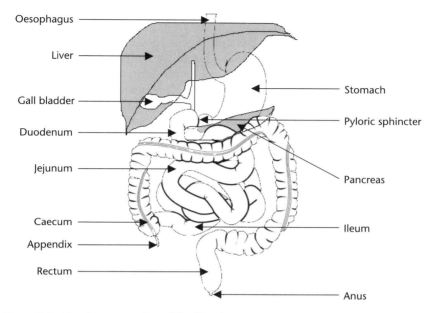

Figure 3.1   Visual representation of the digestive system.

so that it is easier to digest. Different food items require differing amounts of time in the stomach to be fully broken down. This differential time period is known as gastric emptying. Gastric emptying is controlled by a complex interaction between gut hormones and the brainstem (Näslund & Hellström, 2007). It is this complex interaction between the gut hormones of cholecystokinin, peptide YY and glucagon-like peptide 1 and the nucleus of the solitary tract in the brainstem that make an individual feel full and stop eating a meal.

Once the chyme is created, it is released from the stomach into the duodenum where it is neutralized with alkaline digestive juices and enzymes from the gall bladder via the bile duct and pancreas. The duodenum consists of the first part of the small intestine that extends for about 30 centimetres after the pyloric sphincter[1]. Within the duodenum and during its transit through the jejunum[2], the food is digested fully so that amino acids, carbohydrates and lipids can be absorbed across the intestinal wall and into the blood stream in the lower half of the small intestine. The absorption of the important constituent components of the chyme takes place in the ileum[3]. Following its transit

---

[1] This is the smooth muscular ring at the base of the stomach that stops the food from leaving.
[2] The upper half of the small intestine between the duodenum and ileum.
[3] The lower half of the small intestine between the jejunum and the large intestine.

through the ileum, the chyme is excreted out of the small intestine and into the large intestine (or colon). The first part of the colon is called the caecum, where water and salts are absorbed and mucus added. The food then moves through the colon until as much water is removed as possible. At this point, the waste products are formed into faeces and eventually excreted into the rectum and out of the anus. Each significant structure or sub-structure of the digestive system secretes one or more hormones into the blood to signal the rest of the body that it is working and not to let further food through; this usually results in extending gastric emptying time but can act through inhibiting eating behaviour.

For many years, scientists believed that the peripheral organs involved in appetite regulation were limited to a reactionary or inhibitory role in food intake. Recently, a hormone has been found in the stomach that has a similar function to neuropeptide Y by increasing perceptions of hunger. This hormone, named ghrelin, is the only biochemical outside of the brain that has orexigenic properties (Kojima et al., 1999). Due to its unique properties, ghrelin is the best place to begin in any explanation of hormonal changes brought about by eating. The remainder of this chapter is separated into the gastrointestinal phase(s) and the nutrient phase.

Gastric phase

The stomach's involvement in eating behaviour is not just to provide an acidic reservoir for food to be stored in. Whether it is trained in early life to expect food at certain times of the day or whether it is simply responding to the absence of food is open to debate, but we do know that the stomach, through the hormone ghrelin, can attenuate the central release of neuropeptide Y. This suggests that the stomach, in some circumstances, can override the brain to initiate eating behaviour. Indeed, many people associate the 'growling' noise that comes from the stomach as hunger. In most cases, this 'growling' noise is caused by the stomach wall moving when it contains no food, causing the digestive juices to shift. Although this usually coincides with feelings of hunger, it does not always do so.

Intestinal phase: duodenum

It is often assumed by the layperson that the stomach is the 'powerhouse' of the digestive system. This could not be further from the truth. The duodenum, jejunum, ileum and colon are the main organs that digest and absorb all of the necessary nutrients from the food consumed. In addition, these organs release a plethora of hormones into the circulatory system to signal the rest of the body exactly what is being digested, if anything, at that moment in time. This allows the body to coordinate its many essential functions with the imminent abundance of energy.

In the duodenum, several processes occur to begin the digestion of chyme. Both the gall bladder and the pancreas are structurally attached to the duodenum so that they can release digestive enzymes and prepare the rest of the body, and most importantly the adipose tissue, for the imminent increase in glucose in the blood. These preparations are undertaken through the release of insulin and glucagon from the pancreas. Also within this section of the digestive system, another important anorexigenic hormone is released. Cholecystokinin-creating cells are found throughout the small intestine and, when in high concentrations, give the perception of fullness. This occurs as cholecystokinin binds to the vagal nerve[4] and, through a neurocircuit originating in the nucleus of the solitary tract, increases concentrations of CART/pro-opiomelanocortin (POMC) in the arcuate nucleus. More information about these three and other hormones associated with the periphery can be found in Appendix 2. It is important to note that the separation of gut hormones into anatomical sections is not entirely accurate, as cells that produce them tend to transcend the various sections. Therefore, the separation of the hormones into these phases is based on when they are first encountered within the digestive system rather than where they are strictly found.

Intestinal phase: jejunum

Once the chyme released from the stomach comes into contact with enzymes that aid the breakdown of the complex proteins, sugars and fats, it travels through the upper half of the jejunum where the actual digestion takes place. Within this region of the small intestine, cholecystokinin hands over the signalling to glucagon-like peptides 1 and 2 (GLP-1 and GLP-2). The concentration of GLP-1 in the circulatory system will inform the brain whether it can start the next meal or not.

Intestinal phase: ileum

Upon leaving the jejunum, the food has been fully digested and the nutrients are ready for absorption. Absorption occurs across the ileal wall for utilization or storage around the body. Within this absorption section of the small

---

[4] A nerve that descends from the brain and innervates/communicates with the organs in the periphery.

intestine, another hormone is introduced to the blood. Although discovered over twenty years ago, peptide YY has received little research focus – currently this is being rectified. What is now known is that peptide YY inhibits food intake and reduces appetite (Batterham et al., 2002)

Hormonal signalling to the brain and other regions of the body following absorption of nutrients is controlled by GLP-1 and GLP-2. The movement of the waste products out of the ileum and into the colon essentially means that appetite regulation of food intake has stopped, although water and salt absorption continues. This is not the entire description concerning gastrointestinal signalling. It would appear that the digestive system responds to any food in the same way. The biochemicals above, as well as other hormones yet to be discussed, respond to different macronutrients in different ways. Alterations in hormonal profiles brought about by different amino acid, carbohydrate and lipid ratios will now be considered in turn.

The effect of macronutrients on peripheral hormones

Peripheral hormones are unlikely to be able to change food choice, as this is driven by central mechanisms of an individual's preference for specific foods and whether they want them at that time; however, there are noticeable alterations in the concentrations of peripheral hormones in response to macronutrients. It is well known that protein and fat have stronger effects on feelings of fullness than carbohydrates. This can be observed in the strength and magnitude of the hormonal profiles. In response to protein and fat in the small intestine, both cholecystokinin and peptide YY are released in higher concentrations compared with carbohydrates (Orr & Davy, 2005). Alterations in diet can therefore have an effect on behaviour and specifically on perceptions of fullness by varying the concentrations of peripheral appetite-related signals of cholecystokinin and peptide YY.

In addition to the holistic alterations in hormonal profiles, there are additional hormones that are released once specific macronutrients are detected in the digestive system. Indeed, the investigation into macronutrient hormonal profiling is still in its infancy and therefore any evidence offered here should be treated with caution. The information around the three hormones below could change as more research is undertaken and becomes available in the public domain. In addition to the role of insulin, GLP-1 is released predominantly in response to carbohydrate (Lavin et al., 1998; Kong et al., 1999) but is also responsive to fat digestion (Frost et al., 2003; Thomsen et al., 2003). In terms of protein and fat intake, endogenous cholecystokinin is released following the detection of fat and protein in the gut and peptide YY is released following detection of fatty acids and fibre in the gut (Ongaa et al., 2002). The interactional effects of the peripheral hormones are offered in the further reading papers (see p. 185). Lesser-known but equally important hormones are also responsible for protein and fat intake. These hormones are amylin, enterostatin and apoliproprotein A-IV. Only these will be discussed in the following sections.

Responding to protein (amino acids)

Upon detecting protein in the duodenum, amylin is released from the pancreas; thus amylin is a pancreatic rather than a gastrointestinal hormone. In high concentrations, it causes hypophagia (undereating) and targets the brain-stem. Tentative evidence exists that the anorexigenic properties of amylin are selective to dietary protein rather than any other macronutrient (Michel et al., 2007). A lot more research is required before any significant insights to the effects of amylin on eating behaviour can be offered.

Responding to fat (lipids)

Enterostatin is released from the pancreas, duodenum and jejunum in response to fat. Like cholecystokinin, enterostatin also targets the brainstem to alter eating behaviour. It appears to work through altering opioid and serotonin concentrations in response to food (Koizumi & Kimura, 2002), and this appears to remain specific to high fat foods only (Lin & York, 1997). This would suggest that enterostatin works through altering the taste perception of high fat food via removal of the hedonic response to it. Although it would seem to be the main drug target for changing people's high fat diets, the effects of enterostatin on eating behaviour are fairly weak and short-lived (Halford et al., 2003). The functional effect of apoliproprotein A-IV and its possible responsiveness to different macronutrients is a little contentious compared with that of enterostatin. Apoliproprotein A-IV is found in the small intestine and is released into lymph tissue rather than the blood. How it works and whether it targets the brainstem or the hypothalamus are yet to be determined; however, it does appear to respond to fat intake (Lui et al., 2001).

   In both the previous chapter and this chapter, the focus has been on the episodic control of food intake and eating behaviour. This does not consider energy stores. For example, a person who has not eaten for an extended period of time will have used up more of their energy reserves than a well-nourished individual. This will obviously mean there will be a difference in perceptions of hunger and fullness between these two individuals and, there-fore, they will have different endocrinological signals. It would make no sense if the brain had no idea how much energy it had in storage at any one time.

The principal storage area in the body is adipose tissue (fat). Contrary to popular belief, adipose tissue does interact with the rest of the body and is constantly releasing hormones into the blood stream proportional to the amount of fat in storage. Essentially, adipose tissue offers a constant background 'noise' to appetite regulation both centrally and peripherally. This signalling does not respond to food intake directly and as such is known as a tonic influence on eating behaviour.

Tonic signals: adipose tissue

Fat tissue is found throughout the body and varies depending on age and gender. To be considered healthy, females should have a higher percentage of body fat than males, and older people should have more than younger individuals. Differences between the sexes in what is considered healthy are due to the way adipose tissue is deposited between males and females. Females of child-bearing age should have at least 25 per cent body fat to remain healthy, while males should maintain levels at around 15 per cent. Males also tend to store fat around the abdomen, which has been linked to a higher risk of type-II diabetes and cardiovascular diseases. Females, in contrast, tend to deposit fat below the hips and around the thighs. Fat deposits in this area appear to have less morbid consequences. The reason why females have to maintain a higher level of adipose tissue is its role in fertility. Adipose tissue is not currently considered an organ, probably because it is found in multiple locations throughout the body; however, it really should be as it acts just like one. It is an important endocrinological agent that creates and releases several important hormones into the blood and provides an unlimited energy storage facility for the rest of the body. In particular, fat tissue releases gonadal steroid hormones (oestrogens, androgens and progesterone) to signal to the brain that there are or are not enough energy reserves to reproduce. Not having enough adipose tissue will have endocrinological consequences that will make it hard to conceive, as will having too much.

Sexual development and reproduction are important functions of adipose tissue; however, they are not directly related to appetite regulation and eating behaviour. Adipose tissue also releases several hormones that alter the magnitude and duration of other neurotransmitters and hormones involved in energy intake. These signals do not change throughout the day; they remain constant and their concentrations in the blood are directly correlated with the amount of adipose tissue an individual possesses. As they do not vary, they are deemed to be tonic signals, which have a blanket suppressive effect on the appetite system. The primary tonic appetite-related biochemicals released from the adipose tissue are leptin and adiponectin.

Summary

Both this and the previous chapter have discussed the central and peripheral episodic and tonic signals that influence and control eating behaviour. Current opinion in appetite regulation suggests that a complex interaction between the brain and the body exists to control perceptions of hunger and fullness. It would appear that several brain regions and their associated neurotransmitters are responsible for hunger (arcuate nucleus: neuropeptide Y/agouti-related protein; lateral hypothalamic area: orexins), fullness (arcuate nucleus: CART/POMC; paraventricular nucleus: corticotropin releasing factor), taste (brainstem and somatosensory cortex: opioids), liking (brainstem and nucleus accumbens: opioids and gamma-aminobutyric acid) and wanting (brainstem and forebrain: dopamine). The central regions are reinforced and sometimes controlled by digestive and energy storage organs of the periphery and their related hormones. These organs are also involved in the control of hunger (stomach: ghrelin) and fullness (intestines: cholecystokinin, GLP-1 and peptide YY), as well as informing the brain of how much energy it has in reserve (adipose tissue: leptin). Although scientists have made many important discoveries over the past twenty-five years, there are still many unanswered questions that need to be researched before we fully understand the biological underpinnings of eating behaviour.

The appetite regulation system in humans has an extremely powerful effect on behaviour. Studies in which the various biochemicals have been injected into humans and animals have shown an effect on eating behaviour and the subjective feelings associated with it. It is important not to get too carried away with absolute conclusions when considering the relative effects the central regions, peripheral organs and their biochemical agents have. The possible effects and functions that they all have are limited to attenuating or strengthening perceptions of hunger and fullness. Even when people are hungry and have food they like and want in front of them, they still may choose not to eat. Although the system is elegant and considers all components of eating behaviour from the energy needs perspective, it must be remembered that the biological system can be subject to psychological processes. Energy needs are not the only predictor of consuming food. Other more abstract psychological perceptions are also considered when deciding to eat a particular food item. These include the social context and repercussions for eating, cognitions about food, body image and age – all pertinent factors in meal initiation. Essentially, our behaviour is not a slave to biology; rather, the two operate independently and both are responsive to their environment.

4 Learning about food
Developmental aspects of eating behaviour

Children and the development of eating behaviour

The environment plays a key role in human eating behaviour. Although the biological hardwire of the appetite regulation system varies little between individuals, each person's habitual diet and food preferences are unique. Differences in food preferences and tastes are often ingrained during childhood through several arguably covert processes. These influences are compounded with children's ability to learn and their individual processes of learning. Learning is integral to the development of normal eating behaviour. Preferences made at this stage usually remain with the individual for the rest of their life. Children learn about foods in two ways. The first way is through association: the child associates a food with a particular memory or event. Foods associated with good times are liked and foods associated with not so good times are disliked. The second way is through social learning: the child learns through copying or having behaviour modelled for them by other people. Children's diets are also affected by their intellectual development. As the child's ability to make sense of their environment through their mental development (known as cognitive development) grows, they are able to categorize and make inferences and associations about food and eating behaviour. This chapter focuses on these concepts and how children learn to like, or not like, particular foods.

In addition to the theoretical framework surrounding food preference formation in children, other phenomena are also involved in the process of food preference. Exposure, food neophobia, 'picky/fussy' eating and the impact of significant individuals in the child's life all have an important role to play in the development of eating behaviours. *Exposure* is simply how frequently a child is offered a particular food item, but it can also extend to the duration and quality of each experience. *Food neophobia* is a little more complex and is usually defined as the reluctance to eat, or the avoidance of, new foods (Birch & Fisher, 1998). The term was derived from the earlier work of Rozin's (1979)

'omnivore's dilemma', a process described as an evolutionarily beneficial survival mechanism to help children avoid eating potentially poisonous items
(Cashdan, 1998). *Picky/fussy* eating is slightly harder to define as it shares many
similar characteristics with food neophobia; however, it is related to the rejection of foods that are familiar, as well as unfamiliar (Galloway et al., 2003,
2005). While the food neophobic individual will learn to accept new foods
after a distinct period of exposure to them, the 'picky/fussy' eater will continue
to refuse these foods. 'Picky/fussy' eaters are usually described as having very
limited diets in terms of the amount of different foods they find acceptable to
eat and may even have additional psychopathologies associated with food.
Finally, the role of *significant others* can have a marked effect on a child's habitual diet and food preferences. These 'significant others' obviously include
immediate family members and/or caregivers, but can also include peer group
members and even idolized individuals. Idolized individuals do not even have
to be real people, as cartoons and other fictitious characters also appear to be
able to alter a child's food preferences. In this chapter, all of these concepts and
theories will be outlined and their impact on eating behaviour evaluated. To aid
in understanding the formation of food preference, the developmental theories
of Piaget and Vygotsky will be used as a scaffold. Becoming familiar with specific food items is arguably the strongest determinant of whether or not a food
is liked; however, how a child becomes familiar with a food changes markedly
during the first decade of their life. Therefore, this chapter will be loosely
structured around ages based on Piaget's stages of child development. It is
important to note that these scientific observations and theories are not based
on specific ages and there is room for inter-individual differences; however,
thinking of these constructs in terms of age helps to differentiate them and
allows researchers to infer 'normality' in the development of food preference
(e.g. at what age are children most likely to demonstrate food neophobia).

Cognitive development

In psychology, the two most influential writers on child development are Jean
Piaget (1896–1980) and Lev Vygotsky (1896–1934). The intricacies of these
theorists' ideas can be found in many other sources and go beyond the focus
of the current chapter; however, the concepts they offer lend well to how food
preference develops and, therefore, should be considered. Piaget essentially
separates childhood into four stages: sensory motor stage (0–2 years); pre-
operational stage (2–6 years); concrete operational stage (6–12 years); and
formal operational stage (12–16 years). Vygotsky, in contrast, suggests that
significant 'others' aid the child's development. Vygotsky suggests that children's development is shaped by their social environment and that significant
others help them to understand their surroundings by offering 'scaffolding'

(models and structures) to simplify it. As children develop social interaction skills (e.g. linguistic understanding and competence), they are able to impose 'scaffolding' on their environment for themselves.

0–2 years and the importance of exposure

Contrary to popular belief, eating behaviour does not start to develop from when a child starts to eat solid food, which according to the World Health Organization should not occur within the first 6 months of life. Habituation to the environment, and even to the foods within it, starts much earlier than the actual consumption of food. A foetus is exposed to the mother's diet through the amniotic fluid (Hauser et al., 1985) and, after birth, this exposure continues through breast milk (Mennella & Beauchamp, 1999). This form of very early exposure prepares children for the predominant tastants within their environment. Therefore, when they are finally ready for solid food, they have some experience of taste and therefore only have to get used to the sensory components (sight, smell, touch) of the food.

During weaning, exposure to different flavours appears to be important in the development of food preferences. Initial variety, experience and exposure to solid foods also appear to be important in lowering food refusal (Harris, 1993). This short weaning period appears to have a marked effect on future taste preferences (Gerrish & Mennella, 2001), which is not found after this developmental period (Cohen et al., 1995). Very early exposure, through the mother's breast milk, may only work on some specific fruits and vegetables (Mennella et al., 2006), as children can discriminate between, and may have innate preferences for, different flavours of vegetables (Gerrish & Mennella, 2001). A child's exposure to breast milk has been suggested to be critical in increasing acceptance of bitter tasting fruits and vegetables (Cooke et al., 2004), but only if the mother consumes these foods as part of her habitual diet.

Frequency of exposure is also important. Novelty of a particular food still has an effect on a child's eating behaviour for up to fifteen short-term exposures (Birch et al., 1987; Wardle et al., 2003a, 2003b, 2005). This exposure frequency is age dependent, with younger children requiring fewer exposures before accepting and consuming unfamiliar foods. Birch et al. (1998) showed that only one exposure is required to double the intake of a novel food in children aged between 4 and 7 months. This has led some researchers to suggest that this weaning period is critical for getting a child to accept foods. Unfortunately this oversimplifies the process. Although during this period the child will require only a relatively few exposures to accept a particular food, it is still possible to get any child or adult to accept novel foods. Accepting novel foods during and after the weaning process alters because the child has developed more complex categorization schemata (i.e. what is actually food and what is not), as well as survival mechanisms to avoid potentially harmful 'food-like items' in their environment (both are discussed later in this chapter). Therefore, it is unlikely that a critical period for exposure to novel foods exists; it is just that the approach required in achieving acceptance differs with an increasingly complex mind.

The information provided to the child during exposure may also have an effect on acceptance of fruits and vegetables. Wardle and Huon (2000) found that telling children that they should consume certain foods because they are healthy might have led to a lesser acceptance of them. However, this may have been the result of an interaction between parental pressure and health-related information (Wardle et al., 2003b).

Associative learning theory

Associative learning, as the name suggests, explains how a child learns to associate apparently unrelated concepts. Underpinned by the brainstem-mediated processes of liking and wanting, associative learning is the psychological component of reward mechanisms. Whether they are implicitly or explicitly modulated, emotional, cognitive and social reinforcements provide additional impetus on top of the natural 'high' conferred by the biological reward mechanisms. Associative learning theory extends beyond the reaction to specific tastants by offering an explanation of how the environment impacts on eating behaviour. This theory also widens the eating episode past the simple act of eating. Essentially, this theory constitutes the psychological incentive to eat.

Associative learning does not have to be completely explicit. Implicit learning mechanisms arise through the biological consequences brought about by the properties of a particular food, which are learned through association. A child can quickly tell the difference between foods that are high and low in energy. They do this through forming associations between the flavour of a food and the post-ingestive consequences of eating it (Brunstrom, 2007). This is a form of conditioned learning whereby positive consequences are associated with a particular flavour.

A simple Pavlovian type of conditioned learning typically involves the repeated pairing of a conditioned stimulus (CS+) and a particular reward or unconditioned stimulus (UCS) – in Pavlov's case, the bell (CS+) and the food (UCS). Therefore, repeat pairing of stimulus and reward brings about an expectation that the conditioned stimulus will lead to the reward, and so anticipatory responses for the reward are evident upon presentation of the stimulus – the bell rings and the dog salivates.

In eating behaviour this process is a little more complex, as the flavour and the food both have an intrinsic value. Developments to this Pavlovian approach have led to a derivative model based on associative conditioning called the Bolles-Bindra-Toates theory (Berridge, 2004). Bolles termed this process S–S* rather than CS+ and UCS of the Pavlovian psychologists (Bolles, 1972). The difference between S and S* according to Bolles is that S* already carries a value. In Bolles's model, S was essentially the same as the Pavlovian CS+; however, it could be argued that Bolles was suggesting that S is different from CS+ once it is paired with the S*. S* would be the food, which is the animal's energy source. All animals require energy to survive; thus S* has a value even if no learning has taken place, as it is an essential requirement. The pairing of S–S* creates a motivational vector whereby the presentation of S elicits goal-directed behaviour to achieve S*; however, it is questionable whether this motivational behaviour actually occurs (Berridge, 2004).

The Bolles-Bindra-Toates theory is hard to uncouple from the Pavlovian model and there is little to argue that the presentation of S actually elicits motivational behaviour above simple expectancies. This is in contrast to other more psychological rewards where the reward itself has to be learned (e.g. social/emotional rewards). Bindra (1978) extended the work of Bolles through the incorporation of hedonics. In this theory, Bindra suggests that the S does not remain just an association with the S*, but can become a reward in itself. In terms of eating behaviour, S* (food) will have many physiological effects that enhance mood (serotonin) and energy levels – this would be the obvious reward for consuming the food. In the case of food, the initial stimulus also has a desirable reward – the taste perception and opioid release. Therefore, Bindra's addition to the theory is that the flavour promotes goal-directed behaviour in the individual and carries a hedonic value irrespective of its value as a food. An example of Bindra's additions to this theory would be the desire for chewing gum. Chewing gum is flavoured, which makes us buy and chew it. The flavour in itself is desired despite the chewing gum having no value as a food source.

The final addition to conditioned learned associations is that of Toates. Toates (1986) added to the theory by suggesting that the potential levels of reward are attenuated or strengthened by the physiological state of the individual. In the case of food, hunger and low glucose concentrations in the circulation mean that both the sham reward (S) and the actual reward (S*) will be increased. Alternatively, if the individual is satiated, their satiety will elicit less goal-directed behaviour to obtain the reward. The Bolles-Bindra-Toates theory is the cornerstone to associative learning and motivations in eating behaviour research. Current research has extended this theory further, with scientists exploring how flavour interacts with nutrients and the post-ingestive consequences of eating a particular food.

Flavour-based associations with post-ingestive consequences are known as flavour–nutrient learning. The child learns to associate a particular taste with the potential energy, satiation and satiety repercussions of consuming it. This information provides the individual with the relative comfort of being able to predict the energy content of a particular food and weigh up its intrinsic motivational value. Moreover, it gives the individual energy security so that they can concentrate on aspects of life other than the acquisition of food (Brunstrom, 2007).

The focus of associative learning has so far been on the energy value of foods; however, humans also desire and consume foods that have a low or no energy value. These types of foods are equally important in the human diet as they provide the individual with essential micronutrients (vitamins and minerals) to remain healthy. These types of less energy dense foods are learned to be liked or disliked through a process of flavour–flavour rather than flavour–nutrient learning. Flavour–flavour learning is different from flavour–nutrient learning as both the S and the S* are presented at the same time. The new food item (or S) is presented alongside a previously liked food item (S*), which causes a sort of transference between the associations with the S* to the S. This form of associative learning explains how children learn preferences for a meal that contains multiple foods and thus tastes within it.

Associative learning can also extend beyond the flavour–nutrient and flavour–flavour learning. This form of learning is internally driven and fairly implicit in nature. More explicit forms of associative learning come from 'rewards' outside of the actual food item and the physiological consequences of consuming it. These other rewards come from contingencies placed on eating or not eating a target food item. Positive reinforcement is one such contingency outside of the child's control and the physiological repercussions of eating the food item. Most parents try to get their children to eat foods they may not like by using reinforcers (e.g. 'if you eat your dinner you can have your pudding'). This 'negotiation' with the child actually contains several reinforcement processes over and above the contingency of 'eating dinner means I get dessert'. There is also a withdrawal threat implicitly contained within the statement 'if you don't eat it you will not get any dessert', and depending on how it is said it could also contain the insinuation of a potential punishment to be feared.

There are three ways one can 'reward' a child for eating a particular food, and it is these experiences that the child will learn to associate with each other. These approaches are based on the concept of operant conditioning, which consists of three different types of reinforcers: positive, negative and punishment. Positive reinforcement is the addition of something previously liked and is known to elicit goal-directed behaviour in the child to make sure they obtain it (i.e. anything sweet like pudding). Negative reinforcement is the opposite to this with the removal of something disliked following the completion of a particular desired behaviour (e.g. 'I will take away half of the vegetables if you eat the other half in five minutes'). Finally, punishment is the addition of something not liked when the desired behaviour is not forthcoming (e.g. physical harm [smacking], removal of rights and liberties [grounding] or emotional/psychological isolation [the naughty step]). In terms of a particular food and getting children to eat it, it would be easy to suggest that the food should be associated with positive reinforcers; however, it would appear that this is not entirely accurate. Indirect positive associations with contingencies like 'eat your dinner and you get pudding' actually decreases liking for the target food (S) and reinforces the desire for the reward food (S*) even further (Birch et al., 1984; Moore et al., 2007). It could be suggested here that the child sees the target food as an obstacle to overcome to get to the reward rather than associating the target food with the reward. Therefore, the target food is seen as the penalty for gaining the reward, which would suggest that the target food item is negatively reinforced by the attempts to positively associate it. This means that given the choice to consume the target food at a later date, the child will refuse it and not develop a preference for it.

Other types of positive reward appear to have a more profound effect on food preference. Positive emotional contingencies that offer psychological rewards for eating a particular food appear to have a much stronger effect in the medium to long term. Rewards like praise for eating a particular food and not offering any psychological reward are much better (Birch, 1980). Therefore, care should be taken in what is offered as the reward, or consequence, of eating, or not eating, a particular food. In short, offering positive rewards is advisable, while offering another food as a reward is not. Furthermore, it would be beneficial to pair the consumption of a target food with positive emotions through the medium of games. Parents and children who enjoy the 'game' of trying foods are more likely to use the technique more often and for more foods resulting in a higher frequency of exposure (Wardle et al., 2003a). They are also less likely to exhibit frustration towards refusal and so avoid the surreptitious addition of negative reinforcers into the experience. It is imperative that the child does not associate any negative feelings or feelings of disgust with the foods during exposure periods. If this does occur, then it is likely that the child will refuse the food offered and might even transfer, or generalize, this rejection to any foods that look similar to it. For example, if a child associates something negative with cucumbers, it will be hard to get them to accept other cylindrical shaped green fruits and vegetables (e.g. courgettes). Therefore, associative learning can act to ensure independent uptake and liking for foods, but can equally aid in disliking and avoidance.

Associative learning begins early in life and this is the reason for its consideration here; however, it is used as a strategy for the rest of the child's life. Adults can also develop likes and dislikes through associative learning. For example, if someone eats a particular food and then independently contracts an illness that causes vomiting, they are likely to inappropriately associate the illness with the food. This aversive form of associative learning is extremely powerful, as it can occur even if the person is consciously aware that the food did not cause the illness.

Social learning theory, scaffolding and the influence of significant others

Associative learning offers a great deal of insight into how a child learns about food; however, it tends to focus on the individual and neglects the child's social context and therefore the role of others in the process. Parents, older siblings, peer group members and even cartoon superheroes can all have an impact on a child's diet. Parents in particular provide the child with the structure to the mealtime and when they are supposed to eat, especially after weaning.

Social learning theory is based on the work of Bandura (1977) and suggests that children learn through observation or behavioural modelling (copying). This form of learning is based on the cognitive level of the child and their ability to observe and replicate another's behaviour. For this form of learning to occur, the child must have the attentional resources, an ability to retrieve memory, finite motor control of their body and motivation to copy a particular person. Therefore, the ability to copy someone accurately is dependent on the current physical and cognitive development of the child. This would suggest that this form of learning occurs slightly later than associative learning. Although the very young child may not learn more complex skills through observation, social learning can still influence food preference through the child copying some part of the behaviour.

Social influences and behavioural modelling can be predictive of increased dietary variety and food preferences, especially in young children. Children do not eat alone and therefore receive social influences from those around them at mealtimes. If children have a strong bond with the people around them, they are likely to want what the other people are eating and attempt to copy their eating behaviours. This suggests that the caregivers' food preferences and eating behaviours will manifest within the child through the child modelling (copying) their parent's behaviour or the parent not offering foods that they themselves do not like. Therefore, there is a better chance of a child adopting a particular food preference if the people around them also have it and are eating the particular food too. If this modelling is paired with positive reinforcement, the likelihood for acceptance increases further (Rozin & Schiller, 1980). The person being copied also appears to have a role in increasing food acceptance. Mothers are better models than strangers (Harper & Sanders, 1975); older children are better than younger children (Birch, 1980); and superheroes are better than everyone (Birch, 1999).

Parental style also appears to have an effect on food preference formation. Three main styles of parenting have been identified: authoritarian, authoritative and permissive (Baumrind, 1966; Robinson et al., 1995). An *authoritarian* parenting style is where the parent places high demands on the child and controls their behaviour. These parents also tend to show less warmth and be less communicative with the child. *Authoritative* parents score highly on controlling deviant behaviour but are also more communicative with the child, setting clear limits when to respond to the individual child and their current mood. The child is left to control his or her own behaviour, but the parent will respond when the child expresses deviant behaviour. The *permissive* style is the opposite of the authoritarian one, with parents being indulgent to the child, setting no restrictions on what is acceptable behaviour and what is not. This form of parenting is associated with the worst long-term outcomes for the child, as they tend to become immature and irresponsible. Eating behaviour and dietary variety, like all other behaviours, respond best to an authoritative parenting style (Hubbs-Tait et al., 2008). Children of permissive parents tend to be over-reliant on hedonics for making food choices (Cullen et al., 2001) and authoritarian parenting leads to lowered dietary variety when the parent is not around.

Irrespective of overall parenting style, pressure to eat any particular food will be detrimental in the long term. Pleading with or coercing a child to eat a particular food by explaining future health consequences has little meaning to children at this age and therefore has little effect on preference. In fact, the child might reject the food presented because of suggestions of health-related consequences as a form of pressure. Therefore, in terms of 'scaffolding', the influence of others appears to be more effective as a role model rather than as an enforcer.

With the child becoming increasingly more mobile, independent of their caregivers and curious about their environment, other psychological phenomena become evident. The child stops implicitly trusting foods that are given to them or that they find. A 'phobic'-like response towards new foods develops and getting the child to eat becomes harder. In the next section, we consider the phenomenon that begins during the pre-operational stage.

2–6 years and the development of food neophobia

As described at the beginning of this chapter, food neophobia is the reluctance to try, or the avoidance of, new foods. To avoid being poisoned, children will naturally reject bitter tasting foods (McBurney & Gent, 1979), which have been suggested to be reliant on hedonic neurobiological mechanisms that are present at birth (Steiner, 1979) and can persist into adulthood (Stein et al., 2003). Food neophobia aids this avoidance mechanism through the child naturally rejecting potential food sources that they have no experience with. Presentation of a novel food initiates a fear response in the individual (Zajonc, 1968). The natural distrust and fear responses combine to limit the child's diet. Food neophobia is not a psychopathological issue; rather, it is a natural developmental stage that ensures the child does not take unnecessary risks before they have the mental faculties to accurately assess the foods immediately available to them.

Rejection of new foods during this developmental stage does not occur during tasting, but is instead based on sight. Therefore, foods that do not 'look right' to the child will be initially rejected based on vision alone. Evidence for this rejection of foods by neophobic individuals based on visual cues can be inferred from data on willingness to try food items (Bäckström et al., 2004). Within this paradigm, participants are asked if they would be willing to taste different food items. It has been shown that people who have higher food neophobia are more likely to reject food items before tasting them, although it is accepted that previous experiences of other tasted food items may also have a role in this judgement (Pliner et al., 1993). The inference here is that children build up schemata (mental representations) of how an acceptable food should look and so foods not sufficiently close to this stimulus set will be rejected.

Inevitably, if the food is recognized and accepted because of its appearance, it will be tasted. The taste will then be assessed for its subjective value (either positive or negative to the individual), which in turn is associated with the visual image. Successful and continuous positive experiences with the food item will lower the child's reluctance to eat it. Food neophobia is not only a developmental stage but also a personality trait. Children with comparatively strong food neophobia compared with their peers will have a stronger fear reaction to a novel food item. The fear reaction will be by its very nature a negative experience and therefore new foods will be negatively associated and reinforced. High levels of food neophobia will inevitably lead to a diet typified by low variety. As the child becomes more experienced with their environment, the novelty value of new foods will be less pronounced. This is because the child can successfully categorize and compare the new food with other foods they have experienced. With increased experience, exposure and cognitive development, food neophobia diminishes.

It has been shown that the expression of food neophobia decreases with age (Koivisto-Hursti & Sjöden, 1997), with most authors reporting that, from a low baseline at weaning, it increases sharply as a child becomes more mobile, reaching a peak between 2 and 6 years of age (Cooke et al., 2003). This trait then decreases as the individual ages until it is at a relatively stable nadir in adulthood (McFarlane & Pliner, 1997). Contention in the literature can be found, with some authors reporting a general decrease until early adulthood (Rigal et al., 2006), while others suggest food neophobia is stable from adolescence (13 years of age) (Nicklaus et al., 2005). However, it is likely that food neophobia continues to decrease throughout childhood, adolescence and adulthood. Not to decrease would be maladaptive to survival and reproductive rates in our species, as the omnivorous nature of humans means we have diverse nutritional needs that can only be satisfied by an equally varied diet.

The gradient at which this loss of neophobia occurs is probably less pronounced within adolescent and adult populations than in children due to variations in cognitive development (Dovey et al., 2008a).

There is a lot of confusion regarding differences in food neophobia between the sexes. Equal numbers of research studies have suggested that either males or females are more prone to higher levels of this trait. It is likely that differences in personality rather than gender are responsible for variations in the levels of food neophobia; however, more data are required before any definitive conclusions can be offered.

Category representations of food

A very young child, as suggested above, initially learns through associative and social conditioning. As they are exposed to more things, they begin to develop the ability to organize and recall experiences in order to create expectancy. In the case of food, the child learns to associate a food with a particular taste and then through multiple exposures learns to expect the taste before the food is eaten. This organization of thought defines a food as familiar or not. The organization of thought and memory starts from a very early age; however, the actual development of the complexity does not start until after 2 years of age. The complexity of this mental organization is controlled through categorization processes. Three different forms of categorization have been identified: taxonomic, script and thematic (Nguyen & Murphy, 2003). *Taxonomic* categories include items that share common functions or properties. For example, dogs and cats are separated by some characteristics but both belong to the category of mammals and then animals. Such categorization allows an organizational hierarchy to form. The highest level of grouping, in this case animals, is known as the superordinate category. Very young children quickly grasp the highest level of superordinate categories, but struggle to grasp the lower levels until around 2 years of age. Therefore, everything furry and four-legged may be a dog to young children. *Script*-based categorization includes items that have the same role or use a 'count as' approach. For example, rice, pasta and potatoes all have the same role within a meal and therefore are not usually served together. *Thematic* categories are items that are complementary to each other. Whereas script are 'count as', thematic are 'come together'. Knife and fork or meat and two vegetables are examples of thematic categorizations. These items can exist separately, but usually come together.

Organizing food requires a complex interplay between all of these categories. Essentially, the child must learn to cross-categorize foods (i.e. assign multiple meanings to a specific food) (Ross & Murphy, 1999). Early taxonomic arrangements of food occur quite early in a child's development, but they are often flawed. Although the child will quickly learn what is and is not food, their early attempts to group foods are often based on the foods' sensory properties (sight: size, shape, colour; smell: pleasant, unpleasant; and taste: sweet, sour, salt, bitter and umami) (Dovey et al., 2008a). This will undoubtedly fail because foods from any individual group can vary dramatically in their sensory properties. Fruit, for example, is likely/expected to be sweet, but can equally be sour or bitter. Furthermore, fruits come in a variety of shapes, sizes and colours. Therefore, the categorization of foods is often undertaken by other higher-order and more cognitive factors. The complexity does not end in the specificity of the grouping of foods. Food can have meaning beyond its sensory and energy value. Any given food belongs to a taxonomic (dairy, meat, vegetables, etc.), script (snack, substantial, dessert, etc.) and thematic (meat and two vegetables equals a substantial meal, etc.) category, but it can also be defined in terms of its religious, social and health benefits. Most adults will reach a level where they can cross-categorize foods on a taxonomic and script-based level and therefore this would be considered the end of the usual developmental process (Ross & Murphy, 1999). It has been shown that children are able to cross-categorize foods by the age of 4 years and are almost as good as adults by the age of 7 (Nguyen & Murphy, 2003). Individuals who are more accurate in the categorization and cross-categorization process are usually defined as experts. Experts are those people that have a better understanding of the taxonomic, script, thematic and other categorization processes. However, not everyone reaches the level of an expert, and as food is an essential need, everyone will develop cross-categorization schemata for it. Of course, inter-individual differences in cross-categorization exist based on additional factors such as intelligence, strength of food neophobia, and so on. Although the ability to develop new cross-categorization schemata does not end within this age range, children towards the end of this pre-operational stage are proficient in this form of mental representation.

By the age of 6–7 years, the child has had a lot of social influences, learned to associate reinforcers with particular foods and has organized the foods they are familiar with into flexible categories in order to create expectancy. With increased familiarity and expectancy comes a decreased behavioural expression of food neophobia and a varied diet has started to be internalized. Failure to manifest any of these various influences in the child's eating behaviour is likely to lead to psychopathologies requiring professional intervention from a dietitian or clinical psychologist. If a child does not develop normally, irrespective of the cause, they may be at risk of becoming a 'picky/fussy' eater. If they do develop normally, then internal cognitions (perceptions of self, cognitive restraint, disinhibition and mood – discussed in later chapters) and additional social factors begin to exert their influence on the child's eating behaviour.

6–12 years and 'picky/fussy' eaters

When asked, most parents believe that their toddlers and young children are 'picky' or 'fussy' eaters. To the eating behaviourist, these terms mean some-thing slightly different from the general public's perception and usage. 'Picky/fussy' eaters are usually defined as people who have a strong food neophobia and also refuse foods that they are familiar with. Therefore, they require further repeat exposures over and above the 'average' of fifteen exposures. Most parents are quick to label their child as a 'picky/fussy' eater before they have had the necessary experience and exposure. Due to the time requirement, it is difficult to define a child as a 'picky/fussy' eater before one would expect them to be over their natural food neophobic developmental stage. It is not impossible to apply the label 'picky/fussy' eater earlier, as a child can be directly compared with their peer group and, where possible, older siblings; however, the older the child is, the more obvious the poor dietary variety is, making it easier to assume they have adequate experience with different foods.

'Picky/fussy' eating is behaviourally and theoretically distinct from food neophobia (Pelchat & Pliner, 1986). Measures for 'picky' eating are in their infancy, making it hard to quantify this construct (Kauer et al., 2002). Furthermore, 'picky/fussy' eating can extend further than food neophobia through children rejecting food textures and not just a particular food (Smith et al., 2005). Therefore, unlike food neophobia, 'picky/fussy' eating can extend into the realm of the flavour and the feel of foods, as these children are inappropriately rejecting food textures, which can only be completely deter-mined in the child's mouth. In its basic form, 'picky/fussy' eating is differenti-ated from food neophobia through the novelty value of the food presented. Food neophobia can remain as a part of a picky eater's behavioural profile (Pelchat, 1996), while 'picky/fussy' eating is not a part of a food neophobic's profile. This would suggest that 'picky/fussy' eating is more of an abnormality in food preference development, while food neophobia is not.

The diet of 'picky/fussy' eaters appears to reflect that of non-'picky/fussy' eaters in most aspects. There are, however, some distinct differences between the two groups. 'Picky/fussy' eaters consume fewer amounts of foods containing vitamin E, vitamin C, folic acid and fibre, probably due to their lower consumption of fruits and vegetables (Galloway et al., 2005), than non-'picky/fussy' eaters. Lower amounts of these specific nutrients may lead to cell damage (Burton & Traber, 1990; Royack et al., 2000), immuno-logical weakness (Hemilä, 2003) and digestive problems (Bosaeus, 2004). The digestive problems in particular may increase 'picky/fussy' eating through inappropriate negative reinforcement associated with foods that have just been eaten (e.g. constipation). Furthermore, Carruth et al. (2004) reported that 'picky/fussy' eaters were less likely to consume dishes with foods that were mixed together. This makes the parent's job harder, as 'picky/fussy' eaters will also reject foods that they can see may have hidden ingredients in them. Therefore, trying to increase acceptance through 'hiding' fruits and vegetables within other more liked foods may be problematic for these children.

Unlike in food neophobia, it does not appear that 'picky/fussy' eaters compensate for the lack of fruits and vegetables through consuming higher amounts of fat (Galloway et al., 2005). Indeed, some evidence suggests that 'picky/fussy' children have lower body mass indexes than non-'picky/fussy' eaters and yet are not underweight (Marchi & Cohen, 1990). However, other researchers have suggested the opposite (Carruth & Skinner, 2000). Although an interesting finding, these children do not have a behavioural defence to obesity. 'Picky/fussy' eating is associated with essential nutrient deficiency (Galloway et al., 2005) and other forms of inappropriate sensory processing such as tactile defensiveness (Smith et al., 2005). Furthermore, there is some evidence that 'picky/fussy' children may consume more sweetened foods (Carruth et al., 2004). This suggests an over-reliance on hedonic value (i.e. acceptance encouraged by children's innate liking for sweetness). Consequently, there is a risk that such children may establish a habit of over-consumption of energy-dense, highly palatable foods that eventually culminates in excessive weight gain. So far, there is no longitudinal data to support this supposition.

12–16 years and the development of food-related cognitions

Adolescence is a developmental stage characterized by marked physical and cognitive changes. Endocrine changes brought about by the onset of puberty lead to a spurt in physical growth and the preparation for reproduction. Such large growth patterns require larger amounts of energy compared with the formative years. Unfortunately, this stage of development is also marred by increased awareness of social values, concepts of beauty and body image worries that leave these individuals at risk of developing pathological thought patterns towards their bodies and, as a result, their eating behaviour. Social importance by this stage has turned from their parents' and familial view to a higher dependence on societal influences. In essence, the adolescent is now starting to think about food and eating in a wider context, making their eating behaviour much more complex and more reminiscent of that of an adult. Cognitive and affective factors such as cognitive restraint, disinhibition and emotions all begin to impinge on the individual, making their control of their eating behaviour more psychologically dependent.

Research on adolescents is comparatively under-represented compared with other stages of development. Researchers who have focused on this age group have only explored adolescent eating within this developmental stage rather than comparing adolescents with either children or adults. Therefore, the conclusions drawn from this literature are hard to attribute definitively to this developmental stage. Although marked changes are evident, it is likely that these changes started to occur, at least to some extent, earlier in the developmental process. Increasing reliance on peer influence is often associated with this developmental stage alongside a decrease in the frequency of eating meals with the family (Gillman et al., 2000); however, adolescents still report that their parents are important influences on their eating behaviour (Neumark-Sztainer et al., 1999) and those who are given autonomy in their food choices tend to skip meals more often (Videon & Manning, 2003). Research has also suggested that adolescents do not completely understand the concept of a balanced or healthy diet. Instead, they seem to associate a healthy diet with dieting and associate dieting as being healthy (Roberts et al., 1999). This confusion between a healthy diet and dieting also appears to be stronger in females than in males, which could explain the increased prevalence of eating disorders in both this age group and in females. Future research might investigate whether a diet defined by exceptionally low calorific intake is considered healthier among adolescents. Favourable research findings may provide strong evidence for the aetiology of eating disorders.

The internalization of the expression of eating-related differences between the sexes does not stop at the confusion around what constitutes a healthy diet. Although data are available to suggest that there are differences in body image between the sexes in younger children, it is not until this developmental stage that the individual will independently use eating behaviour as a continual and consistent strategy to control weight. At this stage, differences in body dissatisfaction between the sexes often see females in particular begin to skip meals and use dieting as a form of weight maintenance and loss strategy (Wardle & Beales, 1986). Males, in contrast, will often increase food intake, especially snack-based foods during adolescence, giving them the ability to increase their energy intake without having to eat much larger quantities of food during mealtimes (Cusatis & Shannon, 1996). Although this can provide a vehicle that makes a valuable contribution to dietary variety and preferences (Bigler-Doughten & Jenkins, 1987), it is often associated with the consumption of high fat and sugar foods with a lower nutritional quality (Cusatis & Shannon, 1996). This food choice is based on the taste preference of the adolescent and may constitute a significant barrier to developing a healthy balanced diet, especially as there appears to be some form of peer norms and pressures to choose these high fat and sugar foods (Stevenson et al., 2007). This milieu will inevitably lead to food preferences and habits that may lead to a habitual diet lacking in essential micronutrients but rich in energy. This has obvious implications for obesity and its associated pathologies in later life (Kemm, 1987).

Adolescents are almost fully developed in terms of their eating behaviour compared with adults. They may still have developmental-specific errors in their thoughts about the higher cognitive facets of eating behaviour, but the errors are more those of an adult than of a child. Such errors may derive from the increased autonomy to choose their own diets, coupled with insufficient skills to provide adequate dietary variety for themselves. It is not until the adolescent has experienced and developed food preparation and selection skills that they will inherently understand the appropriate higher cognitive schemata associated with food and eating. Other than these very specific errors indicative of inexperience and recent understanding of societal pressures to conform to a socially held ideal in terms of eating behaviour and body image, the adolescents' errors are essentially the same, in terms of their eating behaviour, as those of adults. The concepts indicative of adult eating behaviour will now be considered in the following chapters.

Summary

The development of eating behaviour is a highly complex process that involves many different and, at times, competing factors. Children, in terms of the development of their food preferences, will naturally progress through an open stage during weaning, a closed stage during increased mobility and independence from their caregiver, to a complex interactive stage during later childhood and adolescence. This progression is underlined by learning and overall cognitive development. Learning can be influenced by associations or specific experiences, as well as through behavioural modelling, accuracy of categorization and intellectual ability. Other factors also appear to have a strong effect on the development of eating behaviour: parental style, presence or absence of siblings and the role of significant others can have a strong influence on food preference and eating behaviour from a very young age. Furthermore, the individuality of the child and their personality development can affect eating behaviour through the strength and duration of the natural developmental stage of food neophobia. If any of these factors 'goes wrong', the child may become a 'picky/fussy' eater, which will mean that the child will refuse a lot of different foods.

By adolescence, many food preferences have formed and other factors start to affect eating behaviour. This means that the child moves from a food preference approach to an evaluation of food choice. Here the individual makes decisions about which foods to consume in each eating experience, although others will still control the food selection, and therefore the vast majority of calories, of a child's habitual diet. It is not until the individual starts to cook and buy foods that they start to make active choices among foods on a daily basis. Decisions about food choice are complex and incorporate a plethora of different factors. In the next chapter, the concept of food selection and choice will be explored.

5   Choosing between foods
Cognitive aspects of eating behaviour

Differentiating foods based on energy value

Choosing which foods to eat is a surprisingly complex process that has many latent psychological constructs to it. These constructs go beyond the simple 'I am hungry and so I will eat'; rather, they add new conditions to this statement such as 'what is available?' and 'is it worth the effort?' There are three overarching theories associated with food choice that are differentiated by the intellectual ability of the species to which it is applied. The simple *stimulus–response* type animals use a model of matching principle where the potential food source is linked to effort. As intelligence increases, so does the complexity of the strategy of choosing food. Animals that have to deal with sporadic food sources or have a large base of foods to choose from adopt an *optimal foraging strategy* where the least amount of effort is used to get the maximum potential rewards. Finally, animals with high cognitive ability and abstract value systems employ an *expectancy–value ratio* approach to food choice. Here, the animal compares its belief about its ability to obtain the food against the value to it of having that food. These theories share a common principle that is a judgement about the food and the effort needed to get it. These theories can become quite complex. In this chapter, the role of food choice in eating behaviour will be considered. Humans use all three of the food choice models to make decisions about which food to eat and so all three need to be considered. Once an individual has chosen a food and has successfully obtained it, the decision-making process does not stop there. He or she then needs to decide whether to consume it now, as well as how much of it to take. This essentially relates to the memory for the last meal and indicates habitual portion size. Both memory for the last meal and portion size will be considered.

It is important to remember that the theories and psychological constructs presented in this chapter are not independent of those in Chapter 4. Instead, it is best to see these theories as extensions that go beyond the developmental models. Therefore, learning in all its forms and from the different perspectives precedes those in this chapter. The cognitive theories of food choice depend on the individual having pre-existing knowledge of the value of different foods so that they may make an initial decision concerning the comparative value of these items. However, learning may be limited to knowledge that the item presented is a food and therefore has value as such. This implicit knowledge is integral to the theories of food choice. To reinforce behaviour or to predict food choice, one must offer a reinforcer that has value, and food can only have value if it is recognized as food, otherwise it has no intrinsic attraction and therefore will not elicit motivated behaviours to acquire it.

Before we assess the theories of food choice, there is one overarching contingency beyond learning that underpins all of them. 'Normal' individuals[1] are biologically required to gain weight or at the very least maintain their current weight. The human body, like that of any other animal, does not want to lose weight and so will defend its energy reserves. Therefore, the choice of which foods to eat has the theoretical requirement that the animal will not use up more energy to obtain it than the food intrinsically has. This theory is known as energy balance (see Figure 5.1). Positive energy balance refers to the case in which the individual consumes more calories than they expend. A state in which the individual uses more calories (through effort) than they obtain from consuming food is termed negative energy balance. Positive energy balance leads to the excess energy being stored as fat. Negative energy balance, in contrast, requires a shift in an individual's metabolism so that fat stores are used to compensate for the lack of energy entering the system. Energy balance can be affected by factors other than energy intake. The quality and quantity of food eaten can influence either side of the energy balance equation, although other factors such as physical activity, rest–wake cycles and health can also have an impact. The desire to maintain a positive energy balance underpins food choice, which means that foods that are higher in energy and require less energy reserves to obtain have a higher reward value than foods that are lower in energy. The relative energy or calorific value of one food compared with others is known as energy density. Energy dense foods are those that are high in fat and sugars. These foods are highly palatable to all animals and will be preferentially sought compared with foods that do not contain such high levels of these macronutrients[2]. Therefore, when considering food choice models, it is important to remember that comparative energy values between the foods in question will have a large impact on which are chosen.

---

[1] This basically refers to anyone who does not have a psychopathological thought process indicative of an eating disorder.

[2] 'Macronutrients' is the collective term for the fat, carbohydrate (sugar and starch) and protein in a particular food item.

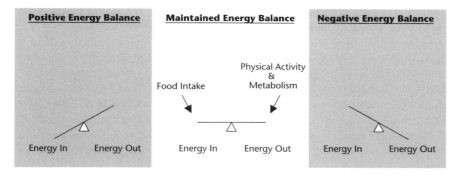

Figure 5.1   Diagrammatic representation of energy balance.

Memory and meals

In addition to the biological feedback of satiety, humans can also consciously recall when and where they had their most recent meal. Recalling the preceding meal has been shown to affect food intake during the next meal (Higgs, 2002). The reliance on memory for the last eating episode is not beyond the realms of expectation, as we rely on our memory processes in all aspects of eating behaviour. If it is assumed that learning is essentially the recollection of past events, then preferences for a target food are actively recalled upon presentation (Higgs, 2008). Without memory systems, humans could not learn about food and therefore make valid food choices. For example, in patients with severe anterograde amnesia[3] it has been shown that they have hunger levels that do not change in response to a meal (Hebben et al., 1985). In extreme cases, such individuals will eat one meal almost immediately after another, if someone does not stop them. Albeit in an abnormal group of people, this would suggest that the memory for the last meal is stronger than state-based physiological feedback brought about by consuming a meal. Taken together, the evidence suggests that memory is integral to eating behaviour.

The model of matching

There have been three key contributors to the theoretical development of the matching principle: Thorndike (1911), Herrnstein (Herrnstein & Prelec, 1991) and Gibbon (1995) (see Figure 5.2). Thorndike's early postulations suggested that all animals adhere to the law of effort. He suggested that through a process

---

[3] Such people can no longer create new memories due to some form of neurological damage.

of trial and error, animals modify their food choice according to the feed-back they receive. More effort is focused on positive feedback and the behaviour becomes reinforced and thus persists. The consumption of a particular food means that the food becomes less abundant. As availability decreases, the effort required to harvest the food item increases exponentially. When the animal perceives the cost (in terms of energy and time) of obtaining the food as unsatisfactory, they will stop gathering and eating it. Essentially, Thorndike's model is simply that the food that requires the least effort to obtain it will lead to a preference for it. Therefore, if two foods of equal value are offered, the animal will automatically choose the one that requires the least effort.

Herrnstein's contributions extended those of Thorndike by considering time and size of the reward. Herrnstein's melioration model considers the effect of both effort and time on behaviour. For example, minimal amounts of effort over a longer period of time can equal a large amount of effort over a shorter period. Furthermore, the size of the potential reward will also impinge on how much time and effort the individual is willing to invest in the food source. Variation in reward compared with effort and time assumes that the individual has learned the intrinsic value of the food in question. This is

---

Thorndike:

$$\frac{FC_1}{FC_2} = \frac{R_1}{R_2} \times \frac{E_1}{E_2}$$

where FC = food choice, R = reward, E = effort

Herrnstein:

$$\frac{FC_1}{FC_2} = \frac{S_1}{S_2} \times \frac{E_1}{E_2}$$

where FC = food choice, S = size of reward, D = delay in receiving reward

Gibbon:

$$\frac{M \times EDT_{(FC_1)}}{(M \times EDT_{(FC_1)}) + (M \times EDT_{(FC_2)})} = \frac{\lambda_{FC_1} \times A}{(\lambda_{FC_1} \times A) + (\lambda_{FC_2} \times A)}$$

where M = previous recent memory for reward at locale; EDT = expected dwell time; FC = food choice; λ = reinforcement rate; A = arousal brought about by consumption of food.

Figure 5.2   Representations of the historical development of the model of matching.

often done through taste perception. All animals have the ability to gain a rough estimate of the energy value of the food based on its hedonic value. Animals that do not have a varied diet and are therefore less reliant on taste perception for choosing between foods will still have to gather their food from multiple sources and therefore will still require a judgement value system. The culmination of Herrnstein's contributions to matching theory is the concept of the equilibrium point. The equilibrium point is the moment when the animal has adapted to its environment and understands the relative reward values of the different foods and food sources within it. The animal is now able to invest the optimum amount of time and effort in gathering it.

Evidence for Herrnstein's melioration model comes from many experiments with pigeons. In this paradigm, the pigeon is given different levers or buttons to peck to receive a small amount of food. From this type of experiment it is possible to work out the effort the bird puts in (the number of pecks), the time it takes to do it (the number of seconds) and its response to the value of the reward (whether it performs the behaviour again). It has been shown that the most important component of this equation is the amount of time it takes. An animal is relatively happy to invest a large amount of effort if the reward is relatively forthcoming. The small amount of time required to obtain the food is integral to the perception of the reward irrespective of the intensity of effort required to get it and its energy value (Gallistel et al., 2002).

The third of the three theorists responsible for updating matching models is Gibbon. Gibbon added several caveats to the law of effect. While Thorndike and Herrnstein suggested that food-choice-related behaviours are a result of the reward earned, Gibbon's model suggests that the behaviour is not sensitive to food reward in itself; rather, it is the individual time frame at each location required to harvest the food. The animal thus holds a heuristic[4] in its mind about the average time frames to find food in each potential food location. This means that the animal's experience of harvesting conditions at each location will indicate the amount of time it will invest, as well as the frequency with which it will visit the locale. Each location, according to Gibbon, will have an inherent value associated with it that will make it richer or poorer than other areas. The allocation of value to location rather than the food received suggests that the behaviour is not responsive to feedback; rather, it relies on a 'feed forward' approach. In terms of the animal's behaviour, it will tend towards visiting richer food sources more often, but will visit poorer locales at times when the richer locations do not meet up to the internally held heuristics about the time it takes to harvest food at them. The fact that the animal will visit multiple locations, and applies a unique set of rules to each of

---

[4] Heuristics is the psychological equivalent of 'rule of thumb'. It is a series of assumptions made about a specific item based on previous experiences.

them, allows for adaptability within its environment and the possibility for contingency plans in times of need. In essence, the amount of time an animal spends at each location is not based on the reward, but is instead a probability-based process whereby it distributes its time between all the potential food sources, visiting the known richer ones first. Thus, if a locale has twice the amount of food in it, it will be visited twice as often. Further caveats are also offered to the theory of matching by Gibbon's proposals. The first is that the animal will not necessarily switch to a richer location straight away. It might persist at a poorer location until its memory has been 'updated' through persistent reinforcement that the locale is not as rich as it once was. Memory can be 'updated' more quickly if the animal is 'lucky' enough to be exposed to a reward that provokes unexpected increased arousal. Unexpected arousal results from a food reward being obtained far outside the realms of expect-ation of the specific locale. Therefore, the animal becomes intrigued by the unexpected reward and repeats the behaviour to see if it has actually changed.

One problem with Gibbon's theory is that it suggests that the animal does not have an impact on its environment, which is accurate for a sustainable organism pyramid where the number of predators is proportional to the num-ber of the prey species. Humans draw from a diversity of potential food sources and therefore are not totally bound by these pyramids. This is a slight weak-ness to Gibbon's model, making its application to humans particularly poor, which is reflected in the extremely limited research applying these models to humans. However, Gibbon's model also suggests that a human will stop visit-ing a locale if the average time frame to harvest a food extends beyond that of another, previously poorer locale. This model could be applied to humans through their tendency to judge restaurants on both the food and the service. If the service is poor or slow, a person is less likely to go back irrespective of the quality of the food. Humans, therefore, are constantly comparing potential food sources on both quality and timeliness to aid them in their choices.

Another problem with Gibbon's model, and matching models in general, is that they do not consider the environmental impact on the decision-making process. Risks in the environment impact on the food choice independent of effort, reward and time. For example, getting honey from a bee's nest up a tree is inherently dangerous. If the same nest is overhanging a cliff, it is even more risky and yet does not affect any aspect of the matching models of food choice. The consideration of additional environmental factors in food choice is the remit of the next theory: optimal foraging theory.

Optimal foraging theory

Humans require a varied diet drawn from many food groups/sources and therefore have evolved a complex decision-making process for deciding what and when to eat. Different foods have different intrinsic values, which include abstract and emotional values as well as the food's pure value – its energy content. Furthermore, the collection of different foods can require different and highly complex harvesting strategies. Adding in the assumption that an individual will not spend more energy acquiring a food item than that food actually has, further increases complexity in the food choice process and means that previous theories based around the choice between two or a few potential food choices can no longer hold up in the face of this kind of more rigorous decision-making. Optimal foraging theory offers some additional assumptions to food choice behaviour. The first is that foods that are currently collected and 'in storage' are worth more than any potential foods that are not immediately available irrespective of their potential value (Nahum & Kerr, 2008). The second assumption in this theory is that the environment plays a key role in the decision-making process of whether or not to risk staying and continuing to search for food in a given location or to move to another location.

Optimal foraging theory brings the element of risk into the equation of food choice. Risk within food choice can come in many forms. For example, the environment can be a source of risk, as can the potential for meeting predators. There are also other forms of risk, such as the consequences to health of eating a particular food and of the decision to stay or move on. The decision to stay or move to another location to search for food is inherently risky, as there is no guarantee that the food will be in greater abundance there. Knowledge of the environment is more important to optimal foraging theory than it is to matching theory. Therefore, an animal will avoid a very rich food source if it carries any potential environmental risks. Moreover, knowledge also allows the animal to adapt to its environment, as it will be able to choose between rich and poor harvesting locations. Within optimal foraging theory, the decision to stay in a given location is known as patch acceptance, and how long an animal stays there gathering food is known as patch residence time. Increases in both patch acceptance and patch residence time are indicative of richer food sources. Once a food source in a particular location is exhausted to the point that it takes an unacceptable amount of time to harvest compared with the time it takes to travel to, and harvest in, a different location underpins the decision to move on to another patch (MacArthur & Pianka, 1966). This decision-making process is known as the marginal value theorem.

For the modern-day human situated in an obesogenic environment, optimal foraging theory finds itself redundant. Humans need only 'gather' food from their local supermarket once a week. The certainty and very low risk of food gathering means that humans do not face the same problems and life-threatening decisions as other animals are faced with (Illius et al., 2002). If optimal foraging theory is taken in a more general sense, as a cost–benefit model of decision-making, then it does still have application. Lieberman (2006) offers an extensive commentary on the applicability of optimal foraging theory to the modern human. Instead of having to worry about the environment and other extraneous factors to the food-gathering process, food quality and content can now contain an intrinsic long-term risk to the individual's health. Furthermore, food has a monetary value for humans in addition to its energy value. Therefore, the modern human's optimal foraging theory and marginal value theorem include the available money to buy the foods needed, as well as the need to provide a nutritionally acceptable diet. In terms of relative importance, it is safe to assume that the monetary consequences are more important than the nutritional ones (Drewnowski & Spector, 2004). Evidence for the continued relevance of optimal foraging theory also comes from observations of the human preference for fast and pre-prepared food. Humans prefer foods that have high energy density (fat and sugar) and are associated with minimal cost (money and time) and effort (obtaining, preparation and cleaning up).

Expectancy–value models

The weaknesses in the matching model and optimal foraging theory are that they are dependent on the physical environment and resources available in it. This does not explain completely the complexity of human food choice, as additional pressures impinge on our choices of what we want to eat. Whereas other models focus on the more animalistic approaches and research paradigms, the expectancy–value model is more specific to human food choices and considers the more holistic pressures on our behaviour. The expectancy–value model of food choice considers individual perceptions of competence, expertise and values. These are important determinants in addition to the reward, effort, time and cost–benefit factors involved in the other models. Using the honey example again, the decision whether to try to gather it not only depends on the factors discussed above, but also requires a conscious assessment of the individual's skill at climbing trees. Moreover, it also depends on the social importance or value that will be gained by gathering it. If the social group considers the honey to be valuable, then an individual is more likely to engage in risk-taking behaviours to obtain it. They will be hoping that they will receive social status and social reward for having the proven skills to successfully gather a food with an high social importance. Essentially, the expectancy–value model extends the reward side of the food choice equation by incorporating the more complex human reward system. Instead of the food only holding a reward value of its potential energy, it also has an increased subjective value based on cognitive, emotional, social, cultural and perceptual factors (Eccles & Wigfield, 2002).

The expectancy–value model suggests that, in addition to its energy reward, the subjective value of a food can be broken down into a further three distinct categories: interest value, attainment value and utility value. The *interest value* of a food considers the emotional consequences brought about by the behaviours required to obtain it, as well as the emotional benefits of eating it. Therefore, a food that is fun to harvest and tastes good will have an intrinsic interest value that is higher than that of other foods. *Attainment values* are related to the social rewards and the relative importance of engaging in the behaviour. Here, the attainment value of a food that is considered harder to gather is likely to have higher rewards than foods that are easier to gather. If a food item has a high energy value but also requires a set of highly experienced and expert skills to gather it, the value of the food and the social status of the individuals with the skills are likely to be high. Finally, the *utility value* of a food item comes from its relation to perceptions of self. For example, if a person is good at gathering food items that others cannot, they are likely to define themselves by that ability. Therefore, they will continue to express the behaviour irrespective of the other factors, as the gathering of that particular food item is related to self-esteem and positive perceptions of the self. A clear modern-day example of this would be fishermen continuing to harvest specific species of fish despite their being on the brink of extinction. Overall, the expectancy–value model suggests that a food item carries more than one value and we expect that these values will bring rewards beyond the simple act of eating.

Specific research into these cognitive decision-making models of food choice is limited. The main reason for this is that these models have been operationalized within a social context and therefore incorporate a more holistic socio-cognitive approach. The application of these cognitive elements has gone through several iterations and will be the primary focus of Chapter 6. Human decision-making models involve many social pressures and components around food choice and it is not until the person's cognitive scripts are captured within the social context that an accurate prediction of their food choice can be made. This social impact is typified most in the expectancy–value model, where decisions to harvest a food are based on the relative social importance of having the skills to harvest it.

Evidence for the wider application of food choice models can be found in the following chapter on social aspects of eating, specifically within the sections related to the theory of reasoned action, theory of planned behaviour and theory of trying. It is important to remember that these theories are socio-cognitive theories, despite their being presented within a chapter related to social psychology, and are therefore derivatives of these more 'basic' cognitive decision-making models.

Food choice models offer insight into the decision-making processes involved in food selection. They consider the role of the food and the effect of negative consequences of obtaining it. Their strength lies in the ability to quantify the process, and when combined together into one predictive model of food choice, they are a good representation of how animals and humans choose which food to collect and eat. The only real weakness is the fact that they are fixated on the food and resources required to obtain it. Humans have the capacity to select from such a wide-ranging potential source of foods that they can actively discard some of them. The meaning of food and how it is collected can be considered in terms of how we would individually like to live our lives. Essentially, food represents part of what we are and portrays how we wish the world to see us. Others can draw inferences about our food choices and make judgements about us based on them. This cognition about food can inform the individual about what is an acceptable food source to eat. Therefore, this extraneous factor can lead to food refusal or acceptance beyond the simple interaction between reward and effort. These internally driven cognitive processes can be summed up rather simply as ideologies.

Food choice and ideology

A food ideology encompasses many factors outside of reward and effort in informing food choices. Usually, this is bound up in some form of individually derived thought process based on what is and is not acceptable to the individual. This additional value is not specific about a particular food, but can incorporate entire food groups and is usually, but not always, seen as an ethical statement to others about the individual's beliefs about 'how we should live our lives'. Therefore, an ideological system is a set of individual values that guide most decision-making processes (Rohan, 2000). In essence, it is an expression of the individual's personality and identity bound up within a belief structure (Bisogni et al., 2002). The most obvious example of a food ideology would be vegetarianism. Here, the individual has made a conscious decision to avoid eating meat. They have chosen to employ an additional set of rules that excludes meat from their diet. The reasons for this are numerous and often tied up in a specific and highly individually significant life event(s) that has had such an emotional impact that they now find the consumption of meat aversive. This can be typified by the variation in extremes of an ideology within vegetarianism. For example, some will not eat red meat, others will not eat any animal meat but fish is acceptable, still others will not eat any animals and, finally, some take it to the extreme by banning any food product associated with animals (veganism).

Vegetarianism is just one doctrine that can be applied to food. Others include the perception of potential risk of illness either to oneself or the environment (e.g. organic diets). Moreover, a more global ideology not necessarily specific to food can also affect food choice. Religious views can ban specific foods from the diet[5], as can beliefs about health[6] and fitness[7]. No food can be excluded from the potential of ideological fixation or refusal in an individual's diet. Lindeman and Sirelius (2001) tried to categorize food ideologies and suggested, based on a series of studies, that there are three types of ideology associated with food, which they named the ecological, health and pleasure ideologies. *Ecological* ideology comprised an individual's values based on universalism[8], stimulation[9], self-direction[10] and animal welfare. *Health* ideologies were associated with belief models beyond just eating healthily. This construct also includes the importance of conformity, tradition, security and familiarity. The final ideology, *pleasure*, was associated with the hedonistic views of the individual. It is simply how much pleasure and positive experiences drive the individual's behaviour.

Ideologies are important components of food choice, as the ethical and belief models of the individual impact on all decisions that they make. The relative importance of food to everyone means that it is particularly vulnerable to belief models. Indeed, it is so vulnerable that some ideologies are specific to food only. In essence, the role of an ideology is to restrict the amount of potential foods available and to show other people that one has specific beliefs about how humans should live their lives. Like the food choice models before them, food ideologies are also nearly always specific to the food item, although this can extend to how the food item is prepared for it to become acceptable. In addition to internally driven belief models about food, the context in which the food is prepared and consumed can impinge on which foods are selected. This will be considered in the next section. The information within this section has been gained almost exclusively through qualitative methods. Furthermore, it is a particularly novel area within eating behaviour, which opens it up to criticism; however, it does offer some interesting theoretical interpretations and insights into the process that other sub-fields have failed to engage with.

---

[5] Examples include the banning of pork for Jews and Muslims and beef for Hindus.

[6] Examples include eating five fruits and vegetables a day, or people who avoid foods because of the metabolic consequences to them (i.e. diabetics and kidney stone sufferers).

[7] Examples include athletes eating carbohydrate-dense diets before running, or weightlifters trying to put on muscle mass by consuming protein-rich diets.

[8] Beliefs about being broad minded, importance of wisdom and equality, social justice and anti-war.

[9] Beliefs about risk-taking, leading a varied life and having stimulating experiences.

[10] Beliefs about the importance of uniqueness, being imaginative and curious, being independent, and freedom of thought and behaviour.

Food choice and the context of the eating episode

Mealtimes can have a context beyond the value of the food and the effort required to make it edible. Both a socially held and individually held schema of appropriateness can define this context. The most commonly held context schema about food is that of meal versus time of day (e.g. breakfast, lunch and dinner) (Blake, 2008). These contexts are so ingrained into the modern individual's thought processes that they are almost completely interchangeable with the act of eating. What is meant here is that the communication of eating between people is not something like 'do you want to go out to eat?' but instead is nearly always defined by the time, as well as the act, of eating. Therefore, 'going out to eat' is replaced by 'going out for dinner or lunch'.

The contextual information of meal/time is also used beyond the habitual separation of eating episodes. Foods can also be defined by the context alone. Basically, if a food is defined by the context it becomes acceptable only when presented within it (Blake et al., 2007). For people from the West[11], the majority of calories are consumed during the evening meal and, as such, this meal has additional values and context-based schemata. The evening meal is often seen as the 'family' meal (Murcott, 1982), which means that the relative status and values of each family can affect the relative investment of the different individuals in the group. The workload is not spread equally among all members of the family and therefore the meal has a different cost–benefit model for different individuals within the group. Blake et al. (2008) offer a qualitative exploration of the different roles individuals have within the evening meal context. They suggest that there are eight formal roles or 'scripts'[12] that adults can assume within the preparation, consumption and cleaning up of a meal:

1   *The provider* – a role usually undertaken by a woman, whereby she controls all stages of the meal. The meals follow a very rigid structure based around a traditional view of eating an evening meal (i.e. at the table where the family talks together).
2   *The egalitarian* – the meal is separated out into tasks and different members of the family stick to their relative expertise. The mealtime is not particularly well structured and each meal tends to develop in its own way.

---

[11] This is not the same for Eastern cultures, where the calorific intake is relatively stable across all three eating episodes.

[12] Scripts are specific thought processes that people follow when engaging in something – in this case, an evening meal.

3   *The struggler* – the person who makes the dinner tries to satisfy everyone's wishes and there is no set structure to eating, with individuals wandering off with their food. One person does all of the work and the others simply eat.

4   *The anything goes approach* – the family is very adaptable and different people undertake different roles each day/week. There is no real structure or set roles for the individuals within the family; everyone is expected to adapt to the situation on a daily basis.

5   *The family cook* – everyone has a set role to play in the meal. It is a well-structured affair. The difference between this approach and the provider approach involves the role of the children. Within the family script, the children have a say, whereas within the provider script they do not.

6   *Head of the table* – a very traditional approach to the meal with very specific gender roles. This script is indicative of a very patriarchal family. Everyone listens to what the 'head of the family' has to say and he is the centre of the mealtime.

7   *The entertainer* – usually reserved for meals when people from outside the immediate family are involved. The guest has more control of the eating scenario and their food preferences and approaches are adopted over the normal familial ones.

8   *Just eat* – little or no involvement by the individual or family. Everyone is expected to look after themselves. The acquisition of food can sometimes be pooled, but the meal is essentially an individual time.

It is important to remember that the eight different scripts are not 'set in stone'; rather, a family is adaptable to circumstances and may change between two or more scripts.

The theories for food choice are complex. Although most animal approaches to eating are straightforward and can be defined by a relatively simple theory, this is not the case for humans. The complex organization of thought creates an even more complex series of behaviours around food choice. Unlike other animals, humans can receive both actual and abstract reward and utilize skill sets that can differentiate the perception of effort. Value judgements about the derivation of food or its source can affect food choice. In addition, the social or cognitive context, as well as the individual's role within the group, can affect what is eaten and when. Once a food choice has been made, the individual now has to decide how much of it to take. This has been discussed briefly within optimal foraging theory, but, among humans, portion sizes are a little more complex than the assessment of available foods for harvesting in a given location.

Portion size

It could be assumed that when we select how much food to consume in a single meal, we make this decision based on our current subjective feelings of hunger. The variation in typical and habitual meal sizes would suggest that other factors are also integral to this supposedly simple process of filling a plate or bowl. Sensory cues, cognitive factors and subjective feelings of fullness and hunger each have a part to play in the process (Kral, 2006). Learned associations about what constitutes a meal formulated by life experiences appear to help create a cognitive script about acceptable portion sizes. Understanding the decision-making processes underlying portion size is important, especially in light of individuals who habitually choose larger portion sizes, as these people are likely to over-consume and therefore will be at risk of obesity (Hill & Peters, 1998). It is important to note that people who are already obese are not more likely to eat bigger portions than their leaner peers (Wansink & van Ittersum, 2007). Indeed, it has been shown that even people with doctorates in eating behaviour are still not immune to the effects of choosing overly large portion sizes (Wansink et al., 2005). Moreover, people, in general, cannot recall their habitual portion size (Burger et al., 2007). This would suggest that, irrespective of societal and intellectual status, all of us are at risk of choosing to eat too much food.

Decisions about how much food to take are initially dependent on how much of it is available, how many people it needs to be shared with, the size of the plates/bowls being filled and the time available to consume it. However, commercial ventures and places where food can be bought can also affect decision-making about portion size. Individually served portion sizes in supermarkets and restaurants have drastically increased in line with the current obesity pandemic (Young & Nestle, 2002). Portion sizes offered by food outlets have significantly changed our consumptive norms, which reinforce the propensity to overeat when faced with food. Our consumptive norms have changed so much that if we were given the same portion that was offered to us twenty years ago we would refuse it and, in all likelihood, complain. It only takes one company to increase its portion size and all the others will quickly follow suit. Companies do this because most of our perceptions of value for money come from quantity rather than the quality of the food we are offered. Therefore, it makes good business sense for a company to offer larger portion sizes than its competitors to get repeat custom. This has led to the scenario where, as a species[13], we continue to consume ever-increasing portion sizes.

---

[13] This is not specific to Westerners, as across the world the same thing is happening irrespective of culture and geographical location.

When choosing how much to eat, people first assess their current feelings of hunger. Although it would appear from the earlier chapters that perceptions of hunger are controlled by biology, that is not completely the case. Environmental cues can affect feelings of hunger and our sensations can make us think we are hungrier than we actually are. Nothing can exemplify this more than the 'bakery effect'. The smells emanating from the bakery will make us more aware of food and activate several processes that will make us ready to eat, which can include increased perceptions of hunger. Moreover, satiation and satiety cues are not totally dependent on how much is eaten (Herman & Polivy, 1984). In fact, two studies have shown that even eating twice as much in one situation compared with a previous one has no significant effect on feelings of fullness (Rolls et al., 2002; Kral et al., 2004). There is also experimental evidence that a larger portion size will also increase perceptions of hunger after a meal (Rolls et al., 2004), which, coupled with the fact that humans are very bad at compensating their energy intake after overconsuming during an earlier meal, means that habitual portion size has a marked impact on the amount of food habitually eaten. In summary, both hunger and fullness can be manipulated by portion size and they are not particularly responsive to the amount of food eaten. Therefore, it is possible to eat larger portions without there being any effect on the subjective perceptions associated with them.

Having made a judgement regarding hunger, a person will then pick up a plate and start to serve up a portion for her or himself. The size of the plate can have a marked effect on how much is served. Most people will simply 'fill up' their plate irrespective of its size. Therefore, larger plates suggest that it is appropriate to have larger portion sizes (Wansink, 2004). Moreover, humans also have a tendency to underestimate the calorific content of food when it is presented in larger portions (Wansink et al., 2005). The continual use of larger crockery is likely to alter our consumptive norms and therefore the amount of food eaten. This derives from a habitual behaviour of eating what is presented, or what some researchers have called the 'clean your plate' script. It is this behaviour that has led to increased portion sizes more than any other factor. Eating everything offered increases the vulnerability to portion distortion, as it is the visual cues of the food that provide the subjective decision-making of how much to eat. However, it is still not appropriate to blame food outlets for offering larger portion sizes. Recent legal cases in which individuals have blamed a specific company for their weight status are inappropriate, as it does not make strategic long-term sense for a business to harm customers. Like all companies, they have a product to sell and want people to buy it. They pander to the customers' demands of value to ensure that they part with their money. It is the value-based system of quantity over quality paired with the 'clean our plate' script to eating a meal that inevitably leads to portion distortion and weight gain. If smaller portion sizes were demanded and potential customers refused to shop in places that served larger ones, companies would change their practices overnight.

Once a decision is made about what food is wanted, how much is wanted and what crockery is going to be used, it will be tasted. The taste of food or the component parts of a meal can also lead to portion distortion. Through processes related to sensory-specific satiety,[14] portion sizes can be increased by offering palatable foods or a wide choice of foods. The presentation of a lot of different foods that are generally liked will lead to larger portion sizes. Essentially, if the food offered is liked, then more will be taken. If a selection of foods that are liked is offered, this will have an additive effect where the process of sensory-specific satiety will be undermined, which in turn weakens the potential satiation feedback processes.

Summary

Choosing what food to eat, as well as how much of it to eat, is based on a complex interplay between biological, sensory, environment and learned influences. Food choice contains a lot of processes that regress down to the fundamental concepts of reward and effort underpinned by energy balance. Once the choice has been made about which food to eat, a new set of decision-making factors will control how much is consumed. Consumptive norms and even factors such as plate size have an impact on how much is eaten. Despite the outward appearance that choosing what to eat is devoid of thought, this is not accurate. State-based circumstances such as the time of day can impact on what is acceptable to eat at that particular time. Therefore, there are many cognitive scripts surrounding mealtime and the process of food selection.

In this chapter we have discussed cognitive involvement in food choice; however, this does not reflect the global effect food can have on people. Although choice involves a decision-making element, when asked, people find it hard to express what made them choose a particular food over another other than a liking for it. Other, more global thought processes that are outside of ideology have a greater holistic role in decisions about what to eat. Food can elicit specific thought processes around it and its content, creating a specific set of beliefs about it. Moreover, when people eat is not always based on how hungry they are. Additional factors such as the presence of other people can lead to eating. In the next chapter, we explore these social determinants of eating behaviour.

---

[14] See Chapter 2 for more details on this concept.

6 The effect of others
Social aspects of eating behaviour

Eating within a wider social context

Being a member of a social group essentially means that each individual shares a similar set of values and has constructed similar schemata, through a process of within-group negotiation, of objects, in this case food, found within their immediate environment (Wagner et al., 1999). To be a member of a particular group effectively means that the individual has, implicitly or explicitly, declared that they share similar values and beliefs to those of the other members of the group. Following this declaration, any subsequent perceived deviation from the explicit values of the group by the individual is likely to lead to some form of social repercussion. Therefore, a person's decision-making processes about which food to choose and how much of it to consume will be bound by perceived social pressures to conform to the group to which they belong. Although this is usually reflected in the refusal to eat specific foods such as those represented by food ideologies, it can also manifest more subtly, such as a desire to portray a specific social image. One example of such behaviour could be the restricted eating portrayed by a woman on a 'first date'. The woman may believe that consuming a perceptually small amount of food will portray a feminine image to the potential partner and thus facilitate a positive social image. Therefore, in some situations, the social context and environment can be the main determinant of food choice.

Within eating behaviour, the majority of the social constructionist approaches to food and eating behaviour have focused primarily on feminist perspectives. The many theoretical commentaries have dealt mainly with eating disorders and how society is constructed to facilitate their development primarily through the strict criteria of beauty and the utility of women (e.g. Hesse-Biber et al., 2006). These approaches allow for the incorporation of perceived body image and social impression into the eating context, which are strong drivers of food choice for some individuals.

A group may hold similar values and beliefs about food and eating, but they may consider specific roles or behaviours to be appropriate only for specific individuals within it. This would suggest that the same social pressures are not equally distributed among all group members and some members may have qualitatively different social representations of appropriate eating behaviour. Feminist writers argue that women have additional pressures inferred on them by society; however, not all women adhere to these values, although some believe these values to be more important than all others. Therefore, the group may hold a similar set of values and beliefs but there is a significant amount of individuality involved, as each member struggles to transform ambivalent information by selecting and simplifying specific messages to make it meaningful to them (Bäckström et al., 2004).

Eating a specific food provides the individual with more than just its nutritional content. Previously, we have explored how food ideologies can restrict food choice; however, food can also provide the individual with a specific social identity. Therefore, the food in itself has a communicative function for the individual. Through social stereotyping[1] and the positive social associations with thinness, positive impressions can be portrayed to others by eating comparatively small amounts or through copying another's portion size (Salvy et al., 2007). The willingness to 'please' others and portray a positive social image suggests that several factors outside of social cognition can also affect eating behaviour in social situations. These include the phenomena of social facilitation, advertising through the media, body image and culture/religion.

Social approaches to food intake

In previous chapters, discussion of the effects of parents and siblings on a child's development of dietary variety has shown that familial groups have a large impact on instilling eating behaviours. This chapter explores in more detail the effect of other people on eating behaviour. Other people can have a profound effect on what and how much a person will eat in a specific social situation. The social situation will affect the decision-making processes and combine with them to alter what food is chosen. This combination with the more cognitive aspects of eating behaviour is known as social cognition and reflects the impact of the environmental context and other people on eating behaviour. In this chapter, the focus will be on several theories that layer one on top of another to provide a better predictive understanding of what people will do when faced with food in a social situation.

Understanding all of the social, contextual and value-based information that enters into the decision-making process around food choice has been

---

[1] These are a form of heuristics that are very simplistic representations of individuals or groups that are widely shared by the general population.

operationalized into three theories: the theory of reasoned action, theory of planned behaviour and theory of trying. These theories incorporate the social context and the relative importance of both the social group and their beliefs/ values within an individual's decision-making around food choice and intake. These models form the basis of most of the rest of this chapter.

Extending food choice into the social world: attitudes, norms and control

Expectancy–value theory[2] suggests that the reward value of a food item extends beyond its energy value. Two of these additional 'values', attainment and utility, are embedded within a social context, suggesting that the reward value is dependent on the other people in the individual's group. Attainment rewards are said to involve the group's celebration for gaining the specific food, while utility rewards are based on the skills that an individual possesses that are better than those of other members of their group. Thus, the utility rewards are embedded in the individual's social identity and what differentiates them in a positive manner from others. In essence, these socially dependent values must derive from socially held beliefs about the particular food item. These beliefs must be consistent among all, or most, members of the group for the food to hold a social value. For example, if a significant minority of individuals within a group do not believe a particular food to be important, the relative social rewards for having the skills to collect it are diminished. In essence, the attainment value of the food is weakened. Beliefs about a specific food can be differentiated into three groups depending on the derivative of the belief: behavioural, normative and control.

Behavioural beliefs relate to when the individual expects to receive a specific reward from others for obtaining the food. This has both an expectation of the size of the attainment reward as well as the type of reward expected. Expectation is also attenuated by the immediate evaluation of the attainment reward upon obtaining the food. Multiple beliefs can be held about a specific food, which must be measured against the individual's personal preferences. Once all of the information about the attainment reward and the expected outcomes of obtaining a specific food have been assessed, this will be formulated into a personal belief model. This overall evaluation of all of the behavioural beliefs is known as an attitude. As in the previous food choice models, attitude has been summed up by a mathematical equation (see Figure 6.1; Ajzen & Fishbein, 2000).

Behavioural beliefs and their derivative attitudes are held by the individual and are involved in cognitive decision-making or learning processes;

---

[2] Discussed in detail in Chapter 5.

$$Attitude \propto \sum_{i=1}^{n} b_i e_i$$

where $\propto$ = proportional to, $\sum$ = sum of, b = outcome belief, e = evaluation of belief, i = one specific belief, n = number of beliefs.

Figure 6.1 Mathematical formula to predict an attitude.

however, they are addressed here within the social chapter because they are evaluated and expressed within the social environment. The outcome of the individual's social evaluation will predict whether or not they will express the behaviour derived from the attitude. For example, when a beer festival comes to town, people will all drink real ale over other alcoholic beverages. Even if the individual prefers other drinks to real ale, during this social occasion they will choose to drink it. The individual's decision-making process will assess the stereotypical social view of real ale to determine the social implications of drinking it ('It is an old man's drink'), as well as personal preferences ('I don't really like it, but I can drink it'). Together, this forms an attitude that is quite poor and would suggest that the individual would not choose to drink the ale. The reason for choosing to drink it is the positive social consequences surrounding the social interaction. By getting together with friends, enjoying time together and collectively experimenting with novel drinks that are not available all year round, they are engaging in the drinking behaviour. This problematic cognitive and social evaluation of the situation poses a problem for psychologists, as it shows that what someone verbalizes does not necessarily predict their behaviour. In terms of eating behaviour, a meta-analysis by Conner (2000) quite convincingly shows that attitudes only predict about 12 per cent of food choice. There are several ways that the predictive value of attitudes can be increased to accurately predict behaviour. These include one or all of the following: improved measurement techniques[3]; consideration of how important or strong the attitude is held; and considering the social rewards or punishments that may result from expressing an acceptable or deviant view to the rest of the group.

To account for the other 88 per cent of behaviour we must address the second type of beliefs. *Normative beliefs* are associated with the perceived social pressure to perform behaviour by significant people in the group alongside the relative importance of the particular social group to the individual. These normative beliefs come together with the general social beliefs to create

---

[3] See Chapter 1 for methodological considerations.

subjective norms. These norms are the perceptions the individual infers the rest of society believes in; essentially, it is the individually perceived common schemas or scripts. The combination of the normative beliefs and subjective norms with the behavioural beliefs feed into the theory of reasoned action (see Figure 6.2). Here, these two beliefs come together to encompass the behavioural intention. Behavioural intention is the motivation a person has to perform a specific behaviour. The interlink between behaviour and behavioural intention is known as a mediator variable because the link between the behavioural and normative beliefs through attitudes and subjective norms via behavioural intention is stronger than the direct link between those variables and behaviour without this mediation.

Research exploring the theory of reasoned action has focused mainly on consumer behaviour (Sheppard et al., 1988), and so for eating behaviour it has been related to food products. Although the spotlight has been on the business end of research, there has been some application of this research outside of this remit. Several researchers have successfully applied the theory of reasoned action to fat (Saunders & Rahilly, 1990), sugar (Grogen et al., 1998) and general healthy eating (Anderson & Sheppard, 1989). From this research, the successful prediction of eating behaviour through the theory of reasoned action appears to be fairly weak, with 28–41 per cent of behaviour accounted for by the variables in this theory. Despite this, research has suggested that there may

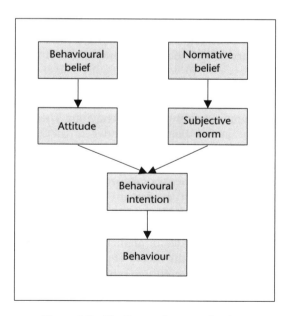

Figure 6.2   The theory of reasoned action.

be differences between the sexes, with women being more susceptible to social pressures than men. Attitudes, in contrast, appear to be relatively stable between the sexes. Recently, it has been shown that this theory has some cross-cultural stability in eating in fast-food restaurants, but does show differences in the action of eating alone (Bagozzi et al., 2000). Chinese people appear to be more willing, in terms of their percentage frequency, to eat out alone than other nationalities[4]. The theory of reasoned action has offered some insight into eating behaviour, although this line of research has been fraught with problems. The applications of this theory to complex behaviour, especially those that require some form of planning, are particularly problematic for the model. Eating behaviour can include a conscious assessment process to the decision to express specific behaviours and therefore must consider additional factors outside of those offered by this theoretical framework.

The third and final types of beliefs involve the important underlying perceptions about *control*. Basically, it is the personality characteristics and current state, including aspects of mood, of the individual that feed into their perceived behavioural control of a specific behaviour. The addition of control beliefs constitutes the theory of planned behaviour (see Figure 6.3). The theory of reasoned action concerns behaviours that are relatively simple to perform. The behaviour must be easy enough that no assessment of one's ability takes place. Therefore, the theory of reasoned action relates to behaviours and food choices that are relatively abundant and easily obtained. Any behaviour that requires a more complex assessment in terms of obtaining the food item will require some form of planning. In the planning stage of the behaviour, an assessment is necessary of the successful completion of the behaviour. The determinants of this assessment will be the ability and the perceived control one has over the situation.

Research on the theory of planned behaviour has almost exclusively focused on the adoption of healthy-eating behaviour. The relative differences in accountability for actual behaviour between the theory of planned behaviour and the theory of reasoned action suggest that the addition of control beliefs adds an extra 12 per cent (Armitage & Conner, 2001). The theory of planned behaviour, like the theory of reasoned action, has also been related to similar eating behaviours with assessments of fat intake (Paisley & Sparks, 1998), short-term healthy eating (Povey et al., 1998) and long-term healthy eating (Conner et al., 2002). This research has shown that the theory of planned behaviour is a good model for predicting behaviour in both the short and the long term. Despite this, the theory of planned behaviour only predicts about 40% of behaviour, leaving 60 per cent unexplained. Moreover, there appears to be differential accountability depending on the 'type' of healthy-

---

[4] American, Italian, Japanese and Chinese participants took part in this study.

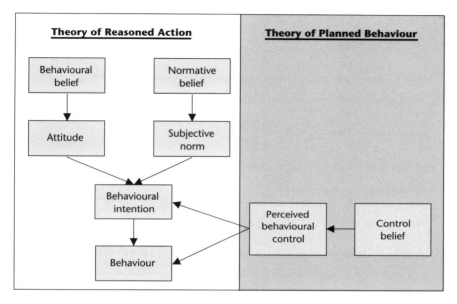

Figure 6.3   The theory of planned behaviour.

eating behaviour. Fat, fruit and vegetable intake appears to fit better within this theory than other healthy-eating targets such as fibre intake.

Each of the belief components defined by the theory of planned behaviour and the theory of reasoned action can be represented mathematically in the same way as attitudes (see Figure 6.4). These can then be combined to gain a mathematical representation of behaviour. This mathematical model is important, as it allows for a complete quantification of behaviour. Unfortunately, this is not an exact science and must consider the inter-individual differences between people or, in mathematical terms, the error inherent in the equation. Therefore, it is geared towards a relationship-type approach. This approach means that the theory of planned behaviour model cannot totally predict behaviour; however, it can provide an indication of what are the most important aspects in the behaviour and evaluate how accurate they are at predicting it.

The final addition to the social cognition theory of food choice is the theory of trying (theoretically similar to the health action process approach) (see Figure 6.5). This aspect essentially replaces the 'behavioural intention' and 'behaviour' part in the theory of reasoned action and theory of planned behaviour. The theory of trying is related to weight control rather than eating behaviour, although weight control requires the conscious control of food selection through awareness about calorific content. Components to this theory include self-efficacy, outcome expectancies and the emotional assessment of performing the task required. Unlike the previous two theories, the theory

$$\text{Attitude or } (A) \propto \sum_{i=1}^{n} b_i e_i$$

where $\propto$ = proportional to, Σ = sum of, b = outcome belief, e = evaluation of belief,

i = one specific belief, n = number of beliefs.

$$\text{Subjective norm or } (SN) \propto \sum_{j=1}^{n} s_j M_j$$

where j = other people or person, s_j = pressure from others to perform behaviour (social),

M_j = motivation to comply with others.

$$\text{Perceived behavioural control or } (PBC) \propto \sum_{k=1}^{n} r_k P_k$$

where k = one factor associated with control, c_k = the belief that a factor associated with

control will occur, p_k = ratio between positive or negative factors which come together

to create the potential power of control.

$\text{Theory of planned behaviour or } TPB = (w_1 A + w_2 SN + w_3 PBC) + w_4 PBC$

where w = specific regression weight.

Figure 6.4   Mathematical representation of the theory of planned behaviour.

of trying offers the additional factor of the pleasantness of the task. Self-efficacy is a component of perceived behavioural control and outcome expectancies are related to attitudes and behavioural beliefs. With the replacement of behavioural intention and behaviour, the theory of trying extends the process to include whether or not the individual is successful. This takes the process beyond the simple act of intention equals behaviour to include some of the cognitive processes of problem-solving. It is not only the intention that is required in complex decision-making processes, but also the individual's decision about how they are going to perform the behaviour (Bagozzi, 1992). As Bagozzi and Edwards (2000) suggest, 'three self-regulatory appraisal processes that function either additively or interactively to determine one's choice of means to an end, depending on the ease or difficulty in implementing goal-directed or instrumental behaviours'. Increasing the complexity of the intention behaviour process may, in time, offer an additional accountability within the food choice model; however, as the original components to the theory

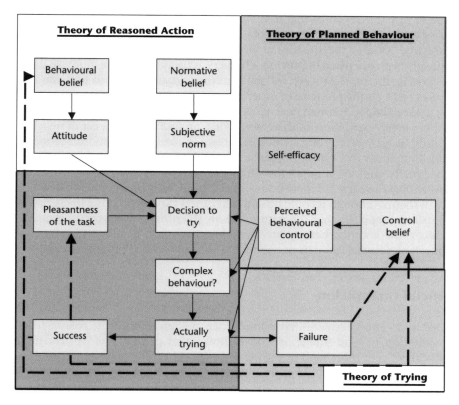

Figure 6.5   The theory of trying.

focus on the interaction between intention and behaviour the theory is limited to those behaviours that are complex to perform. The theoretical strength of this approach may help in the performance of behaviours that are more long term in nature. Therefore, its role in food choice in the short term (i.e. one meal) may be limited. However, this long-term approach may help to explain how beliefs may alter in the longer term[5].

Social situational factors: the effect of others when eating

Thought processes have a marked impact on behaviour; however, it is important to remember that not all aspects of eating, either in one meal or over a longer period, are conscious in nature. All behaviour incorporates the more

---

[5] This is shown by the dashed arrows in Figure 6.5.

latent situational factors that have no conscious elements to them. It is all too easy to assume that humans are totally cerebral in their choices. This is simply not true. One of the situational effects that can alter food intake, and has already been discussed in previous chapters, is palatability. The more palatable a food is, the more of it we will eat. Another situational factor that can also affect eating is the presence of other people.

According to Herman et al. (2003), other people can affect an individual's eating behaviour in one of three ways. First, an individual can eat more when eating as part of a group, which is known as social facilitation. Second, if the individual eats with another person, he or she can model behaviour – essentially copy or emulate the other person's eating behaviour. Third, the individual can eat less if there is someone else watching them rather than eating with them. Although it could be said that others can affect eating in every way possible, it appears that the nature of how the others interact with the individual who is eating has a relatively stable effect on how they will eat. Let us now look at social facilitation, modelling and impression management in turn.

Social facilitation

De Castro and colleagues have done extensive research on the role of social facilitation in food intake and have shown that participants will consume 40–50 per cent more food in the presence of others (de Castro et al., 1990; de Castro, 1991, 1994; Bellisle et al., 1999). It has been suggested that social facilitation leads to eating more; however, it would appear that the 'type' of 'others' has an effect on the magnitude of how much more the individual will eat. If the 'others' are not members of the individual's family, it is less likely they will have an impact (de Castro, 1994). Hetherington et al. (2006) also found that eating with friends had a marked effect on the amount eaten, while eating with strangers only had a marginal effect compared with eating alone. Differences between the sexes are also apparent within this interaction. Females appear to eat more when part of a couple, while males tend to eat more when with friends (Salvy et al., 2007). As well as the 'quality' of the people eating, the 'quantity' of people also appears to have an effect on the amount of food consumed. The more people that are eating together, the more food each person will consume. This is not a proportional relationship though, as each additional person added to the group has an exponentially smaller impact compared with the last.

The evidence to date suggests that the effects of social facilitation on eating behaviour follow quite closely with the rules of social impact theory. This theory assumes that that an individual's feelings, attitudes and behaviours can be manipulated by the presence of others. The theory comprises three factors and the 'impact' it has on behaviour can be summed up by the perceived closeness to the group (proximity) or how 'connected' the individual feels to the group and the members within it. The evidence from social facilitation research would suggest that social impact theory has a very strong effect on an individual's eating behaviour; however, limited research has explored directly the impact of this form of social influence. Although eating behaviour may not have been investigated directly using this model, drinking behaviour has (Pedersen et al., 2008). Preliminary evidence suggests that larger group sizes have a much larger impact than smaller ones. When group size interacts with connectedness, the effect of the smaller group appears to strengthen. This postulation would be consistent with social facilitation research in eating behaviour, as additional people increase the amount of food consumed and the presence of family members and friends has a marked effect, especially for males.

The way that social facilitation appears to increase food intake is by increasing the amount of time a meal lasts (Pliner et al., 2006). This is known as the time-extension hypothesis (de Castro, 1990), whereby the additional people increase the length of the meal through the socializing that occurs during the meal compared with when eating alone. The increased time spent around the table increases individuals' exposure to food and its cues and so they overeat.

Modelling

Social influence does not always lead to overeating. Through the use of confederates[6], experimenters have shown that social influence can decrease food intake as well as increase it (Nisbett & Storms, 1974). In this early study, it was shown that when the confederate ate less so did the participant, compared with when the participant ate alone. Furthermore, when the confederate ate more so did the participant. Several researchers have replicated this finding but have also added some caveats to the relative strength of the confederate on the participant's eating behaviour. The original study by Nisbett and Storms (1974) found that the confederate only affected participants of normal weight, while both overweight and underweight participants remained unaffected. Moreover, the confederate must be present and eating alongside the participant, as simply informing the participant that others ate more or less does not appear to affect their eating behaviour (Roth et al., 2001). Conger et al. (1980) offered another caveat based on the sex of the confederate. They suggested that the confederate has to be a suitable person for the participant to model. For example, males will not emulate a female confederate as they

---

[6] Confederates are individuals who are brought into the experiment to manipulate the social interactions between participants. They know the hypothesis of the experiment and will perform the same predetermined behaviour in each of the tests.

expect them to eat less, while children tend to rely more on 'connectedness' to the confederate for an effect to be observed (Salvy et al., 2008). The interaction of a female participant with the confederate appears to be more complicated. Several studies have shown that the attractiveness or 'slimness' of the confederate appears to have an interactive effect with the amount consumed (Salvy et al., 2007; Hermans et al., 2008). If the confederate is thin, they are less likely to be copied in the overeating condition. To further reiterate the power of the modelling effect, Goldman et al. (1991) showed that even participants who had not eaten for 24 hours were still susceptible to modelling effects. This suggests that the social influences are much stronger for short-term food intake than biological influences in well-nourished individuals.

Little is known about the theoretical underpinning of modelling behaviour within eating. The only real explanation offered to date has been that the participant matches the confederate to increase their potential social acceptance and self-image (Roth et al., 2001). Therefore, if the confederate is someone who is an acceptable model, and the participant wishes to impress upon them or the experimenters, they adhere to both social norms and eat similar or less than the model. For females, this is further complicated by the perceived body image of the confederate. Restrictive eating[7] as a feminine social impression appears to be the norm among female participants and even the thin confederate overeating cannot alter this.

Impression management and social judgement

Impression management is the attempt by the individual to control the views of other members of the group through socially acceptable behaviour even if they do not habitually express such behaviour. To control one's social impression, (1) there must be a set of socially held stereotypes, which (2) one must be aware of, and (3) be motivated to adhere to. All behaviour has a stereotypical correlate, including eating behaviour. In terms of the socially held stereotypes around food and eating behaviour, Vartanian et al. (2007) sum up the concepts well under the titles of you are *what* and *how much* you eat. In essence, other people will judge us on the type and amount of food we eat. Each aspect of these stereotypical judgement criteria is underpinned by socially held gender, appeal and health beliefs.

Gender stereotypes encompassing definitions of self by *what* is eaten are bound in the social beliefs about what is a 'good'[8] and 'bad' food. Diets that are

---

[7] Restrictive eating is discussed in detail in Chapter 7.

[8] Usually determined by its fat content, with less fat being considered a good food item; however, this is slowly changing as the general population becomes increasingly aware of what constitutes a healthy diet.

indicative of foods that are low in fat are generally considered to be more feminine diets, while masculine diets more often than not contain foods higher in fat. Moreover, the stereotype appears to be stronger in females than males (Oates & Slotterback, 2004). Therefore, the definition of self through food within the social group appears to be more dominant in females than males, suggesting that food plays a much more important role in female rather than male identity. The effect of food stereotypes and the observations of what others eat also appear to transfer into a more global view of an individual. By eating foods that are considered 'good' within a social group, an individual will be considered to have other positive attributes that make them more socially appealing. People who eat 'good' foods are associated with being more attractive, likeable and moral (Stein & Nemeroff, 1995). However, the situation is not completely straightforward, as there appears to be some self-defence mechanisms to prohibit associations with people who eat 'good' foods. Although people will universally associate the 'good' foods with morality, some people will not choose to associate themselves with those that eat 'good' foods (Mooney & Amico, 2000). These 'good' food eaters are also associated with being unhappy and antisocial compared with individuals who eat high fat foods (Barker et al., 1999). It would appear from this research that food selection has an impact on social perceptions. Specific foods are stereotypically associated with gender and attractiveness. Therefore, it is important to consider that when someone is eating in a social context, they will alter their behaviour according to perceived social pressures, especially if the food has a high fat content. The reason they do this is to ensure that others will view them in an acceptable, socially attractive way.

The *how much* stereotypes also consider gender and social appeal remits. As expected, eating smaller amounts is associated with more feminine roles (Chaiken & Pliner, 1987). What would perhaps be less expected is that masculinity is not judged by how much is eaten. Unfortunately, therefore, gender stereotypes are specific to females. Following the early work of Chaiken and Pliner (1987), several studies have explored gender stereotypes and meal sizes but the findings have been inconsistent. More research is required in this area before firm conclusions can be drawn. Due to the specificity of the gender stereotype to females, social appeal has focused on female physical attractiveness (Chaiken & Pliner, 1987). In terms of relative importance of meal size on female attractiveness, it would appear that it only has an effect when the target person is not in the room (Basow & Kobrynowicz, 1993). This is to be expected, as the participant may be inferring long-term behaviours of food intake and therefore body shape from the size of the meal. When the person is in the room, they will be able to judge attractiveness based on the direct measure of physical appearance.

If someone is aware of these social stereotypes, it would be expected for them to portray them in group situations. Although the research is very limited on this topic, it is evident that the process is a little more complex than the simple social desirable belief equals behaviour expressed. This is because it is not always favourable to portray gender-specific roles in all social situations. In terms of attractiveness to the opposite sex, portraying a feminine eating style may be positive, but in a business or social environment it can be perceived as weak and of a lower social status (Vartanian et al., 2007). It is therefore important that the individual judges the social situation accurately and that not all situations require the same portrayal of stereotypical gender roles. One thing that is certain about stereotypical behaviour and impression management is that, compared with other research, it is poorly represented in the literature. A lot more research is required, especially in terms of social interactions and the decision to portray gender-specific behaviours, before anything definitive can be offered about this field of research. It is likely that this research will become much more convoluted in the future with many other additional factors being considered in this aspect of eating behaviour.

Media influences

One of the main ways that stereotypes are perpetuated throughout modern society is through the media. The popular misconception is that the media is to blame for these beliefs. Simply put, the media is in the business of selling products, just like any other business. They are also the largest target and all too often take the blame for causing disordered eating behaviour. The stereotypes that are portrayed in the media, especially those concerning body image, are not their own creation; rather, they are views held by the general population. If anything, the media are guilty of perpetuating and reinforcing these stereotypes. Although they are not responsible for the stereotypical behaviour itself, it could be argued that they have the strongest influence on social behaviour. Images and models of acceptable social behaviour are taken from all forms of media[9]. Companies that wish to exploit this influence can do so through the use of advertising. Mass marketing strategies can quickly alter people's perceptions about food products and can create a desire to want them. This can have a direct influence on the individual's food choice or it can influence a group's decision-making behaviour through making the food item an object of social appeal, where having and consuming the food in a group context contributes to the positive impression.

Before considering the effects of media on eating behaviour, it is worth noting that some effects that have been previously attributed to the media are confounded by factors intrinsic to the process. For example, Hetherington

[9] Forms of media include, but are not limited to, television, radio and periodicals (such as newspapers and magazines).

et al. (2006) showed that just watching TV during a meal could increase food intake even if the content of the programming contained no reference to food[10]. Furthermore, TV viewing is a sedentary behaviour and thus affects the energy output side of the energy balance equation, which in turn increases the likelihood of weight gain (Viner & Cole, 2005). Despite the effect of TV viewing on overall individual energy use, this form of media has been shown to alter children's eating behaviour and specific food requests. This has been assumed through the effect of advertising to children rather than the TV viewing in general. Increased TV viewing can affect food choice, as those who watch it have been shown to eat less fruit and vegetables and eat more snacks (Boynton-Jarrett et al., 2003; Matheson et al., 2004). It would be expected that exposure to adverts manipulates food preferences through branding of a food product and then associating the brand with positive outcomes. This is not the entire story, however. In a series of experiments, Halford et al. (2004b, 2007, 2008b, 2008c) have shown that exposing children to food adverts increases food intake irrespective of the adverts' content. This 'beyond-brand' effect is postulated to work through the advert being a food cue and leads to a desire to eat all similar foods, rather than a desire to eat the specific food item advertised, especially in the case of young children. Children do not understand the advert as a product and the desire to eat the product is a misunderstanding that the name of the product itself is not related to all similar foods. For example, a TV advertisement for a burger by a fast-food chain elicits desire for all burgers and not the specific product. Therefore, the child may demand a specific brand of burger but be placated with any burger. It is not until concrete associations of a particular product are made with 'treats', toys or positive social appeal that the branded product itself is desired. Furthermore, it is important to remember that children's categorization approaches are quite rigid and therefore the replacement product would also have to look similar to the desired advertised product.

Although many intrinsic factors could be considered to contribute to increased energy intake, these factors are not true for all people and ages. The principal aim of the advertising industry is to manipulate the target audience's perceptions and/or attitudes towards the product in question; however, it is possible to alter subjective norms through advertising. The direct approach is to advertise to adults and change their beliefs about continuing to use a specific brand, to switch to a new brand or to inform the potential customers of additional uses of a brand (i.e. to get them to use more of it). This approach is likely to alter behaviour through the theory of reasoned action. Altering the individual's attitude about a specific food item can have repercussions for food preferences (Coon & Tucker, 2002) and can eventually lead to a distrust of food items that are not of a specific brand. In fact, the *Wall Street*

---

[10] This is likely to be through a process of disinhibition, which will be considered in Chapter 7.

Journal found that the branding of food is the most important factor on deciding between food items. This would suggest that all foods that are not branded are not even considered. This effect is not specific to eating behaviour, as it has an important role in all forms of purchasing, but it does have a profound effect on it. Nearly every item in a supermarket is available in a branded and unbranded version. In the majority of cases, and particularly for those brands that have been around for many years, the branded versions outsell the unbranded versions by many fold in terms of the number of products sold as well as total revenue received. In fact, the brand can become so entrenched in the social psyche that the name of the brand replaces the name of the product. For example, many people use brand-specific words such as Coke™ for cola drink, Wotsits™ for corn cheese snack, Bisto™ for gravy granules and Oxo™ cube for concentrated beef stock. This list is not exhaustive and will vary between nations and markets.

The media do not just have a direct effect on eating behaviour through the manipulation of attitudes towards the product. They can also have an indirect effect through the perpetuation of stereotypical images of beauty. Although the reason that advertising agencies use 'beautiful' people is in order not to divert attention from the product to the model, the constant use of this tactic over the decades has left society with a rather narrow view of what constitutes beauty. Although this view is unlikely to have been created by industry, it has perpetuated it. Currently, we have an unhealthy, and arguably pathological, social schema about the perfect body image. Body image concerns lead inexorably to alteration in food choice and preferences. Size-related fixations on specific body parts, either being too small or too big, will lead to a desire to gain weight or restrictive dietary practices (dieting[11]).

Body image

Having and displaying a 'good' body image is the ultimate in impression management. Individuals with a socially determined preferable body image will be sexually desired and, as a result, will be associated with positive attributes. They will have many friends and will be successful in many, if not all, aspects of their lives. Our bodies are quickly and easily analysed by others and, rightly or wrongly, can be used as a tool to interpret what the person's personality is like and even what their values are. Being associated with or actually being considered physically attractive is a social marker for success, and as a marker it will attract success. As discussed already in this chapter, having a thin body image is an expression of control and intelligence. Currently, mainstream society considers being lean and having few obvious signs of fat tissue to be

---

[11] Discussed later in the book.

desirable attributes. This has not always been the case. Evidence from prehis-
tory[12] suggests that being obese was considered attractive, and through the cen-
turies every possible image has been held up as an object of desire. Most
emphasis, in terms of body image, has been placed on the female form. This has
led some authors to suggest that it is a female-specific phenomenon; however,
although arguably to a lesser extent, men have also been subject to body image
alterations. While female body image concerns have been targeted towards
being smaller, those of males have been towards being bigger – bigger in terms of
muscle mass and height rather than perceptually heavier. It would appear that
body image changes over time and, more importantly, tends to be unachievable
and incongruent with the current environmental demands. In times of few
resources, humans associate being larger with attractiveness, and in times of
plenty being lean is held up to be desirable. This incongruence between
environment and human views of attraction could be argued to be pathological.
It is inherently unachievable and with perceptions of social self-worth being
dependent on the portrayal of a good body image, it may lead to individuals
engaging in dangerous behaviours in the attempt to achieve such an image.
Basically, the ideal is simply unachievable for the vast majority of the population
(Cusumano & Thompson, 1997). The only reason it could not be considered
pathological and therefore abnormal is the simple fact that we all share it.

The role of body image within eating behaviour has primarily focused on
the propensity to diet because of dissatisfaction. Although body dissatisfaction
is considered by many as a strong driver for food choice, very few studies have
explored this in detail. Those studies that have investigated food choice in
participants who are dissatisfied with their bodies have found that these individuals have consistently healthier food choices in terms of their consumption
of fruits and vegetables (Contento et al., 2003). However, even these studies
found it difficult to discern the primary reason for the alteration in food
choice. It is reasonable to assume that the individual who is dissatisfied with
their body is attempting to rectify this by dieting; however, such a direct
measure is notably absent within the literature. Due to the lack of evidence on
this subject, the rest of this subsection offers an introduction to the drivers
behind body dissatisfaction. Interested readers on this topic should refer to
Grogen (1999) for a more detailed examination of body image and dissatisfaction beyond its relation to eating behaviour.

The holistic approaches to body image whereby individuals judge themselves as meeting the right body image or not are important to eating behaviour.
Research has shown that females tend to focus on chests (to be bigger), stomach, hips, thighs, bottoms and overall silhouette (all to be smaller); while males
are more concerned with arms, chests, shoulders (all to be bigger), stomachs
and overall silhouette (to be smaller) (Ogden & Taylor, 2000). The only option

---

[12] For example, the Venus of Willendorf.

available to alter one's appearance without resorting to surgical procedures is to alter current energy balance. Adverts aimed at altering the energy balance are invariably produced and employed by the diet industry. These adverts always appear to suggest that altering body size, shape or even specific areas of dissatisfaction is relatively easy to accomplish (Brownell, 1991). This portrayal will, even if inadvertently, suggest that those who are overweight should feel ashamed, while those who are not should believe that it is easy to lose weight. Restricting the amount of calories consumed is commonly used as a strategy to lose weight for both sexes. Women tend to diet more than men, with the majority of women partaking in a diet at some point in their lives. Men, in contrast, tend to engage in exercise to improve body image, although many will also alter or restrict their diet. Grogen (1999) has suggested that the primary reason for exercise is not to be healthier, but to lose weight or improve muscle tone or mass.

Body dissatisfaction is influenced by a number of factors outside of the media. These include low self-esteem (Ghaderi & Scott, 2001), depression (Stice et al., 2004a) and more socially derived influences such as friendship groups (Hutchinson & Rapee, 2007) and peers (Stice, 1998). In terms of the effect of social groups on body dissatisfaction, it would appear that friendship groups provide a protective role for females: friends provide an additional comparison source, as well as the socially held representation of body image. However, it does appear that other less desirable behaviours around eating are shared among friendship groups. Females who do not have large friendship groups are more likely to adhere to the media representation and be more dissatisfied with their bodies.

Most research in this area has focused on Caucasian women. Therefore, other ethnic groups and males are somewhat under-represented within the body image literature and theory. Early researchers suggested that women of African descent had fewer body image concerns and tended to be heavier (Abrams et al., 1993). Later studies on these and other ethnic groups have shown this not to be the case. Lee (1993) showed that Chinese women are concerned about their body image. This has been taken further to suggest that other ethnic groups may be at increased risk of body image dissatisfaction (Robinson et al., 1996; Field et al., 1997; Sjostedt et al., 1998). The differences between these groups may be related to the complex social situation that ethnic groups have within the Western world. It could be the case that studying ethnicity effects within a society that has one predominant ethnic group is different from studying the same ethnic group in another country where they are not the dominant group. It would be the case that studying ethnic minorities within a society that has one predominant ethnic group is different from studying the same ethnic minority group in another country where they are the dominant group. These discrepancies could therefore be a result of cultural or religious differences.

Cultural/religious impacts on eating behaviour

The final aspect to affect eating behaviour within a social remit is culture/religion. Both culture and religion inevitably affect an individual's self-identity. These two factors provide the individual with a set of ethical and value-based criteria of what behaviour is and is not acceptable. The obvious effect of religion is the prohibiting of specific foods or preparation methods within eating behaviour. This ideological belief about specific foods or food types restricts food consumption in a variety of ways, from not eating during certain periods of the year or times of the day to enforcing the selection of specific foods. The impact of culture and religion does not stop with ideological beliefs about specific foods. These factors also impact on other aspects, such as body image/dissatisfaction, which can indirectly affect food intake and feelings of self-worth. Previous investigations have focused on the ethnicity of the participant; however, this is arguably a crude measure of cultural or religious beliefs (Kim, 2007). These ideologies extend beyond the ethnic or skin colour domains and are more likely to affect behaviour than these rather simplistic categorizations of people. A lot of evidence has shown that Western cultures differ little in terms of their eating behaviour compared with other less Westernized regions. Furthermore, differences that have been observed within ethnic minorities in Western countries are likely due to the amalgamation of religion and culture or two separate cultures rather than being anything to do with skin colour. It has been shown that religion is a much better predictor of weight beliefs (Kim et al., 2003) and risk of eating disorders (Smith et al., 2004) than ethnic divides. Essentially, in the same way as friendship groups may provide protection from the societal views of body image and eating behaviour, the value-based norms that religion provides to its adherents may also protect the individual from dissatisfaction with their weight status or perceived body image. It may even go as far as preaching acceptance through the body's functional role rather than as a social judgement of the individual.

Data from research conducted on religion and eating behaviour/body image offer some interesting insights into the protective role that this socio-cultural factor has. Women with greater religious commitment[13] and men with greater religious application[14] appear most likely to underestimate their body weight (Kim, 2007). It also appears that the commitment to religion for women in particular provides a strong protective role for disturbed views about weight (Kim, 2006). Unfortunately, much of the research on religion and eating behaviour, like most research in psychology, has focused on Christianity and its various denominations. Therefore, there is a need for

---

[13] How important religion is to someone's life.
[14] How important religion is in making everyday decisions in daily life.

research into other religious convictions as well as less officially recognized spiritual beliefs. It is highly likely that this field of research will expand hugely over the next decade, as religion appears to have a much stronger effect than other sociocultural factors.

Summary

The effect that social cognitive factors have on eating behaviours, especially the role of 'others' in food selection and intake, is profound. To avoid social judgements, a person may completely alter their behaviour socially compared with when they are alone. To understand the relative effects of social factors on eating behaviour, we must understand the component parts of the decision-making process. This can be summed up rather well within the theory of reasoned action and its various theoretical expansions. The most important components to social eating within these approaches is the attitudes the individual has about a specific food, the perceived social pressure they feel about eating it and whether they feel they have the ability to obtain and consume the food item.

In the presence of other people, the individual will usually overeat. Factors that predict whether the person will overeat include whether the person knows and feels an attachment to those people they are with, their sex and whether they feel they have to please the other person. In a social environment, the individual will feel they have to manage their social image and whether or not the other people will judge them on what or how much they are eating. To avoid negative judgements, people tailor their eating behaviour. If other people in the social group are eating smaller portion sizes, it is likely that the target person will do so too. Which foods are chosen in a group setting, as well as the size of the portions, will be dictated by social stereotypes often perpetuated by the media through targeted advertising. The type of friendship group and/or religious conviction an individual has can confer some protection from these social stereotypes.

Drawing this chapter to a close completes our exploration of the different individual aspects or psychological components to eating behaviour. In the remainder of this book, we will explore the holistic interaction between these various independent components to psychology when people are confronted with food. In the next chapter, the focus will be on 'types' of eaters. The concepts explored in this chapter will combine the various core aspects of psychology to offer the reader an insight into how people react and interact with their food.

7 Getting inside people's heads
Restraint, emotional eating, disinhibition and their combined effects

So far in this book we have looked at the effect of various core areas of psychology on eating behaviour. Although interesting to the academic and practitioner of psychology, and which with the right interpretation could be incorporated into a wider theoretical context, it does not really fulfil the layperson's expectations about a person's thought processes when they are thinking about, or confronted with, food. It is the interaction between all of the core areas of psychology that offers a better explanation of the process of eating. The cumulative effect of the psychological-related disciplines is likely to offer the most insight into the process. Most eating behaviour research has been conducted with adults, particularly young adults and their interaction with their food.

The information considered in the previous chapters should not be seen as separate from the concepts presented here; rather, it should be thought of as the foundation on which they are based. When the average layperson talks about food, they might say: 'I spend a lot of time thinking about the content of my food'; 'When I am down I just eat'; 'I am eating away and I get to the end of my meal and I cannot remember eating it all or that I was near the end of it'. All of these statements refer to specific phenomena in this field of study. Adults' interactions with food can be broadly categorized into three groups: dietary restraint, emotional eating and disinhibition.

Dietary restraint refers to the concepts around the purposeful restriction of food intake or calorie intake to control one's image or prohibit weight gain (Herman & Mack, 1975). In essence, it is the premature termination of eating before the full activation of the physiological feedback processes of satiation. This process is about what individuals think they should eat and the quantity they should eat it in rather than what their body is telling them they need to consume. Of course, this thought process shares similarities with eating disorders, especially anorexia nervosa, but it is important not to confuse this concept with pathological behaviour. Instead, it is more accurate to consider dietary restraint on a continuum of behaviour. At one extreme are those individuals with a restrictive form of anorexia nervosa and at the other are individuals that rely totally on biological feedback processes of satiation and satiety to control their food intake. In reality, most people employ, to a greater or lesser extent, some form of psychological processes to limit food intake. Dietary restraint is exercised by all of us to some extent and without it we could not respond to the environmental pressures around food intake. In evolutionary terms, restraint theory allows the individual not to consume too much if resources are not abundantly available. In the West today, we do not experience the scarcity of food resources that our ancestors were confronted with. Instead, restraint is now used to limit food intake to preserve or improve social identity, maintain body image and therefore adhere to current societal views of beauty, as well as being the most common form of weight-loss strategy.

Emotional eating refers to eating because of alterations in mood. In short, it is the attempt to improve or stabilize mood through eating. Such individuals experience intense emotions in response to most food and mood-related stimuli (Heaven et al., 2001). These people will eat when feeling 'down', anxious or self-conscious. Although emotional eating is usually associated with negative mood, there is evidence of over-consumption during positive moods (Cools et al., 1992), especially when restraint is incorporated alongside emotional eating.

Disinhibition or *disinhibited eating* refers to an individual's 'distractibility' from their food or the amount they are eating. The classic example of disinhibited behaviour is eating popcorn while watching a film. When watching a film, people consume large amounts of popcorn without consciously realizing how much they are eating; this is because the film requires all of their attentional resources. Without consciously attending to their food, people do not register how much they are consuming.

These three concepts dominate this area of research and indeed provide the cornerstones to eating behaviour in adults. It is unlikely that a research paper on eating behaviour will not consider at least one of the three concepts. Here, we consider them in depth. However, these psychological components do not act independently. Everyone has an individually set level of all of these and it is their combination that predicts food choice and the amount consumed. And they are not all-or-nothing concepts; rather, they should be considered on a continuum. At one end we have disordered individuals, while at the other we have those that do not think about these concepts at all when around food. Both extremes are quite rare. Most people sit midway along this continuum.

Dietary restraint

Dietary restraint is a complex behaviour. Although it is the attempt to restrict or control food intake, it is often used to predict over-consumption rather than under-consumption. This prediction may seem incongruent, as it is contradictory to the individual's intentions. However, the best way to understand this concept is to explore its overarching theory – the Boundary Model. The seminal work of Herman and Polivy (1984) offers insight into the perceptions of hunger and fullness in different types of people. In this theory, the referents were initially based on dieters and non-dieters; however, this was later expanded to refer to 'restrained' eaters. In essence, individuals who have high levels of dietary restraint, such as individuals who are trying to lose weight through calorie restriction, impose almost unachievable goals regarding their food intake.

The Boundary Model suggests that 'normal' eaters – who have no pathology or self-imposed rules around food intake – respond to their physiological needs regarding energy and digestion. They are comfortable with waiting until they are hungry and eat when they feel they need to. Once they have started a meal, they will eat until they feel full and then stop. This response to eating does not change – each eating episode follows a similar pattern. If a preload[1] challenges their hunger and fullness systems, it will have comparatively little effect on their food intake during a meal. What this means is that if the individual is given an appetizer of some kind, their subjective feelings of fullness will compensate for the additional energy intake and they will eat less accordingly. Furthermore, the normal person has some flexibility in their 'boundaries' that allows them to eat when less hungry and, at times, to eat more than they normally would. People who place self-imposed rules on the amount of energy they consume are said to be 'dieting'. The successful adherence to these rules requires some form of cognitive interference with the natural progression of fullness within an eating episode. This interference is based on some form of hyper-awareness about the calorific content of the food being eaten, as well as some restriction on the types of food eaten. Therefore, this process is about both food selection and the amount consumed within a meal. Selection will be along the lines of 'good' and 'bad' foods, and the categorization of a food item will be based on whether or not the item violates individually self-imposed rules. To ensure that they do not perceptually 'overeat', dieters psychologically control the termination of their meals without adhering to subjective feelings of fullness (McLean & Barr, 2003). Moreover, they are likely to ignore feelings of hunger for longer periods than 'normal' eaters. If dieters are challenged by a forced violation of their diets, they will overeat through what is termed 'counter-regulation'. Here, the dieter will violate all of their rules during that meal and eat until they feel full. However, because they are often in a slightly energy-depleted physiological state, they will consume more than the average person (see Figure 7.1). Irrespective of whether they are disordered or not, it is

---

[1] Preloads are often liquid-based 'starters' given before a test meal and will, because of the calorific content of the drink, purposely violate the restrained eater's self-imposed rules.

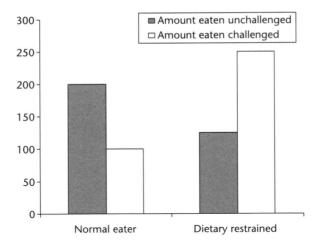

Figure 7.1   Response of dieters to preloads.

the presence or absence of dieting rules, and variations in perceptions of hunger and fullness as well as when satiation and satiety are reached that differentiate eaters.

Dietary-restrained individuals act in a similar way to those on a diet. Because such individuals use cognitive rules to regulate their food intake, a variety of scenarios, such as distraction[2], can lead them to overeat. Other factors that will lead dietary-restrained individuals to violate their 'diets' include the consumption of alcohol, social pressure and larger portion sizes.

Recent advances in our understanding of dietary restraint suggest that not all people who share this behaviour express it in the same way. For some individuals, the rules they use are flexible and they are able to respond to the various environmental or emotional situations they find themselves in. They can compensate for overeating one day by restricting intake on another. Such individuals are referred to as flexible restrainers. The flexibility in their dietary restraint protects them from the negative consequences, such as feelings of failure, brought about by perceptually violating their 'diets'. Other dietary restrainers are less flexible in their approach to their dietary rules and are thus known as 'rigid' restrainers. Rigid restrainers view their rules as all-important and any violation is likely to be considered a personal failure irrespective of the reason for the violation. The rigid approach to dietary restraint and eating defines those at risk of overeating and most likely to respond to factors that will allow them to violate their diets (Westenhoefer, 1991). In effect, the difference between flexible and rigid restrainers is the way they perceive their

---

[2] This would be considered part of disinhibition and will be discussed later in the chapter.

rules. For rigid restrainers, the rules are all-or-nothing self-defining regulations to their eating; they are to be upheld at all costs and during every meal. Flexible restrainers, in contrast, view their rules as general long-term guidance to their eating behaviour. Flexible individuals view their eating behaviour over the long term rather than focusing on each and every meal.

Being flexible about dietary restraint appears to be important in avoiding developing eating pathology and being successful at losing weight (Pudel & Westenhoefer, 1992; Smith et al., 1999); however, there are negative consequences associated with this behavioural trait. Individuals who exhibit high levels of dietary restraint have been found to experience greater depression (Dewberry & Ussher, 1994) and lower self-esteem (Gendall et al., 1998). They are also less emotionally stable (Tiggermann, 1994), more preoccupied with their body image (Geschwind et al., 2008) and are more easily distracted (Herman et al., 1978). Increasingly, dietary restraint has been linked with smoking and continual dieting. Highly dietary-restrained individuals often use nicotine to limit food intake (Mitchell & Perkins, 1998) and are habitual dieters (Weinstein et al., 1997). Interestingly, dietary restraint has also been reported to be a stable cognition in children (Hill & Pallin, 1998) and has been shown to be a contributing factor in over-consumption in younger people (Roemmich et al., 2002), suggesting that this concept may be comparable to a personality trait. All of these negative associations with dietary restraint suggest that the individual who has this behavioural trait will fail to adhere to their own dietary rules.

Recently, research has suggested that there may be problems with the concept of dietary restraint. These problems stem from the way dietary restraint is measured. In the published research, three different psychometric questionnaires are employed to measure dietary restraint: the Restraint Scale, the Three Factor Eating Questionnaire Restraint subscale (TFEQ-R) and the Dutch Eating Behaviour Questionnaire Restraint subscale (DEBQ-R). Each questionnaire measures the same alleged psychological construct, but they do so in different ways. The Restraint Scale focuses on chronic levels of dieting, the DEBQ-R investigates how often the individual employs weight loss or maintenance behaviours, and the TFEQ-R explores the same areas as the DEBQ-R but also includes the importance of thinness and body image concerns. Thus it is likely that differences between study findings may be due to differences in the measures used to define people as restrained or not. Indeed, in the field of dietary restraint it has been shown that none of these scales may be very reliable at assessing this concept (Stice et al., 2004b). It is also noteworthy that these scales predict weight gain, whereas individuals who say they are 'on a diet' exhibit weight loss. Therefore, if the premise is that those who are dietary restrained gain weight, then these scales are valid at differentiating dieters from those who are restrained. Perhaps the situation could be resolved if we view these individuals not as 'dietary restrained' but as having intentions of restricting food intake while also at risk of not being able to do so.

Emotional eaters

In Chapter 2, it was shown that eating food, especially food that we find palatable, gives us a 'feel good' boost by the release of endogenous opioids. Therefore, eating food can have a direct effect on our moods. Nearly everyone learns the mood-enhancing property of foods at an early stage in their life. Some people may come to rely on this effect and may learn to eat when they are feeling down or anxious. Eating in such situations provides the person with several methods to negate their negative moods. In addition to direct mood-enhancing properties, food can also provide a distraction from emotion through switching attention to the finding, preparation and consumption of food. In essence, the reliance on food can become an avoidance-coping mechanism whereby the individual associates being down with eating, and during similar situations in the future they will turn to food to cope. In psychology, such people are deemed to be emotional eaters.

Emotional eaters view foods as having an additional component. For emotional eaters, some food items have a restorative or mood-enhancing property irrespective of their macronutrient content. Such foods can, in essence, combat feelings of low mood and anxiety. The foods that emotional eaters use to enhance their mood will be specific and personal to them. Irrespective of the type of food a person habitually chooses, all foods that are potential targets for emotional eaters share similar characteristics. They are nearly always comparatively high in sugar or fat. These properties result in an increased likelihood of activation of the opioid system. Opioids are released upon ingestion of foods that are palatable, and foods that are palatable are high in carbohydrates and lipids. Some carbohydrates have an additional mood-enhancing property in that they contain the metabolic precursor to serotonin[3]. Eating lots of carbohydrates will eventually increase endogenous concentrations of serotonin and thus increase the individual's perceived mood. When eating, therefore, an emotional eater receives a psychological improvement to mood through the act of eating a liked food or through diverting attention away from the source of the anxiety that resulted in an altered mood state, as well as a very small biological improvement through the opioid and serotonin pathways.

Emotions can affect eating behaviour in one of five different ways depending on the intensity of the emotion, the situation and the person involved (Macht, 2008). First, emotions alter food choice. Emotions initiate cravings and motivate the person to choose foods that are energy-dense. Individuals who have a propensity to eat to regulate their mood will alter their food choice more profoundly than those who score lower on the emotional eating

---

[3] The neurotransmitter that is responsible for elevating moods, among its many other roles.

continuum. Individuals in this state will choose foods that they usually 'forbid' themselves and are very likely to overeat. Second, if the emotion is extremely strong it will lead to a suppression of, not an increase in, eating behaviour. If the emotion is very profound, such as the loss of a significant other or fear, it will override the individual's normal appetite system and they will refrain from eating. This is an appropriate response, as the emotion is associated with such a significant event that eating would simply 'get in the way'. For example, when confronted with an imminent biological threat it would be inappropriate to think about food or start eating. It would be counterproductive to survival and therefore has evolved not to happen. Third and fourth, eating habits interact with the emotional state. Irrespective of their direction, emotions undermine cognitive controls of food intake; negative emotions will elicit eating behaviours in an attempt to return emotions back to a steady state. Therefore, individuals who are highly restrained will find it hard to maintain their 'rules' about food when they have particularly strong emotions and emotional eaters will eat to regulate their mood. Finally, emotions will feed back into perceptions of the food by increasing or decreasing perceptions of pleasantness congruent with the emotion itself. Therefore, negative emotions will decrease the perceived pleasantness of the food and positive emotions will increase it. This five-way model (Macht, 2008) is a relatively new addition to the field of eating behaviour and, as yet, has received no research support. However, each of the five factors within the model has received support and the model is likely to become a cornerstone to the field. The most immediate criticism of this model is that it relies on a lot of research focused on restrained rather than emotional eaters, thus it is likely to be a little confounded and will lose some of its specificity to emotional eating in time.

Disinhibition

The propensity to disinhibit is not really a separate construct of eating behaviour; rather, it is associated with both dietary restraint and emotional eating. Disinhibition can be defined as a situation, subject or stimulus that diverts attention away from a task or thought. It is any form of distraction that leads to eating more than usual. For the restrained eater, anything that encroaches on their strict control of food intake would be considered a disinhibitor. An example of this would be the consumption of alcohol (Yeomans et al., 2003), which decreases attentional resources and intellectual capability around self-awareness and the ability to control food intake, leading to over-consumption (Haynes et al., 2003). Specifically for the emotional eater, it is the negative emotion that acts as the 'disinhibitor'.

Other psychological constructs that appear to increase the likelihood of disinhibited eating behaviour independent of the other two constructs explored in this chapter are attribution style (Ogden & Wardle, 1990) and impulsivity (Lowe & Eldredge, 1993). Attribution style encompasses the type of cognitive reasoning that people adopt in an attempt to understand why something has happened to them. There are three possible dimensions to the attributions that people tend to use: internal–external, stable–unstable and global–specific. *Internal* attributions are associated with people that believe the reason for something happening to them is the result of their own doing: they were in control of the situation and therefore are responsible for any consequences. *External* attributions are the antithesis to internal ones, with the person believing that fate is responsible and this is the predominant force in controlling the situation. *Stable* and *unstable* attributions are associated with the changing views over time: if the attribution is stable it will not change over time. Global attributions are views that are held towards a variety of scenarios and can extend beyond the specific experience that led to the formulation of the view. The global view is often summed up by the 'no matter what I do . . .' prefix. *Specific* attributions are, as the name suggests, specific to the situation, scenario or individual circumstance.

Impulsive eating refers to unplanned eating or starting to eat without forethought. Impulsivity is generally associated with engaging in behaviours without truly thinking of the consequences. In this situation, eating a large quantity of food or consumption of something that is harmful could be considered dysfunctional. When impulsivity is twinned with other eating behaviours, especially those of the more restrictive types of eaters, it can lead to problems in controlling food intake through the impulsivity undermining psychological control.

Although disinhibition may be an important component of eating behaviour, there is one component of disinhibition that has received a disproportionate amount of attention – external eating. External eaters are individuals who disinhibit in response to environmental cues to eat. Most people eat more food if it is freely available in their environment or if sensory cues to eat are in their immediate surroundings. It is important that external eating is not considered a separate construct, as it is simply a specific form of disinhibition.

External eaters

External eating is the inability to resist food when in its presence or if there are sensory cues to eat (Braet & Van Strien, 1997). It is the disinhibition of eating behaviour through attention shifting to the food in the immediate environment. The external eater consumes food when it is immediately available despite receiving few or no physiological incentives to start eating. The motivation to eat among strong external eaters is reliant on external cues such as hedonic value, texture or smell (Heaven et al., 2001) rather than internal, physiological cues (Marcelino et al., 2001). External cues for food can elicit a physiological reaction to them, which leads to an increased food intake. Essentially, the sensory processing of food cues in the environment overrides the normal physiology of meal initiation. The theory of externality has consistently been linked with obesity (Herman et al., 1983). The role of externality, which overrides any cognitive or biological control of food intake, has become a mainstay in the eating behaviour literature, almost becoming a separate construct in its own right. Inter-individual differences in gaining weight are likely to be dependent on variability in response to environmental triggers (Blundell & Finlayson, 2004). Therefore, external eating provides an important and separate measure of eating behaviour, as it is the only measurable aspect that has routes within environmental triggers. The derivation of external eating comes from the work of Schachter and colleagues (Schachter, 1968; Schachter et al., 1968).

Early work on externality and eating was based on animals and stemmed from experiments with a limited definition of external cues (Herman & Polivy, 2008). Furthermore, the idea was based on explanations or observations in obesity. Differentiating obese from normal people based on whether they have different/deviant behaviours has since been dropped as a theoretical concept; however, the concept of externality has remained owing to its application to all people rather than specific subsets of individuals. Historically, Schachter and colleagues did specify that external eating was specific to obesity, as they suggested that external eaters do not learn to associate gastric contractions and extensions with feelings of fullness and hunger as normal-weight individuals do. Schachter et al. (1968) suggested that lean individuals who have learned to associate gastric feelings with subjective hunger reduce their consumption, whereas those who have not will continue to eat and eventually become obese through their reliance on emotional and external cues to control their appetite. Several studies have been conducted to test this hypothesis, with some providing supporting evidence (McKenna, 1972) and others not (Lowe & Fisher, 1983). The reason for this confusion is probably related to the fact that the evidence to derive this theory was based on the internal construct of eating behaviour and associating everything that did not back this premise with external cues. In essence, the theory was that obese people are less internal, not more external. Modifications to the externality theory then culminated in three separate viewpoints (Herman & Polivy, 2008):

1   External cues affect people's food intake, and do so equally for all individuals, regardless of their body composition.

2   External cues affect the food intake of obese people but not that of normal-weight individuals.

3   External cues affect everyone's food intake, but especially that of obese individuals.

It was not until Rodin (1981) that the concept was first said to be applicable to all individuals with little or no variability in current weight status. In effect, it is a personality trait that makes someone responsive to external cues that include, but are not exclusive to, food. Currently, externality is viewed as a sensory initiation of eating. It is often referred to as the 'bakery effect', whereby a person passes a bakery and smells the food cooking and feels hungry. Here, the smell of the food will initiate perceived hunger. However, it is important to remember that it is not limited to just one sense; rather, stimulation of any of the five senses can lead to external cues to eat.

Combined effects

It is important not to assume that the psychological concepts discussed within this chapter do not interact or have cumulative effects. All 'types' of eating feed into one another and even have additive effects. It is possible for an individual to experience dietary restraint, be an emotional eater and have the propensity to disinhibit. In short, any combination of these behaviours is possible. Indeed, recent studies have suggested that an interaction between dietary restraint and disinhibition is integral in predicting those who will over-consume in specific circumstances, such as stress (Haynes et al., 2003), while other researchers suggest there are important links between emotional eating and restraint (Wallis & Hetherington, 2004). Most researchers now measure multiple components of eating behaviour. Only through the complete charac-terization of an individual's eating behaviour is it possible to predict how that person will react to and interact with their food. It has been reported that certain combinations of eating behaviours will predict general psychological well-being and weight status. For example, a rigid dietary-restrained individual low in emotional eating and disinhibition will have a relatively stable weight, usually at the lower end of what would be considered healthy. Emotional eaters who are high in disinhibition and low in restraint will often suffer from fre-quent episodes of overeating, which will impact on their sense of general well-being leading to negative mood. It is thus possible to infer that each individual will react to food based on the relative strengths of these three traits.

Escape from self-awareness theory

One theoretical framework that is based on the interaction between or com-bination of cognitions and emotions in eating is the escape from self-awareness model. Although often applied to the more pathological end of binge eating, it is a cognitive-affective model[4] of overeating. It has been suggested that the motivation to eat during periods of negative mood is based on the desire to escape from self-awareness. Heatherton and Baumeister (1991) argue that during periods of negative mood, people will focus on their identity and may start to globalize their negative feelings, making it aversive to remain in the negative emotional state. To avoid thinking about negative emotions, they will focus on a small aspect of their environment and avoid 'thinking' too much. In the case of emotional or binge eaters, this 'focus' is food. Within this model, the food provides a short-term respite from the cognitive and social environment by allowing the individual to become wrapped up in the immediate present without thought for cause, consequence or identity. If the person does not engage in this behaviour, it is likely that they will turn in on themselves and become hypercritical of their self-worth and ability. Therefore, rather than being thought of as a negative coping mechanism, it should be considered as a way of preserving self-esteem. The only difference between this coping mechanism and other forms of coping is that escape from self-awareness through eating is often accompanied by additional ego-threats immediately after eating. These ego-threats are brought about by feelings of failure and guilt associated with overeating. This can be compounded further if the individual has high dietary restraint. Eating as an escape inadvertently causes a violation of the dietary 'rules', which results in even more feelings of guilt and loss of self-worth through not being able to adhere to one's restrained diet.

Limited capacity theory

Another combined theoretical framework for eating behaviour is limited capacity or resources theory. The approach is based on Lazarus and Launier's (1978) cognitive transactional theory. Limited capacity theory is dominated by the cognitive approach, although it does incorporate other aspects. It is believed that there are limited attentional resources and that complex schemata use up more of them than simple schemata do. Therefore, the restrained individual uses up more attentional resources to control their eating than an unrestrained person. Key to the cognitive transactional model is that perception of environment is affected by both the personality traits and emotional state of the individual. Considering these factors allows the cognitive transactional model to capture the person-in-context (i.e. the specific individual at a specific time results in a specific behavioural response). This gives the theory much more fluidity. The model's necessary complexity and specificity

---

[4] These models suggest that an interaction between the individual's internal thought processes or schemata and their emotional state are the basis of their behavioural response.

to context and individual gives it strength, but also makes it much harder to test. In effect, the overloading of the attentional resources by the combination of dietary restraint with any other factor means that it is impossible for the individual to maintain their rule set. They will only be able to do this in very stable situations when they are in a stable mood, in a familiar environment and alone. Any variation from this strict set of criteria will lead to the person violating their diet's strict rules.

Summary

The psychology of eating has three main overarching concepts that provide researchers and interested parties with anchors to explore the behaviour. Dietary restraint, emotional eating and disinhibition are used in the explanation of every aspect of eating behaviour. Although these approaches are heavily biased towards the cognitive school of thought, they are not wholly reliant on it. In the reality of the everyday meal, it is these three components to eating that control when and when not to start eating. Each of us has a highly individualized set of 'rules' for food and eating. For most people, this will be bound to food preference whereby the foods liked are those that are chosen. However, for a large proportion of the population, additional factors also underpin how much and what is eaten outside of the simple food preference domain. Some people apply additional rules about calories or other rules that limit the amount they eat. In essence, they use their psychological attentional processes to prematurely terminate meals in an attempt to control their weight. The use of such measures to control food intake is known as dietary restraint, which is a concept that has received much research attention over the last thirty years.

In addition to dietary rule sets, eating behaviour can also be affected by the individual's emotions. Some individuals attempt to control their mood through selecting and consuming foods high in fats and sugars. For the emotional eater, food has an additional meaning through its ability to control their mood and in particular allow them to cope with or defeat negative states of mind. The brief respite gained through the consumption of mood-improving food may also be an attempt to preserve self-esteem by allowing the person to escape from self-awareness.

Environmental cues to eating also play a role in controlling eating beyond normal social interactions with others. The presence of food or its cues can lead to the individual disinhibiting and over-consuming, a specific form of disinhibition known as external eating. Disinhibition is not limited to its role within external cues to eat. Any factor that overloads or causes an individual not to adhere to their normal dietary rules or habitual amount of food consumed is known as a disinhibitor. In this way, emotion could be considered to be disinhibiting the person from maintaining cognitive control of their food intake. Therefore, this complexity is indicative of a combined approach to these three concepts. Each person has a specific combination of these concepts as part of their personality and this remains fairly stable throughout life. To date, research of these concepts has focused on females more than males probably due to the greater variation in eating behaviour exhibited by females. In short, when considering dietary restraint, emotional eating and disinhibition, it is better to see them as part of a continuum and working in combination rather than as individual phenomena. For accurate prediction of eating behaviour, it is important to have an understanding of how each of these three concepts is manifested within the person in question, especially since intentions and thus what is said may be undermined by other eating behaviours. For example, a highly restrained individual will say that they tightly control their eating behaviour; however, if they are also a strong emotional eater, their mood will play an equal if not more prominent role in perceived control.

8 Dealing with obesity
Dieting and drugs

Obesity has become a pandemic of global proportions. In just thirty years, the prevalence of obesity in adults has quadrupled and does not appear to be slowing (National Audit Office, 2001). However, it is not just adults who are at risk of developing obesity; children's rates have also increased exponentially in recent years (Rudolf et al., 2001) and even our pets do not appear to be immune (Laflamme, 2006). Thus, obesity has become a worldwide concern for healthcare professionals and governments alike.

Obesity is associated with a number of non-communicable diseases[1], including cancer, diabetes and cardiovascular disease. It is the increased prevalence of these diseases that concerns the already overstretched health services and those that have to subsidize them. Moreover, unlike communicable diseases, obesity is perfectly avoidable, which means it is unnecessarily drawing on consumable resources. There is ever-increasing demand to receive treatments for all types of illness, which, combined with recent medical advances, places pressure on the finite resources available. This has led some people to suggest that obese individuals should be considered the same as smokers and alcoholics. However, obesity is different from smoking and alcohol abuse. Many paths to becoming obese exist and different people achieve this status in different ways, which requires a highly individualized way of intervening to treat obesity.

In this chapter, the causes and consequences of and treatments for obesity will be discussed. The various biological and psychological theories and consequences for how someone becomes obese will be addressed. Emphasis will be placed on dieting and the psychopharmacological treatments for the condition. Brief evaluations of physical activity and surgical treatment for obesity will also be considered. However, we must first understand how obesity is defined.

---

[1] These are illnesses that cannot be 'caught' from someone else. They are a result of biological [dys]function rather than a bacterium or virus.

Defining obesity

It is difficult to define what constitutes being obese. Several measures are used to diagnose an individual as obese or to categorize weight status. The two most common means of assessing obesity are body mass index (BMI) and waist-to-hip ratio. Methods of weight percentiles and percentage body fat are also used in some specific populations.

Body mass index is a simple calculation based on an individual's height and weight (see Figure 8.1). A person's weight in kilograms is divided by the square of their height in metres. The outcome of this equation allows the interested party to 'band' the individual into a category based on BMI. A person with a BMI of less than 17.5 would be considered to be at risk of a restrictive type eating disorder such as anorexia nervosa;[2] between 17.5 and 25 is considered normal weight, above 25 but below 30 overweight, between 30 and 40 obese and above 40 morbidly obese. Body mass index is the most common method of characterizing obesity. Although popular, it is not without its problems. For example, the BMI approach often provides false-positive results or is too conservative depending on the situation. By taking a rather crude measure of weight without considering the individual's physique means that some people with high muscle mass are considered obese. Using BMI to characterize obesity is both adult- and female-dominant. One way to overcome the limitations of the BMI equation is to consider waist-to-hip ratios.

Waist-to-hip ratios consider the amount and location of adipose tissue in an individual. Based on the BMI approach, individuals with a high muscle mass would at first be considered obese, only for this diagnosis to be withdrawn when assessed based on their waist-to-hip ratio. A low waist-to-hip ratio indicates that an individual is at low risk of the diseases associated with obesity. As with BMI, however, there are issues surrounding the accuracy of the waist-to-hip ratio. Anatomical differences between males and females mean that men cannot be compared with women and therefore a different criterion of assessment is required. Furthermore, the waist-to-hip ratio does not consider an individual's overall weight, thus people who 'preferentially' store fat

$$BMI = \frac{Weight\,(kg)}{(Height\,(m))^2}$$

Figure 8.1   An equation for assessing body mass index.

---

[2] Although other criteria are required for a full diagnosis of an eating disorder (see Chapter 9).

in areas other than the abdomen will avoid being considered obese. Females are more likely than males to store fat in non-abdominal regions, making this approach more male-oriented. To overcome these problems, some researchers have suggested that only waist measurements should be considered. For men, the cut-off value that suggests they need to lose weight is a waist circumference of more than 102 cm, while for women the value is 88 cm (Lean et al., 1998). Again, this approach may result in false-positives, especially in anatomically larger individuals (Hubert et al., 2008).

Focusing on the abdomen is an appropriate method considering that high abdominal adiposity is associated with an increased risk of health problems (Despres et al., 2001). Moreover, it has been shown that measuring this type of obesity using BMI or waist-related measures is sensitive enough to predict risk factors – with waist circumference being slightly more sensitive (Hubert et al., 2008). Together, BMI and waist measurement are the preferred way of diagnosing obesity.

Recent technological advances allow direct measurement of an individual's fat mass. This has led to a relatively new way of defining obesity. Fat mass assessment or 'percentage body fat' has resulted from advances in bioelectrical impedance analysis (BIA). With this technique, the total amount of water in the body is assessed and fat mass calculated. As fat prohibits the passage of an electrical current, the amount of electrical signal 'lost' within the body provides an indication of how much fat is in the system. There are two types of bioelectrical impedance analysis: single-frequency and multi-frequency. Multi-frequency BIA is more accurate, as it is better able to account for the variation in biological material. Single-frequency BIA suffers from the inability of the electrical current to pass through the cell membrane; therefore, a lot of fat and water is not measured. Multi-frequency methods are not limited by such problems (Kyle et al., 2004). A healthy amount of fat mass is also related to gender, with males having stricter criteria for percentage body fat than females. Age adds additional complexity to the use of bioelectrical impedance analysis as a method of defining obesity. Age-related differences confound the measurement of fat mass because of the natural development of sarcopenia[3], while gender differences are bound up with female fertility[4]. A healthy range for women is between 20 and 35 per cent body fat mass and for males it is much lower at between 10 and 25 per cent (see Figure 8.2). Due to its high cost compared with simple height, weight and waist calculations,

---

[3] This is a process whereby the individual loses muscle mass and replaces it with fat tissue. This is a natural process that starts to occur in humans after the age of 30.

[4] As briefly mentioned in Chapter 3, fat tissue releases oestrogen, a hormone related to female fertility. As women age, their ability to produce fertility hormones from their sex organs diminishes. At this point the additional fat tissue (around 5% increase in percentage body fat) compensates for this loss.

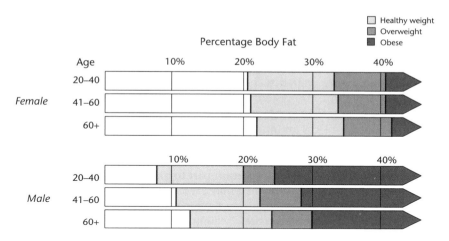

Figure 8.2 A quick guide to working out healthy percentage body fat.

this method is somewhat limited in its application. Therefore, it is usually reserved for clinical practice and for those patients currently undergoing medical interventions (Horie et al., 2008).

The final method used to define obesity is weight percentile scores. With this method, all members of a group are measured for height and weight and placed on a continuum. Those individuals who score in the highest percentiles are considered obese. This type of measurement is usually reserved for groups who are still growing (i.e. children). Several obvious problems exist with a model based on cut-off values. First, some individuals will be considered obese even when none are. Furthermore, the number of obese individuals in a given population will not change, as it is always set at above 85 per cent of the group. This blurring of the diagnostic boundaries makes this model hard to apply. A relative strength of this approach is that it does allow comparisons within groups that are rapidly changing in size and shape; this is because it imposes some stability on the population in terms of where an individual stands, in terms of their weight status, compared with their peers. Recently, it has been shown that waist circumference is a better predictor of obesity in children (Hubert et al., 2008), and thus it is likely that the percentile approach will diminish in popularity.

Causes of obesity

In its most basic sense, obesity is simply the storage of energy over and above that expended over a long period. Thus an individual need only consume more energy than they expend on a daily basis to gain weight – in short, they need to maintain a positive energy balance. This is a rather simplistic explanation of the cause of obesity, which would lead to the inevitable conclusion that it is the fault of the individual for their current weight status. The true causes of obesity are related to potential influences on the energy balance equation. Energy into the system comes predominantly in the form of food; however, the type of food and more specifically its energy density play a major role in weight gain. How an individual processes this food can also affect the energy input side of the equation. Metabolic rate, genetic and other biological factors will define how well an individual absorbs the energy and what they do with it. Energy use also has an important part to play in the development and onset of obesity. An obese individual may eat a lot less than a lean person, but if they do not utilize the energy they have consumed they will still have a positive energy balance and thus gain weight.

Most early explanations for obesity were based almost exclusively in the biological domain. One of the first was set-point theory. Stemming from the work of Kennedy (1953), set-point theory suggests that dysfunction in the hypothalamus results in excessive weight gain, as this region controls eating behaviour. This relates to dysfunction to an individual's individually set, biologically predetermined weight. Thus individuals are born to be a certain weight and irrespective of what they eat or how they exercise, their biology will control their weight status. Thus, if an individual has a high 'set point', their body will do everything it can to ensure that they reach it; a low set point has the opposite effect. In short, it is a 'destiny' approach to weight status. This rather simplistic approach suggests that people are the weight they are supposed to be and that they will find it difficult to maintain another weight. Although set-point theory once received support from both academics and clinical practitioners, it has more or less been rejected as an adequate explanation of obesity (Levitsky, 2002). The main problem with set-point theory is that it cannot adequately explain the sudden increased prevalence in obesity over the latter half of the twentieth century. Modern interpretations of the set point suggest that biology offers a 'range' of weight status called 'settling point'. Where an individual currently lies within their settling point is controlled by environmental cues. With ever-increasing numbers of people becoming obese, it would appear that this 'settling point' is very large. Such diverse ranges limit the applicability of this theory compared with environmental explanations.

Another theory that has been consigned to history is that of (s)low 'metabolic rate'. Metabolic rate is the base amount of energy that is required to stay alive. The mammalian body requires a relatively large amount of energy to perform all of its essential functions: this baseline value is known as resting metabolic rate. Each person's metabolic rate is highly heritable, with family members sharing similar rates. Initial metabolic theories suggested that obese people have low metabolic rates because they use less energy to remain alive and therefore have the potential to store more energy following each meal. The main problem with this theory, and the reason why it has been all but discredited as an explanation of obesity[5], is that the 'larger' a person is the higher their resting metabolic rate. This is because resting metabolic rate is associated with lean muscle mass and obese people require more muscle mass to carry their excess weight around. Therefore, the more fat mass a person has, the more lean muscle mass they must have and thus the higher their resting metabolic rate. Recently, this theory has received some minor research focus following the discovery of the Thr54 allele of the FABP2 gene that codes for both obesity (Hegele et al., 1996) and resting metabolic rate (Takakura et al., 2005). The mutation of this gene appears to cause lower *comparable* resting metabolic rates that are associated with visceral obesity. As visceral obesity has few health consequences compared with abdominal phenotypes, it is still relatively unimportant for explaining the negative aspects of obesity and remains on the periphery of this scientific research.

Biological explanations for obesity have also included dysfunction of most, if not all, of the biomarkers of appetite regulation (discussed in Chapters 2 and 3). But each of these explanations has failed to account for current levels of obesity. Very few individuals have been diagnosed with obesity as a result of problems in genetic mutations or biological dysfunction. A famous example was the rural Pakistani family who displayed mutations to their leptin genes, which meant that their bodies were unable to create leptin[6] naturally. This led them to overeat and put on excessive weight. Administration of synthetic leptin rectified their obesity. The vast majority of obese people have very high concentrations of leptin and so this explanation did not hold up to scientific investigation and rigour.

Exercise scientists target the energy output side of the energy balance equation by encouraging people to increase their energy expenditure. Their argument is that a combination of factors has led to us becoming more sedentary. The ownership of cars and the advent of computers have meant that both travel and work require less physical activity. Until the mid-twentieth century, most jobs involved manual labour, whereas data processing and computers define modern jobs. The widespread use of computers began in the 1980s, which coincided with the rapid increase in the prevalence of obesity. This technological advance did not occur in isolation. Other labour-saving gadgets and multimedia devices have flooded the market. Multimedia devices in particular mean that leisure-time activities – watching television, playing

---

[5] It remains in popular consciousness though and is a source of great frustration for practitioners. This explanation allows for learned helplessness to permeate a person's attempt to lose weight. Proponents of this belief say that they can do nothing about their weight status as their biology governs their energy storage.

[6] Leptin is the tonic biomarker for the amount of fat currently stored in the body (see Chapter 3).

computer games, and so on – are nowadays much more sedentary. Thus we now spend less time burning calories both at work and at home. Such an extreme change in habitual physical activity[7] in just one generation has meant that humans in the developed world have lost their natural behavioural defence against obesity. A longitudinal investigation of children suggests that lower levels of physical activity in the obese are likely to be a consequence rather than a cause of obesity (Wardle et al., 2007). Wardle and colleagues found that the incidence of obesity in children when exposed to one episode of physical activity a week rose from 4 per cent to 6.1 per cent; with two episodes it increased from 3.9 per cent to 5.7 per cent, and with three episodes it rose from 3 per cent to 4.2 per cent. Therefore, over time, the incidence of obesity increased even with higher levels of physical activity. This suggests that physical activity is a protective factor to the development of obesity. If obesity is not due to a sedentary lifestyle, it must be the result of differences in food choice (the consumption of energy-dense alternatives), the amount of food eaten, and/or a change in the environment.

A calorie provides the same amount of energy no matter how it is consumed. Concurrent to the increase in obesity, there has been a significant increase in the amount of sweetened drinks consumed (Sturm, 2008). The average 500 ml beverage of cola contains around 10 per cent of a person's recommended daily intake of calories. Research has also shown that the habitual consumption of these beverages is a significant predictor of weight gain (Ludwig et al., 2001; Raben et al., 2003). Furthermore, the price of fresh produce has increased while the cost of confectionery and sweetened drinks has decreased compared with the average family income. This has inevitably led to the selection of cheaper foods, which suggests that economic and commercial factors are also pertinent to the development of obesity.

At the same time as technology countered the need for physical activity, changes in eating behaviour were also observed. Compared with the past, people now eat out more (Jekanowski, 2001) and the type of food on offer outside the home is often higher in energy, requires less effort to prepare and is offered in much larger portions (Prentice & Jebb, 2003). Compared with the previous two generations, energy intake has in fact decreased; however, there has been a simultaneous decrease in physical activity and the modern diet is also associated with a higher percentage of fat (Prentice & Jebb, 1995). Moreover, the modern diet is characterized by the absence of foods rich in micronutrients (Popkin et al., 2005). Based on these data, it would appear that people do not necessarily eat *more* now than they did in the past, but that they eat *differently* from how they once did.

---

[7] This would be considered habitual, as this previous form of physical activity was part of everyday life rather than having to be a purposeful behaviour requiring forethought and planning (e.g. going to the gym).

Obese people have more energy stored in their bodies than lean people and the only way that they could have obtained that energy was by consuming food. Thus they must have overeaten to achieve a positive energy balance. It is wrong to assume that such overeating is due to greed or poor self-control. The mechanisms for why someone over-consumes are not that simple. In Chapter 7, Schachter's theory of obesity was discussed in relation to external eating, but there are many other factors involved. For example, at least 7 per cent of obese people may suffer from binge eating disorder, which is a psychopathology similar to bulimia nervosa (Wade et al., 2006).

The causes of obesity are multifaceted. Obesity arises due to the maintenance of positive energy balance over an extended period. All of the factors that influence one side or other of the energy equation can lead to increased adiposity. What is essential to understand is that simple explanations of the causes of obesity, such as gluttony or sloth, are partly or wholly inaccurate. Both biological and psychological explanations have merit; however, when environmental and social factors are incorporated, we have a highly complex situation making it almost impossible to offer any meaningful conclusions. Offering simplistic explanations leads inevitably to inappropriate stigmatization of the obese. Such social repercussions are wrong, unhelpful and liable to lead to discrimination. Furthermore, much of the evidence is based on associations with, rather than direct measurement of, obesity. Therefore, only conservative estimates of the causes of obesity can be offered. It will come as little surprise, therefore, that most research has focused on the consequences of obesity rather than the causes and, as such, most clinical applications and practices are focused on these repercussions.

Consequences of obesity

As with the causes of obesity, its consequences are split into the biological and the psychological. Taking the biological consequences first, the ultimate cost for carrying excess weight for a long period is premature death. Being obese, depending on its severity, takes between 3 and 13 years off of one's life expectancy (Jebb, 2004). Other consequences that will require medical intervention include: fertility problems, metabolic syndrome, type II diabetes, cardiovascular disease, respiratory dysfunction, cirrhosis of the liver and cancer (Finer, 2006).

Metabolic syndrome (also known as syndrome X) refers to a collection of symptoms that have not reached a pathological state but will do so in the near future. This syndrome is an early diagnosis and therefore allows medical intervention before other more serious morbidities manifest. It is characterized by high abdominal adiposity and by insulin resistance. Insulin resistance is the early stage of type II diabetes and is when an individual has started to become less responsive to concentrations of insulin in their blood. This inexorably leads to higher concentrations of circulatory sugar, which in turn has ramifications for blood pressure and cardiovascular function. Ford et al. (2002) offered the first complete characterization of metabolic syndrome (see Table 8.1). Importantly, this syndrome is fully reversible upon the loss of excess body weight. Therefore, it is imperative to diagnose people with metabolic syndrome so that they can take action before they develop diabetes. Diabetes, in contrast, is not reversible and will require a lifetime of medical support.

Diabetes, or more specifically type II diabetes, occurs when persistent and consistently high concentrations of blood glucose place ever-increasing pressure on the β cells of the pancreas to secrete the hormone insulin, which functions to remove glucose from the circulatory system. As in all animals, these cells can only take a certain amount of pressure before they denature (cell death). The eventual degradation of these cells leads to an inability to create insulin. This results in the individual having to inject synthetic hormones to compensate for their inability to produce insulin naturally: if

Table 8.1 The central features of metabolic syndrome

Symptom	Explanation
Central adiposity	High levels of fat deposited in and around the abdominal wall
Dyslipidaemia	High levels of fat in the blood Low levels of high-density lipoprotein cholesterol, which help to protect against the effects of low-density lipoprotein cholesterol
Hyperglycaemia	High concentrations of glucose in the blood
Hyperinsulinaemia	High concentrations of insulin in the blood. High concentrations of insulin are supposed to protect against high concentrations of glucose. The job of insulin is to 'switch fat cells on' and make them absorb glucose from the blood. Clearly, in this state they are not responding or are too full and cannot respond. Either way, this is the beginning of diabetes
Abnormal glucose tolerance	A glucose test is used to diagnose diabetes. People with metabolic syndrome will respond to this test somewhere between normal people and diabetics
Hyperuricaemia	High concentrations of uric acid in the blood, suggesting that either the kidneys are starting to fail or that there is too much sugar in the diet
Hypertension	High blood pressure due to abnormal blood composition. A combination of all of the above

they fail do this, they will eventually fall into a diabetic coma and die. Although a relatively easy condition to monitor and control, diabetes has become so prevalent that it is absorbing increasing amounts of government funding and subsidies. Most, but not all, people who develop type II diabetes could have avoided doing so by leading a healthier lifestyle.

There has been a concerted effort by governments, charities and non-government agencies to increase awareness of the health consequences of a poor lifestyle. Cardiovascular disease is the build-up of plaque in the arteries in and around the heart, which prohibits blood from reaching the essential muscles within this organ. Loss of blood flow to the heart muscles causes the death of these cells and eventually leads to a heart attack. The only way to overcome this is either to insert stents[8] into the arteries or to perform bypass surgery. Respiratory dysfunctions due to obesity include breathlessness, obstructive sleep apnoea and asthma. Excessive fat in, on and around the chest cavity makes it hard to maintain a consistent oxygen supply to the blood. While awake this leads to problems in breathing and while asleep it leads to snoring or a cessation in breathing altogether. Sleep apnoea occurs when an individual stops breathing, resulting in the need to wake up to start breathing again. Sufferers experience disturbed sleep patterns and excessive sleepiness. People with sleep apnoea may fall asleep at inopportune times, such as when driving or during the day when not physically active.

The final common medical consequence of obesity is cirrhosis of the liver. High fat deposits in the liver cause it to become inflamed and degrade. Although the liver has remarkable regenerative capacity, it is not capable of surviving high blood pressure, glucose and insulin in the blood in the long term. If a patient does not lose weight immediately, the organ will fail and he or she will require a transplant. Loss of liver function was previously almost always the result of alcohol abuse; however, obesity is fast becoming the main reason for liver failure in the West.

Obese individuals suffer discrimination on a daily basis. Both obese men and women are less likely to get married and both – but especially women – suffer prejudice and discrimination in all aspects of the workplace, including hiring, placement, compensation, promotion and firing (Cossrow et al., 2001; Hebl & Mannix, 2003; Wade & DiMaria, 2003). The main reason for this discrimination is that obese people are believed, wrongfully, to have poorer working habits as well as emotional and interpersonal problems (Finer, 2006). Such discrimination has psychological consequences, which include higher rates of depression as well as low self-esteem and self-worth. The psychological consequences of obesity are often overlooked or given little emphasis

---

[8] Stents are small metal mesh tubes that are inserted into the artery to force it open. By compressing the plaque against the arterial wall, blood flow is no longer restricted and normal function returns.

compared with medical problems associated with the condition. This dis-crimination undermines the individual's self-belief, and psychological empowerment for obese people who are trying to lose weight is a potent mechanism in helping them to change their lifestyle.

Treatments for obesity

The House of Commons Select Committee (2004) estimated that the total direct and indirect cost of overweight and obesity in England in 2002 was £6.7–7.4 billion. Despite this considerable investment, relevant organizations have failed to curb the rise in the prevalence of obesity, indicating how difficult it is to tackle this condition. Although most learned people call for a multidisciplinary approach to obesity, this has not happened. The onus is still, in the main, on the obese individual to seek help.

The first step for an obese person trying to lose weight is to contact their general practitioner or private weight loss clinic. Relying on the individual to be proactive in seeking treatment means most cases referred for intervention initially present with one or more of the co-morbidities of obesity. Often, it is not until obese individuals become aggrieved by their weight status, in terms of developing diabetes or sleep-related problems, that they motivate them-selves to seek help. Relying on a physical illness to provide motivation to act means that the damage resulting from the excess weight is already irreversible and the individual will remain in the healthcare system indefinitely.

In cases of serious co-morbidities, referral to a specialist clinic is usually the second step in the process. Although the primary reason for referral is to receive medical help for their co-morbidities, obese individuals will also be examined by a medic, a dietitian and a clinical psychologist. The medic will test for and diagnose additional complications and illnesses and usually pre-scribe some form of weight loss drug or treatment regime for the presenting co-morbidities. The dietitian will examine the patient's current diet and provide advice for changing their habitual diet to aid in a healthier lifestyle and strategy for weight loss. The clinical psychologist will check for additional psychological illness such as binge eating and depression. They will also try to uncover in what circumstances the patient over-consumes and offer behavioural strategies to avoid doing so. After this initial assessment, the patient will have to return to have their medication checked and to find out whether they are progressing as expected. Psychological treatment will also be provided for those diagnosed with an additional psychological morbidity. Outside of these bi-monthly or monthly visits, patients are left to control their treatment for themselves and receive little social support.

Often, in addition to a medical intervention, obese individuals will join weight loss groups where they receive the social support they require. The remainder of this chapter will explore each of these potential strategies for treating obesity.

Pharmacological treatments for obesity

The best practice guideline for prescribing weight loss drugs to obese people is that they have previously failed to lose 10 per cent of their body weight through behavioural and nutritional interventions. When an obese individual visits their general practitioner, this criterion has usually already been fulfilled. Once the drug has been prescribed, it should be carefully monitored over a period of three months. If an additional 5 per cent of body mass has not been lost, the treatment should be terminated (Royal College of Physicians of London, 1998). The drugs that are prescribed by medics to aid weight loss are sibutramine and orlistat. Each drug works to lower weight in distinct ways.

Sibutramine is a selective serotonin and noradrenaline[9] re-uptake inhibitor (Halford et al., 2004a). It works by stopping the neuronal cells in the brain that make serotonin and noradrenaline from 'reabsorbing' these chemical messengers. This means that they have a greater chance of communicating with other cells in these two systems to ensure that the pathways maintain a high level of activity. Both of these neurotransmitters stop the individual from feeling hungry and so decrease their biological-based motivation to eat. Sibutramine therefore works as an appetite suppressant. Specifically, it increases feelings of fullness so that when the individual starts to eat they become satiated more quickly (Halford et al., 2008a). It also has the advantage of being an anti-depressant. Therefore, individuals who present with depression as well as obesity may receive additional benefits from taking sibutramine. The drug is up to 40 per cent effective, that is, 40 per cent of people on sibutramine will lose between 5 and 10 per cent of body mass while taking it (McNulty et al., 2003). The side-effects of sibutramine are the same as those of most other anti-depressants and include insomnia, nausea and constipation.

Orlistat is a pancreatic lipase inhibitor, which works by preventing the absorption of lipids (fat) across the intestinal wall (Hauptman et al., 1992). Therefore, orlistat targets the periphery. Because it targets the intestinal wall, orlistat needs to be taken in high doses. However, the benefits of this are that only a very small amount of the drug enters the blood stream. Orlistat should be the drug of preference because of its low potential to alter the biochemistry of the blood, brain and peripheral organs; however, this is undermined due to the poor efficacy of the drug. The only real side-effects to taking orlistat are oily stools and faecal urgency. This inability to control bowel movement means

---

[9] Both of these neurotransmitters are discussed in Chapter 2.

that at least half of patients will fail to complete their treatment. Of patients who do complete the course, up to a quarter will lose between 5 and 10 per cent of body weight. Handled appropriately, the side-effects can serve to act as a behavioural modifier of the patient's diet – lapses into eating high-fat foods while on orlistat will result in discomfort. Unfortunately, the potential perceived social embarrassment of the inability to control bowel movement means that most people stop taking the drug.

Whatever pharmacological intervention is offered, it is clear from the data that efficacy is poor. In all cases, more patients taking the drug will not achieve the recommended weight loss than those who do. It is essential that patients follow a total lifestyle intervention alongside taking any weight loss drug to achieve maximum benefits. Such a concerted effort to overhaul an individual's entire life is obviously quite daunting and is likely to end in failure. But failure can have far-reaching negative consequences for their psychological well-being, as it may reaffirm their negative self-worth. Furthermore, most patients have overblown expectations of the efficacy of weight loss drugs stemming from overconfidence in medical interventions. It is important therefore that the person's expectations of how quickly and effectively their weight loss will be achieved are carefully managed so that they do not wrongly interpret perceived slow progress as failure.

If a pharmacological intervention is unsuccessful, there is one other medical intervention that can be offered. An obese person may elect to undergo bariatric surgery to physically stop them from eating.

Surgical treatments for obesity

Currently, there are four different 'approaches' to surgically altering the digestive system, all of which aim to dramatically reduce weight by restricting the amount of food that can be comfortably eaten. They all do this through altering the stomach and duodenal regions of the upper digestive tract. The most popular techniques are laparoscopic adjustable gastric banding (LAGB), vertical banded gastroplasty (VBG), Roux-en-Y gastric bypass (RYGBP) and bilio-pancreatic diversion (BPD). The most common procedures used today are laparoscopic adjustable gastric banding and Roux-en-Y gastric bypass (Cummings et al., 2008). However, general guidelines state that the surgical approach and technique used should be tailored to the individual. Figure 8.3 shows how these different approaches are undertaken. Although it could be argued that this is a drastic measure to take for a relatively benign issue, it is an elective surgery and so is not an enforced medical treatment. The reason why so many people elect to take this surgery is that their general quality of life is very poor and they believe that they have tried everything else possible to lose weight (Dixon et al., 2001). Therefore, elective surgery is a last resort only to be taken if the patient wants it and has tried all other avenues of treatment. Such drastic interventions are not without risk and a small proportion of patients will pay the ultimate price for electing to have this treatment (LAGB = 0.05 per cent; VBG = 0.5 per cent; RYGBP = 0.31 per cent). Unlike other interventions, however, successful bariatric surgery almost guarantees weight loss. In terms of average weight loss, the reversible surgeries like laparoscopic adjustable gastric banding have poorer efficacy than the irreversible ones. Instead of assessing these techniques using percentage body weight like other interventions, it is easier to use total BMI average weight loss (LAGB = 10.4; VBG = 14.2; RYGBP = 16.7; BPD = 17.9), as they have such a massive impact on weight status. If measured against the criterion of being morbidly obese (BMI of 40+), then all

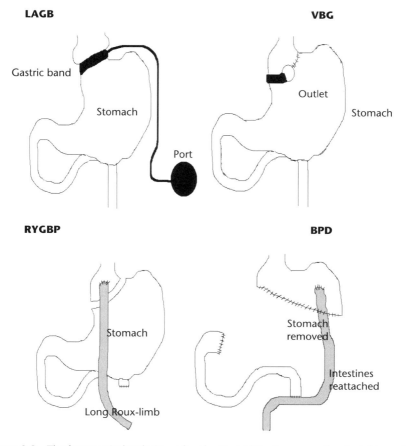

Figure 8.3 The four surgical techniques for obesity. LAGB = laparoscopic adjustable gastric banding, VBG = vertical banded gastroplasty, RYGBP = Roux-en-Y gastric bypass, BPD = bilio-pancreatic diversion.

but the reversible laparoscopic adjustable gastric banding would give people back a healthy weight status (Pontiroli, 2008). Dramatic weight loss of this magnitude has obvious benefits for all co-morbidities of obesity, whether biological or psychological. The long-term efficacy of surgery is so good that even after eight years patients will still have a 16.5 per cent lower body mass, while those on diet-based interventions will have gained 0.7 kg (Torgerson & Sjöström, 2001).

Nutritional treatments for obesity – dieting

Of all the possible treatments for obesity, dieting to lose weight has the longest, and most turbulent, history. Standard scientific advice would be that any diet designed for weight loss purposes should consider all of the following issues. On any diet there should not be a trade-off between quality, in terms of micronutrients (vitamins and minerals), and quantity. Thus any diet that proposes the consumption of less than 1200 calories will require vitamin and mineral supplementation. In terms of macronutrients, protein should not fall below 50 g, carbohydrates below 100 g and fibre below 30 g over the course of a day. These quantities of macronutrients and roughage are needed for healthy function; anything less will likely result in adverse side-effects. Furthermore, 'dieters' should increase their fluid intake to compensate for the loss of water that they would otherwise obtain from their food. In addition to these more scientific demands, there are psychological considerations. To ensure that the diet is adhered to, food preferences should be considered and elevated hunger or loss of energy avoided. Ignoring any of these three factors will ultimately lead to the dieter withdrawing from the intervention. To ensure long-term weight loss and avoid weight regain, any potential diet must also educate the individual to make more healthy habitual food choices; they must not revert to their 'old ways' following attainment of their target weight. A diet also has to be able to be followed within a normal social context and, most importantly, the diet must not cause any harm to an individual's health, either psychological or biological (Rock & Coulston, 1988).

Following any diet may require some cognitive restructuring in terms of how long the process of weight loss will take. Most people who opt for dieting to lose weight have completely inappropriate time frames in which to achieve their target weights. It is important that dieting to lose weight is seen as a first step on a path towards total lifestyle change, otherwise even the most successful interventions will only work for as long as the diet is adhered to; following completion of the diet, the individual will start to regain all of the weight lost.

Many commercial ventures have tried to provide consistent and predictable weight loss regimes to the general public. Most have now been consigned to history, although such diets often come back into to vogue before disappearing again. These diets have been variations on a similar theme work-ing through excluding one or more food types from the diet. The more reput-able diets focus on limiting total calorie intake while still providing a balanced diet. Others proclaim to work through altering macronutrient intake, specific-ally limiting carbohydrate or fat consumption. However, those diets that have withstood the test of time have almost always focused on a total lifestyle adjustment, incorporating the needs of the individual and accepting that there will be lapses. Irrespective of the type of dietary intervention, their aim is to provide a rule set for the individual to follow by creating additional schemata around the holistic experience of eating. These rules are an attempt to make the unrestrained person act like a rigid, restrained individual. In essence, they try to re-educate the individual into relying on psychological perceptions of food over biological or environmental feedback in controlling food choice and portion size. Thus any factor that competes for the dieter's attentional resources will inadvertently lead to over-consumption. This is especially the case if obese people start eating for reasons other than hunger (such as as a pallia-tive agent for negative emotions; Kaplan & Kaplan, 1957). Currently, the diet industry is thought to be worth billions of pounds each year, and it is set to grow as the prevalence of obesity continues to rise.

Despite all of the arguments in and around dieting, judgements can only be based on efficacy. The evidence suggests that dieting decreases weight in the very short term, but increases it in the medium to long term. Most experts on the subject believe that dieting leads to weight gain not weight loss and that early dieting predicts the early onset of obesity (Birch & Fisher, 1998). This is a relatively complex process. It would appear that cognitively restricting diet leads to an increased prevalence of binge eating (Meno et al., 2008), meal skipping leading to increased hunger (Calderon et al., 2004) and rebound weight gain following completion of a diet (Stice et al., 1999). When meal skipping, breakfast is the meal usually skipped (Neumark-Sztainer et al., 2007). Traditionally in Western societies[10], energy intake varies throughout the day. Breakfast constitutes the lowest amount of energy intake and the evening meal the largest, with the midday meal in between. By skipping breakfast, an indi-vidual will be hungrier come midday. With more energy-dense foods being eaten at midday than at breakfast, the individual is likely to consume more calories than if they had eaten breakfast. Therefore, skipping meals will lead to an increased calorie intake.

Although the efficacy of dieting is relatively good in the short term, diet-ing may be directly linked to obesity in the long term. Even when weight loss is relatively great, and this will depend on the type, duration and intensity of the diet, each time the patient reaches a target weight they will often revert to

---

[10] Meal skipping is less common in societies where individuals do not vary their calorific intake throughout the day.

their old eating patterns and regain all of the weight lost. Although this means repeat custom for businesses that offer weight loss interventions, this will not help dieters to avoid the negative implications of obesity. As an intervention, dieting is a double-edged sword. Members of the general public believe that dieting is highly effective, especially if they have lost excess weight in a relatively short time; however, diets are actually highly ineffective at what they are supposed to do (i.e. combat obesity).

Physical activity interventions for obesity

The theoretical underpinnings to interventions that focus on physical activity are unique in their preferential targeting of the energy output side of the energy balance equation[11]. Compared with the other weight loss interventions, physical activity is a relative newcomer. It has long been known that physical activity promotes psychological well-being by increasing endogenous concentrations of opioids and serotonin. These neurological changes lead directly to positive influences on depression, anxiety, mood state, self-esteem, well-being and personality (Opdenacker et al., 2008). However, increased physical activity can potentially enforce a state of negative energy balance and thus weight loss. Exercise-based interventions are often described in terms of mode, frequency, duration and intensity; therefore, when considering any physical activity weight loss regime it is important to consider these 'anchors'. The American College of Sports Medicine (1995) has offered guidance for designing treatments for excessive weight loss. They suggest that the intensity should be relatively low (burn 300 kcal per session) and that the recipient should engage in exercise three times a week. The goal here is it to increase energy expenditure through relatively low-impact exercises, such as walking, swimming and cycling. This mode of exercise will avoid injury to the joints and potential muscular and bone problems. The guidelines also suggest that social stigmatization should be avoided through specialist sessions or in activities that will not attract negative attention to the individual who is trying to lose weight. As the fitness of the individual develops, the intensity of the sessions can be increased (2000 kcal a week).

The efficacy of physical activity as a weight loss intervention is weak. Most recent studies have suggested a total weight loss in the range of 0.4–2.6 kg (Curioni & Lourenço, 2005). This is unsurprising, as the guidelines of the American College of Sports Medicine state that the maximum potential weight loss through structured exercise should only be 2000 kcal. Moreover, physical

---

[11] Of course I refer here to *legal* interventions. Previously, other interventions, including the medicinal use (and subsequent abuse) of amphetamines, would also have been used to target pharmacologically the energy output side of the equation.

activity as an intervention for obesity is reliant on the participant's confidence (Riebe et al., 2005). Confidence, however, is inhibited by the co-morbidities of obesity (e.g. poor-self esteem, poor perceived quality of life, depression). Therefore, the efficacy of physical activity is inhibited by the condition itself. Other types of interventions (e.g. pharmacological, nutritional and psychological) actively engage with these co-morbidities in addition to the symptoms of obesity itself, rather than being inhibited by them. Despite this, physical activity has benefits for treating the co-morbidities of obesity post-intervention, although the likelihood of an individual engaging in physical activity is diminished by the very symptoms that characterize it, thus weakening the potential success of this type of treatment. A caveat to this conclusion would be the very small proportion of obese individuals who are highly motivated, confident and do not have of any of the psychopathological co-morbidities that often accompany high levels of adiposity. Essentially, physical activity may be used in conjunction with other types of interventions for its physical well-being benefits and most importantly as a weight maintenance strategy, but not for weight loss.

Physical activity does provide some additional value as a weight maintenance tool to prevent weight regain, which other interventions do not. Once a patient comes off a drug or diet, they will regain a large proportion of the weight lost. Increasing physical activity and, in particular, weekly structured exercise programmes will provide a partial defence against overeating. By seeing 2000 kcal as a margin of error in the habitual diet rather than as a weight loss strategy, an individual will have more short- and medium-term flexibility and thus control of their energy intake. This is especially helpful in an appetite system that promotes positive energy balance and habitual over-consumption. Evidence for the effectiveness of physical activity and structured exercise has been reported in both children (Wardle et al., 2007) and adults (Pavlou et al., 1989). Pavlou and colleagues showed that physical activity has a very powerful function in avoiding weight regain (see Figure 8.4). Using various permutations[12] following weight loss, structured physical activity on average stopped the weight regain observed in individuals who did not exercise. Exercise allowed the recipient to return to similar eating patterns to those before intervention but inhibited the progressive weight gain that was previously observed.

Psychological treatments for obesity

The psychological treatments for obesity should not be considered in isolation of the other treatments, as each type of intervention has a crucial

---

[12] These permutations included reinitiating physical activity at different times post-intervention. For example, some participants continued with their exercise regimes while others stopped. Of those who stopped, some were asked to start again after 8 months and vice versa.

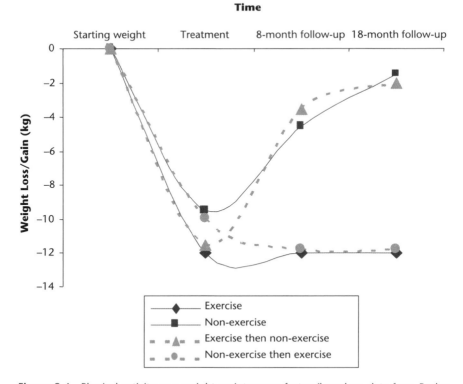

Figure 8.4   Physical activity as a weight maintenance factor (based on data from Pavlou et al., 1989).

psychological component to it. Unlike the other treatments, psychological interventions also offer additional factors and are individually focused rather than prescriptive. Bound within the concepts of food selection, preference and triggers to eat, psychologists try to identify the situations and behaviours that risk violating the diet, as well as any psychopathological phenomena that may have led to the weight gain in the first place (e.g. depression and binge eating). In addition, psychologists can offer behavioural therapy to empower the patient to lose or maintain weight, although the efficacy of these therapy-based interventions has been shown to be relatively weak (Perri et al., 1988; Baum et al., 1991).

Several important facets of psychological treatment programmes have been identified. First, confidence in one's ability to refrain from eating at times other than when hungry, known as self-efficacy, is very important (Jeffery et al., 1984). Stress also appears to be a significant problem within successful long-term obesity treatment. An inability to cope with stress leads to overeating through associated negative emotions interfering with cognitive control of food intake (Wallis & Hetherington, 2004). Continuous vigilance is needed to make sure that weight regain does not occur. It would appear that to prevent weight regain, previously obese individuals have to use cognitive resources to monitor both their food intake and current weight status (Westerterp-Plantenga et al., 1998). Lapses in concentration around food over the medium term will lead to weight regain. The final thing that psychology offers independent of the other fields is a trait/state analysis of behavioural triggers to eating behaviour. Various levels of emotional eating, disinhibited and external eating can lead to loss of dietary control. By increasing awareness around these issues, it is possible to arm an individual with expert knowledge regarding their own triggers to eating. By knowing these triggers, they may be able to avoid situations that are likely to lead to eating in the absence of hunger.

The practical application of psychological-based therapeutic interventions in obesity has been almost completely within a behavioural domain and context. Little research has attempted to incorporate other schools of thought and approaches. In other investigative endeavours, cognitive and psychoanalytical approaches dominate. Both of these approaches are noticeably absent from the obesity literature. The reluctance to offer these psychological interventions for obesity may stem from the belief that obesity can be rectified through behavioural manipulation, and that only the specific co-morbidities associated with the development of excess weight (depression, binge eating, etc.) will respond to these therapies. Current efficacy rates are at odds with this viewpoint.

There is little evidence in the literature for psychoanalytical approaches to obesity except in those cases where specific experiences (i.e. abusive experiences) are uncovered as significant contributing factors (Felitti, 1993; Felitti et al., 1998). Therefore, these interventions are aimed at trying to resolve the impact of these experiences rather than the more holistic reasons behind weight gain and the factors that prevent weight loss. Cognitive behavioural therapy-based interventions are also relatively under-researched. Cooper and Fairburn (2001) have outlined a cognitive behavioural therapy intervention for obesity; however, efficacy rates from detailed long-term studies with sufficient power are lacking. Recently, relaxation therapy has also been employed with individuals considered at risk of emotional eating (Manzoni et al., 2009). Although no replication has been performed and the study suffered from high dropout rates, the results obtained provide tentative evidence that this form of intervention may help in weight loss over a three-month period. Future clinical investigations should attempt to rectify the deficiency in this area of research to ensure that the best obesity intervention services are offered to individuals trying to lose weight; currently, the focus is almost entirely on nutritional, pharmacological, surgical and physical activity-based interventions. All of these interventions (with the exception of surgical) have been found to be ineffective for a large proportion of the obese population in the medium to long term.

It would appear that each type of intervention on its own has little impact on weight loss and maintenance with the exception of surgical interventions. Although surgical interventions are the most effective solution to the obesity pandemic, they are also the most costly. Moreover, the removal of stomach tissue appears to be counter-intuitive. The removal of an organ that is functioning properly prohibits adaptability to future circumstances and there may also be significant, if not terminal, repercussions. Beyond surgical solutions, the best approach to helping people lose weight is through a combination of methods. Alterations in habitual diets to provide a calorie-restricted yet nutritious alternative should always be the first point of reference. Together with this nutritional guidance, psychological and medical interventions can help magnify the effect of the weight loss and prohibit weight regain. Once these three interventions are under way, holistic lifestyle advice should be offered together with an exercise regime and dietary food choice advice to protect against future weight regain. When treatment for obesity is from a multi-dimensional perspective, it ceases to be a 'diet' and becomes a total lifestyle change that needs to be adhered to for life. It is not until an obese individual understands that such drastic changes are required for successful weight loss that they actually become protected from the obesogenic environment. Simply put, the average individual is under attack from all sides in terms of weight gain. The appetite system is geared to over-consumption, the modern environment is littered with labour-saving devices and energy-dense foods and our psychological control of eating can be undermined in a number of relatively simple, yet frequently encountered, ways. In light of the research suggesting relatively small gains made in the treatment of obesity over the last thirty years, it is likely that prevention will be better than a cure in this case.

Preventing obesity

Similar to the treatment of obesity, the prevention of obesity is anchored in the same fields of nutrition, physical activity and psychology. For prevention, pharmacology would be inappropriate; we cannot offer drugs to stop people gaining weight. In the case of prevention, pharmacology is replaced by the more active involvement of politicians (Harkin, 2007). Public initiatives to pseudo-protect children from the obesogenic environment by banning directed advertising of high-fat, nutritionally poor foods, increasing physical activity, sending letters to parents of children considered overweight and threatening to remove children from their parents under child protection laws have met with limited success. The banning of directed advertisements to children meant that only television advertising was included in the voluntary legislation, which led to companies switching their advertising strategies to more subtle means via other forms of multimedia (e.g. the internet). Until government agencies are willing to employ more draconian measures, any intervention is likely to have little effect. Unfortunately, few weight loss services are available, especially for children. It is counterproductive merely to inform parents of their children's overweight, threaten them with court proceedings and yet provide little or no means of helping their children to lose weight. Currently, there are many private and public agencies that focus on weight loss in adults; in contrast, beyond educational seminars on nutrition and physical activity clubs, there is nothing for children. Recently, plans were released by the Welsh Assembly to offer funded and focused weight loss interventions for children, but other political and private groups are less forthcoming.

Research evidence to date indicates that a limited preventative effect has been observed with various interventions for children. Wardle and colleagues (2007) showed that increased physical activity results in a limited effect on rates of obesity, while Jeffery and colleagues (1995) showed similar effects when providing nutritional information. This leaves only one real measure for the prevention of obesity – government and legal interventions. The prevention of obesity must emanate from changes in the environment. Unless banned outright, the heavy taxation of foods considered to be luxuries or nutritionally poor convenience foods will offer an additional monetary dimension to the decision-making process of choosing healthy foods. This should be followed up with directed 'life cycle' interventions where, at each stage of life, from conception to death, targeted tactics are used to dissuade over-consumption of food and promote physical activity (Johnson et al., 2006). Such interventions need to be run by dedicated professionals who are non-profiteering and specialized in one aspect of the life cycle. It is likely that such interventions will cost a lot of money. However, it will require fewer resources in the long term as interventions are successfully implemented in the general population. Moreover, this kind of intervention is likely to draw upon similar or comparable amounts of funding as the current NHS treatment regimes of obesity surgery and diabetes clinics. Future policy makers and consultative experts are likely to face an uphill struggle and a significant chance of failure. This conclusion is based on previous attempts to intervene in the same biological and environmental conditions.

Summary

Defining obesity is notoriously hard and depends on the method used and the reason for using it. The many approaches have their own strengths and weaknesses and should be used in conjunction with each other rather than in isolation. Because of the difficulty defining what obesity is, it should be left to the medical profession to decide who is and is not obese and thus who requires intervention. Therefore, the definition is likely to be based on metabolic syndrome leading to a consequence-based symptom-led service. This 'medicalization' of obesity will mean that interventions will not take place until after the consequences of the excess weight have been manifested. It would be better if a more preventative and screened definition is used so that action can be taken before ailments arise. The difficulty defining obesity is not helped by its number of potential causes. Most aspects of modern life, coupled with our evolutionarily generated appetite system designed to cope with periods of famine, mean that we are all predestined to put on weight unless we actively and strictly control our eating behaviour.

High adiposity is responsible for a plethora of complications usually culminating in diabetes. However, diabetes is not the only consequence of obese weight; there is also an increased risk of mortality through cardiovascular disease, cirrhosis of the liver and cancer. These complications make intervention in obesity through structured weight loss programmes necessary. The principles behind successful weight loss are obvious: an individual should consume less energy than they expend on a daily basis – that is, maintain a negative energy balance. The mechanisms and means of how this is achieved are complex, with many academic fields claiming to have a successful method for achieving short-term negative energy balance. A robust and multidisciplinary approach to the potential causes and consequences of excessive weight gain and obesity is necessary.

All discipline-specific interventions can to some extent influence both sides of the energy balance equation, although most would be considered to affect one side or other of the equation. For example, the two drugs currently licensed for the treatment of obesity, sibutramine and orlistat, both target the energy intake side of the energy balance equation by, respectively, artificially terminating a person's meal and specifically prohibiting their absorption of dietary fat. In contrast, exercise scientists target the energy output side of the equation by encouraging individuals to increase their energy expenditure. Recent systematic reviews of drug treatments (Arterburn et al., 2004) and exercise (Curioni & Lourenço, 2005) place the potential additional weight loss at between 3.6 and 5.3 kg for drug interventions and between 0.4 and 2.6 kg for exercise, compared with 6.4–12.1 kg for short-term dietary interventions (Curioni & Lourenço, 2005).

Getting overweight individuals to lose weight is only half the battle, as it is equally important that weight is not regained post-intervention. Evidence on weight regain following various interventions suggests that, in the long term, people will usually put on a proportion of the weight they had previously lost (van Aggel-Leijssen et al., 2002; Borg et al., 2002). Therefore, understanding the motivational and psychological underpinnings of why this regain occurs is essential to solving the obesity crisis. Habitual over-consumption (portion distortion) (Hill & Peters, 1998), psychological (self-efficacy, vigilance, coping strategies, cognitive restraint, disinhibited eating, emotional eating or external eating) and psychopathological (binge eating and depression) factors are candidates for why weight regain occurs (Byrne, 2002).

9 When eating behaviour goes wrong

Anorexia nervosa, bulimia nervosa and eating disorders not otherwise specified

What constitutes an eating disorder?

Research on eating behaviour is dominated by what happens when it goes wrong. In fact, so much is known about eating disorders that we could dedicate a book to each disorder. For a good text on eating disorders, the interested reader is referred to Fairburn and Brownell (2002). The objective of this chapter is to provide an introduction to the topic rather than an in-depth analysis. To understand what it is to have an eating disorder, we must first address how we define such disorders. This begins with a complex interplay between internationally recognized diagnostic criteria and the expertise of the practitioner involved.

The diagnosis of abnormal eating behaviour is necessarily complex. Such wide-ranging ideologies and inter-individually derived rules around food and eating exist that some essentially harmless behaviours could be considered abnormal. To aid in this diagnostic process, mental health practitioners refer to diagnostic manuals, the most well known of which are the *Diagnostic and Statistical Manual of Mental Disorders-IV-TR* (DSM-IV-TR; American Psychiatric Association, 2000) and the *International Statistical Classification of Diseases and Related Health Problems*, 10th edition (ICD-10; World Health Organization, 2007). These books contain essential criteria for all accepted psychological disorders and characterize each disorder based on the measurable behaviours/symptoms expressed. To be diagnosed with one of these disorders, a patient must exhibit a specific number of symptoms. Eating disorders come in many different forms, although the best known and researched are anorexia nervosa and bulimia nervosa. The criteria for these two eating disorders are shown in Table 9.1. These diagnostic criteria are rigid and the patient must fulfil all of them before they can be officially diagnosed with a specific eating disorder. Although these diagnostic criteria are rigid, the expertise of the clinician is important for assessing the current state of the patient. The severity of symptoms, usually physical symptoms (e.g. weight

Table 9.1   Criteria for eating disorders

Anorexia nervosa	*Bulimia nervosa*
1. Refusal to maintain body weight at or above minimally normal body weight (for sex and age); weight less than 85 per cent of norm	1. Eating an amount of food that is *definitely* larger than most individuals would eat in similar circumstances
2. Intense fear of weight gain and fatness despite abnormally low body weight	2. Lack of control over bingeing episodes
3. Disturbance in experience of own body weight or denial of seriousness of current low body weight	3. Following the binge, a sufferer must employ *inappropriate* compensatory behaviours (including vomiting, laxatives, restrictive dieting, excessive exercise)
4. In post-menarche females, amenorrhoea (i.e. absence of at least three consecutive menstrual cycles)	4. Minimum of two bingeing episodes a week for 3 months
Specify type	5. Obsessive behaviours and thoughts about one's body image
• *Restrictive type*: Person does not binge eat at any time during the development of the disorder	*Specify type*
• *Binge/purging type*: Person engages in regular cycles of binge eating followed by purging behaviour such as vomiting or the abuse of laxatives	• *Purging type*: Person uses purging-type behaviours to cope inappropriately with binge
	• *Non-purging type*: Person uses restriction or excessive exercise to cope with binge

status), will help to determine both a diagnosis and what intervention should be offered.

Other less well known eating disorders include: binge eating disorder; eating disorders not otherwise specified; and feeding disorders. The DSM-IV-TR diagnostic criteria for each of these disorders are shown in Tables 9.2–9.4. Eating disorders not otherwise specified and feeding disorders cover many eating and food-related disorders and, until such time as a full characterization of the various disorders is made, they will continue to be based on generic diagnostic criteria.

How common are eating disorders?

Around 0.1 per cent of the population develops anorexia nervosa during their lifetime. There are also distinct gender and age interactive effects, with around 1 per cent of females developing anorexia nervosa between 15 and 25 years of age. Anorexia nervosa affects females more than males, with 90–95 per cent of adolescent and adult cases being females; however, among 8- to 14-year-olds, 25 per cent of cases are males. This suggests that childhood onset anorexia

Table 9.2   Diagnostic criteria for binge eating disorder

Binge eating disorder
1. Regular and persistent episodes of binge eating
2. Binge-eating episodes at least twice a week for 6 months
3. Inappropriate compensatory behaviours do not follow binge eating episodes
4. Binge eating is associated with at least three of the following: eating faster than normal; eating to the point of excessive fullness; binging when not hungry; feelings of embarrassment and distress accompany binge eating; feelings of guilt immediately after binge eating

Table 9.3   Diagnostic criteria for eating disorders not otherwise specified

Eating disorders not otherwise specified
1. All diagnostic criteria for anorexia nervosa are met, except that menstrual cycle or weight is normal
2. All diagnostic criteria for bulimia nervosa are met, but the frequency of binges has been less than twice a week for less than 3 months
3. There are recurring efforts to compensate (such as self-induced vomiting) for eating only small amounts of food, but body weight is normal for height and age
4. Regularly chewing and spitting out large quantities of food without swallowing

Table 9.4   Diagnostic criteria for feeding disorders

Three types of feeding disorders

Pica	Rumination disorder	Early infant feeding disorder
1. Persistent eating of non-nutritious substances for more than one month	1. Repeated regurgitation and re-chewing of food for at least one month after normal function has been previously observed	1. Persistent failure to eat properly resulting in an inability to gain weight or maintain weight over a period of at least one month
2. Eating substances that are inappropriate to developmental stage	2. The behaviour is not associated with a previous or current medical condition	2. The behaviour is not associated with a previous or current medical condition
3. Consuming a substance that is not part of a cultural ritual	3. The behaviour is not associated with a previous or current eating disorder	3. The behaviour is not associated with a previous or current eating disorder
4. If it exists alongside another disorder, it is so bad that it warrants independent attention and intervention	4. If it exists alongside another disorder, it is so bad that it warrants independent attention and intervention	4. Age of onset before 6 years of age

is the result of a different mechanism from that for adolescent/adult onset anorexia[1]. There are also cases of pensioner onset anorexia nervosa.

One public perception about anorexia nervosa as an eating disorder is that it affects predominantly middle-class teenage girls. However, this is not the case and it could be a diagnostic bias. Historically, practitioners were likely to diagnose malnourishment in people from lower social economic groups and so such individuals were not diagnosed correctly. Another belief is that this eating disorder is most common in Western (Caucasian) women. Although this may once have been true, rapid globalization has seen the prevalence of anorexia nervosa increase markedly throughout the world. Rates of anorexia nervosa comparable to those in Caucasian women have recently been reported in Japan (Yasuhara et al., 2002), and very tentative evidence from China suggests a prevalence of 0.56 per cent, which is much higher than that in the West (Huon et al., 2002).

Intelligence is also often associated with anorexia nervosa. This factor is reflected in the epidemiology of anorexia nervosa, with university populations having higher rates (3 per cent). Furthermore, an increased risk of developing anorexia nervosa has been observed in individuals who work in industries that are more image conscious, such as models, actors, dancers, beauty therapists and athletes. This disorder also has a strong genetic component. Having an identical twin with anorexia nervosa increases the chance of developing the disorder oneself to 56%; having a non-identical twin with anorexia nervosa will increase it to 5%. A mother with anorexia nervosa also increases the risk of her children developing the disorder.

Bulimia nervosa is prevalent in about 1–3 per cent of the population at any one time, and around 20 per cent of Western women admit to having uncontrollably binged at some point in their lives (Hoek, 2002). Of those that have binged, 3 per cent admit to vomiting afterwards as an attempt to control weight gain. Like anorexia nervosa, bulimia nervosa also has a gender bias with only one in thirty bulimics being male (Fairburn & Harrison, 2003). The symptoms of bulimia usually develop in adolescence, often when dieting for the first time. There are several risk factors for bulimia nervosa (see Table 9.5). The more of these risk factors a patient has, the more likely they are to develop bulimia nervosa and the more severe it is likely to be. Bulimia nervosa shares the same ethnicity biases as other eating disorders, with Caucasians displaying the highest rates. However, this too is a diagnostic bias as Eastern cultures (especially Japan) have rates comparable to those in the West (Yasuhara et al., 2002), with early indications of a rate of 1.1 per cent in China (Xiao et al., 2001).

Regarding binge eating disorder, some commentators suggest that as many as 33 per cent of people seeking weight loss treatment suffer from the

[1] Discussed in detail later.

Table 9.5 Risk factors associated with the development of bulimia nervosa

Risk factors associated with bulimia nervosa	Risk factors associated with triggering a binge
• History of childhood obesity • Familial tendencies towards obesity • A close family member with bulimia • External locus of control • Lower than average ideal body image • Depression • High levels of neuroticism • Drug-taking	• Negative emotions (i.e. being in a bad mood) • Stress (psychological stress is the worst) • Intense hunger (i.e. dieting or skipping meals) • Presence of food • Food craving (usually caused by denial of a particular food) • Alcohol • Social facilitation (i.e. eating with other people)

disorder, while medical practitioners suggest that only 7 per cent meet the DSM-IV-TR diagnostic criteria (Williamson et al., 2004a). It is believed that within the general population, the prevalence of binge eating disorder is about 3 per cent (Lilenfeld et al., 2008). This makes binge eating disorder much more prevalent than anorexia nervosa and bulimia nervosa. There is a slight gender bias to binge eating disorder, with female sufferers outnumbering male sufferers by 1.5 to 1. Most individuals with binge eating disorder are also obese and therefore suffer from complications due to excess weight. It has also been suggested that people with binge eating disorder are likely to have suffered from bulimia nervosa at some point and are more likely to present with other psychological problems such as anxiety disorders and depression. Like anorexia nervosa and bulimia nervosa, there appears to be a strong familial component to binge eating disorder. Having a family member with binge eating disorder could triple the likelihood of developing it oneself (Hudson et al., 2006). Binge eating disorder is much more common in adults than in children and has no known ethnicity biases. Compared with other eating disorders, binge eating is a relative newcomer, based on a description of bulimic-like symptoms without the inappropriate compensatory mechanisms. Due to its recent addition, there are many conflicting accounts of prevalence rates, and until longitudinal cross-sectional studies are performed, epidemiological data should be treated with caution.

Pica is the Latin for 'magpie' and this disorder is associated with the craving for and consumption of non-food items. A person with pica has an irrational desire to find and eat things that have no real nutritional value. Common items include ice, dirt, clay, chalk, rust, paint, plaster, soap, wax and crayons. Pica is harmless until it begins to block or irritate the gut. In all cases, it should be explored further to make sure the items that are being consumed do not contain any toxic elements. It is most commonly observed in pregnant women, children under the age of 5 years (over 50 per cent of children go through developmental pica) and people with developmental disorders. However, it has also been reported in patients with eating disorders (Yalug et al., 2007). In pregnant women, the craving for non-food items is often a sign of iron deficiency, and iron supplementation will stop the behaviour. For children, pica is a developmental process as they learn what is and is not edible. If the item they choose to consume is harmless, it can be ignored, as the disorder will usually diminish with age. The treatment for anxiety or re-establishing a better diet will eliminate pica. Dieting is also associated with the severity of pica. Therefore, it may in some cases be an attempt to satisfy biological hunger signals without consuming calories.

Ruminators regurgitate food and either re-chew and swallow it or spit it out. Ruminators often report that the regurgitation is preceded by a gentle burp that does not taste bitter. They state that they never gag or retch when the food comes back. Rumination syndrome can be under both voluntary and involuntary control and may cause halitosis, indigestion, chapped lips, dental problems, damage to tissues of the mouth, growth retardation, pneumonia and weight loss. It is a very secretive disorder and so practitioners are unaware of its true incidence in the general population. Most ruminators have some level of mental or emotional dysfunction and its severity is increased with depression or anxiety. The cause of rumination syndrome is still unknown, although it is likely to be a biological disorder of the upper digestive system; however, neurological explanations cannot yet be discounted.

Feeding disorders are the most common of all the eating disorders. It is believed that up to 25 per cent of children under the age of 6 years will develop an eating problem and about 1.4 per cent will meet the diagnostic criteria for a disorder (Dahl & Sundelin, 1986; Reilly et al., 1999). Despite the high prevalence of feeding disorders, there is confusion within the literature. Multiple labels exist for problems or disorders that are almost identical, making it hard to characterize them. Until such characterizations are possible, their true incidence will remain unknown. This may in fact be the intention, as having such loosely defined criteria allows the application of the term 'disorder' to a variety of possible problems. For an in-depth analysis of feeding disorders see Dovey et al. (2009b) or Chatoor and Ganiban (2003).

The causes of eating disorders

Like all psychological disorders, eating disorders do not usually manifest for one reason only. A complex interaction between biological, individual and environmental factors leads a vulnerable person to develop pathologies in their eating behaviour. Most researchers believe that the causes of eating disorders can be separated into two groups: organic and non-organic. However, it is important to remember that although eating-disordered individuals may exhibit a series of very similar behaviours, why they developed such a disorder will be highly individualized. Therefore, the causes of eating disorders should be considered as 'themes' in an individual's life. The best explanation of the causes of eating disorders should embrace all of the different schools of thought.

Organic causes of eating disorders

The organic or biological explanations of eating disorders include genetic dysfunction, differential activation or both. *Genetic dysfunction* suggests that people who suffer from an eating disorder are genetically different from those that do not. Such people have a very minor mutation somewhere in their genetic make-up, and they experience problems producing certain bio-chemicals such as receptors and neurotransmitters. *Differential activation* is the belief that eating-disordered individuals experience different brain acti-vation and blood flow around their brain compared with other people. Most research into the organic causes of eating disorders has focused on anorexia nervosa and bulimia nervosa. The other eating disorders described above either have no organic explanation associated with them or their biological cause is so obvious that it does not require in-depth medical analysis. For example, a tube-fed child may develop a feeding disorder, but this can be directly associated with poor development of muscles in the digestive system to accommodate solid food. Therefore, when reading this section it should be remembered that the focus is on anorexia nervosa and bulimia nervosa.

Many genes that have undergone selective mutation have been suggested to be responsible for anorexia nervosa and bulimia nervosa. Before searching for a candidate gene, it is important to narrow down the search to regions within the DNA. Current evidence suggests that regions on chromosome 1 are responsible for anorexia nervosa (Grice et al., 2002) and changes to chromo-some 10 are responsible for bulimia nervosa (Bulik et al., 2003). This evidence suggests that eating disorders do not necessarily share the same genetic com-ponents. Instead, they are separate disorders that manifest within eating behaviour rather than similar disorders that have a different individual expres-sion. Armed with this evidence, it is possible to search for genes that are associ-ated with each disorder.

The genes proposed to explain eating disorders are derived from those associated with appetite regulation. The two main groups of genes associated with eating disorders are serotonin and dopamine – specifically, the receptors for serotonin (5-HT_{2A}) and dopamine (D_3, D_4) (Schmidt, 2005). Genetic theory suggests that eating-disordered patients, especially those with anorexia nervosa and bulimia nervosa, have dysfunctional neurochemistry; the evidence for this, however, is inconsistent at best. Theory dictates that serotonergic dysfunction is associated with restricted eating and dopaminergic dysfunction with binge eating. What is known is that, even after recovery, anorexics (all sub-types[2]) show dysfunctional and reduced 5-HT$_{2A}$ activity in several regions of the brain (Frank et al., 2002; Bailer et al., 2004). The classic counter-argument to the genetic approach is one of cause and consequence. The main problem with genetic explanations of eating disorders is that the research evidence is not consistent. Taking 5-HT$_{2A}$ and anorexia nervosa as an example, some studies have reported a strong link between the two, whereas others have suggested no link. Thus even though serotonergic dysfunction is offered as a cause of eating disorders, it is more likely to be a risk factor. High dopamine activity has also been associated with bingeing-type anorexia nervosa and bulimia nervosa (Frank et al., 2005). The argument for this candidate gene also draws upon the link between dopamine and addiction. Anorexics in particular are hyperactive and binge-eating anorexics and bulimics are strongly linked with substance misuse/abuse. As with serotonin, there is evidence both for and against a link with dopamine.

The regional activation hypothesis suggests that patients with eating disorders use their brain differently from those that do not have such a disorder. The hypothesis is based on differences in regional blood flow within the brain, which indicate the regions that are being used at any particular time. Some aspects of eating disorders have been associated with different or ineffectual blood flow in the frontal and parietal[3] regions of the brain (Goethals et al., 2007). Although an interesting method for exploring eating disorders, these activation studies do not really enlighten us about how to correct the problem and again cannot differentiate between cause and consequence. Furthermore, differences in regional activation may be due to genetic dysfunction of the serotonin and dopamine pathways, both of which are very wide-ranging pathways in the brain and responsible for many different functions. All that can be concluded from this theoretical explanation is that anorexics and bulimics show different brain activation patterns from those seen in non-eating-disordered individuals and this may mean that they have formed different strategies and perceptions about the world around them.

Several problems with the organic explanation have to be addressed when proposing a biological model for eating disorders. Over the last few decades,

---

[2] Discussed later in this chapter. Essentially, there is more than one type of anorexia.

[3] The cerebral cortex (or outer layer) of the brain has four lobes: the frontal, parietal, occipital and temporal lobes. The frontal lobe as the name suggests is at the front. The temporal lobe is on the sides underneath the temple region of the skull. The occipital lobe is at the back and is associated with visual perception. Finally, the parietal lobe is between the frontal and occipital regions, on the top of the head.

the prevalence of eating disorders has increased. As our genetic make-up has not changed during this time, it must mean that genetics cannot be entirely responsible for the disorders. Also, genetic assessments cannot differentiate between genetic traits passed down from parents to children and familial behavioural interactions. Although geneticists believe that some gene is of paramount importance, it cannot be discounted that the interaction between family members who share the same genetic material is not the cause. Behavioural factors could also account for sudden changes in prevalence, such as alterations in the way society perceives the family and how family members should interact. Although familial factors are arguably not organic causes of eating disorders, they cannot be disassociated from the obvious shared biological material that all members of the family share. Thus, familial factors believed to be related to eating disorders are considered here, although they might be discussed in the non-organic section, especially since this approach is associated with the social psychological perspective.

A close family can provide an individual member with physical and mental support, as well as a place of refuge from the negative aspects of society. In contrast, a poor family structure can make individual members more anxious and provide little or no protection. If significant members of the family hold strong views on what constitutes attractiveness, this could have a serious impact on someone's becoming anorexic. The first study to suggest that the family could be the root cause of eating disorders was that of Minuchin et al. (1978). They suggested that 'anorexic families' were more polarized in their approaches to right and wrong, as well as being more rigid in their views. Such families also contained fathers who were more protective than normal (Stuart et al., 1990), parents who were over-involved with their child's problems, and family members who had difficulty expressing emotional intimacy. The final aspect to family involvement in eating disorders is an inability to resolve conflicts: arguments in these families are to be avoided at all costs, leading to passive coping mechanisms and internalization of emotions. Humphrey (1986) stated that such families were weakly bonded through poor intra-family communication.

There is some evidence to support the role of the family in eating disorders, whereas other evidence suggests that the family dynamic leads to pathologies associated with eating disorders rather than eating disorders themselves. Recent research indicates that the family does have a role to play in about 8 per cent of cases of disordered eating (Kluck, 2008). Table 9.6 provides a summary of familial theorists' beliefs about eating disorders.

Familial theorists do not offer a specific cause for eating disorders. The geneticists, in contrast, believe a specific candidate gene causes the disorder. Multiple influences on the family from individual members and the way they interact constitute a large proportion of inter-family variation. Therefore, like most non-organic causes of eating disorders, a mix of psychology and

Table 9.6 Summary of the familial theorists' beliefs about eating disorders

Familial factors and what they mean in eating disorders

- **Eating disorders are an expression of many behaviours and problems**
  - ➢ Provides a way to avoid conflict
  - ➢ Provides a way of communicating with the family something that cannot be expressed normally
  - ➢ Provides a way of coping

- **Eating disorders are a way of expressing emotions**
  - ➢ Extreme emotions within the family are not tolerated or expressed
  - ➢ Conflict within the family group is not tolerated, so problems are not discussed and resolved

- **Eating disorders are an expression of poor boundaries**
  - ➢ The eating-disordered individual does not know what their role is within the family and so does not know how to interact with other family members

environment means that familial theorists tend towards description rather than explanation. The fact that family members might not know they are responsible for manifestation of the disorder compounds the matter; therefore, proponents of the familial perspective tend not to suggest to family members that they bear any responsibility. This serves two purposes. First, by not attaching blame, the family are more likely to be involved in the healing process and may address the issues responsible for manifestation of the eating disorder. Second, if some members of the family were to be blamed, they could be driven away thus isolating the anorexic. The final criticism of this approach is that it provides little or no explanation as to why an eating disorder develops instead of any other psychological problem. This may go some way to explaining the conflicting findings (Fairburn et al., 1997).

Non-organic causes of eating disorders

In addition to the organic causes of eating disorders, there are many more social and psychological approaches, including psychodynamics, cognitive behavioural theory, the sociocultural models and significant events theory. Each of these approaches explains eating disorders from a purely psychological, environmental or cultural rather than biological perspective. The psychodynamic and cognitive behavioural schools of thought have the most proponents and the largest evidence base.

Based on Freudian views, the *psychodynamic approach* focuses on how the patient experiences the disorder and what feelings and thoughts are associated with it. It is an attempt to understand the individual's experiences and how this understanding can be applied to others. Practitioners of the psycho-dynamic approach believe that eating disorders are bound up with fear – that these psychopathologies, and in particular anorexia nervosa, are anxiety dependent. The fear itself is related to becoming an adult and everything that that entails: weight gain, puberty and sexual contact. Restrictive practices around food are a behavioural attempt to avoid adulthood, allowing the suf-ferer to regain control of their biology and thus reduce fear of developing into an adult. This control then feeds into an anorexic's feelings of self-worth and provides them with a sense of identity (Williamson et al., 2004a). To treat the disorder, psychodynamic practitioners focus on the conscious and unconscious representations and manifestations of specific symptoms. The focus tends to be on the patient's childhood, familial interactions and trans-ference of these experiences onto present relationships with significant others (Dare et al., 2001), although there is much diversity between approaches and thus between published material (Fonagy et al., 2005).

According to the psychodynamic approach, eating disorders are also char-acterized by contradictions regarding social interaction. Patients with eating disorders crave relationships with others yet will withdraw when offered one. This may stem from their hypersensitive nature and egocentric interpretation of other people's attitudes and beliefs (Corcos & Jeammet, 2001). This leads them both to desire and to detest social interaction. Although they want to be around people, they place a negative interpretation on what others say and apply that interpretation to themself. Owing to the dependence on case stud-ies within the psychodynamic perspective, some phenomena are applicable to each eating-disordered individual whereas others are not. Therefore, this model does have several restrictions. The theory does not hold up to scrutiny if the trigger for the eating disorder does not manifest within a significant child-hood or relationship experience[4]. Equally, the model does not explain why this disordered development manifests specifically as inappropriate feeding practices rather than any other form of psychopathology.

One of the earliest theories of eating disorders and, in particular, anorexia nervosa grew out of the psychodynamic approach and was related to the indi-vidual's fear of becoming an adult. This was the maturational model. Based on the work of Crisp (1967), anorexia nervosa was considered a morbid fear of gaining weight based on an unwillingness to become an adult. Therefore, the disorder itself was thought to manifest through a heighted sense of fear, even-tually becoming a phobia fixated on weight and food. As research into eating disorders has expanded, new types and sub-types have been discovered. The specificity of the maturation model to anorexia nervosa and prepubescence, as Crisp (1980) himself acknowledged, means that it cannot be applied to other

---

[4] Although proponents of this theory would argue it is in the subconscious, so the person would not be consciously aware of it.

eating disorders or even to sub-types of anorexia nervosa. Although the maturation model has not withstood modern interpretations of eating disorders, it is considered a cornerstone in the development of a theoretical understanding of eating disorders. It moved explanations of anorexia nervosa beyond the psychodynamic explanations of the symptoms and allowed for more detailed examination of the other symptoms that characterize the disorder. Together with the concurrent work of Bruch, the maturation model allowed for detailed description of the affective and cognitive components of the disorder.

The antithesis of psychodynamics is the *cognitive behavioural approach*. Instead of being bound by Freudian views of the mind, cognitive behaviourists believe in thought patterns or schemata. These theorists extend the explanations into a world beyond childhood and consider faulty thought patterns and personality characteristics. Advocates of this perspective suggest that people with eating disorders have internalized a faulty way of thinking specifically about weight and body image. The constant fear of gaining weight means that the act of restriction provides respite from the anxiety about gaining weight. Cognitive behaviourists also suggest that eating-disordered individuals have some form of visual disturbance regarding their own body image and 'see' themselves as being larger than they actually are. The personality characteristics around eating disorders proposed by this school of thought are the perfectionist tendencies and the need for order. Things, thoughts and actions must all have their place, and deviations from this order will be considered incorrect and cause anxiety. The final significant component to this theoretical perspective is the internalization of social/media ideals of beauty. People with eating disorders believe that only extremely low body weight is considered beautiful and draw upon specific 'role models' within the media as evidence for this. They then strive to achieve this weight status, but often fall below it through dysfunctional views of their self-image. It is only when all of these factors combine within the individual that an eating disorder is manifested (Williamson et al., 2004b).

Cognitive behaviourists believe that eating disorders arise through dissatisfaction with all forms of mental and physical development. Eating-disordered individuals believe that they cannot be autonomous and do not wish to be independent from significant others. They attribute their perceived continual failure to become independent to their own lack of ability. For the person with an eating disorder, this dissatisfaction is brought about not by their circumstances but by their perfectionist tendencies. Therefore, irrespective of the outcome, the eating-disordered patient will consider themself a failure unless they achieve what most would consider impossible. Another cognitive factor is preoccupying thoughts about their appearance and food, which lead to the overloading of their cognitive resources, and results in an inability to deal with additional psychological and environmental demands. Thus, few resources are left for problem-solving capabilities. Table 9.7 provides

Table 9.7   Summary of the cognitive factors involved in eating disorders

---

Cognitive factors in eating disorders
- *Selective attention*: only listening to very specific aspects of the information one receives
- *Black and white thinking*: only thinking in extremes, there is no grey area
- *Over-application of conclusions*: applying one's thoughts to a far too wide array of phenomena
- *Exaggeration of thoughts*: making ideas and thoughts that should be considered less important integral to one's perceived existence
- *Inappropriate interpretations*: coming to the wrong conclusions and refusing to change them
- *Egocentric thinking*: obsessively thinking about oneself before others
- *Anxiety issues*: in a perpetual state of anxiety about an array of issues
- *Perfectionism*: need to avoid all perceived mistakes
- *Obsessive-compulsive thoughts*: all-encompassing thoughts that are acted out in a ritual fashion
- *Narcissism*: a focus on body image and shape to the point of obsession about appearance
- *Sociotropy*: a desperate need for social acceptance and approval of others
- *Poor self-esteem*: low opinion of self and one's ability

Bulimia nervosa only
- *Impulsive and sensation-seeking*: engaging in behaviours without thinking about the potential consequences and the need to experience new thoughts, feelings and sensory situations

---

a list of cognitive behavioural factors associated with eating disorders. This list was derived from the work of Fairburn et al. (2003), Cassin and von Ranson (2005) and Cooper (2005).

Similar to psychodynamics, the cognitive behavioural approach suffers from being unable to offer a complete explanation of eating disorders. This approach is only able to offer its own characterization of phenomena observed in individuals with eating disorders. Furthermore, this school of thought does not differentiate those people who are disordered from those who are not: the thoughts, schemata and coping responses of the eating-disordered are viewed as being similar to those of individuals who are merely cognitively restrained. This is damning criticism: an inability to tell the difference between disorder and normality means that a diagnosis can be made only once the individual is in danger. In the case of eating disorders, this is reflected in the patient's current weight status. Intervention before full manifestation of the biological consequences of an eating disorder would be unlikely, thus increasing the severity of the disorder while decreasing the potential for recovery.

The *sociocultural model* of eating disorders is based on the belief that eating disorders manifest because of changing societal ideals and/or rapid changes in how society functions. Marked social and cultural changes cause confusion to younger individuals through being exposed to and judged by an outdated way of living perpetuated by their parents, which is incongruent with the modern environment. For instance, globally, we are undergoing rapid economic development based on industrialization and mechanization of the workforce. Furthermore, developing countries are experiencing rapid urbanization. These changes in living arrangements result in changes in how individuals and groups function, which leads to changes in attitudes around social interaction. Modernization means that women are no longer viewed purely as caregivers and mothers; rather, they are now considered major contributors to the work-force and can be the equal of their male peers. Industrialization also allows for global communication and the potential for cross-cultural pollination of beliefs, ideas and social norms. Within this theoretical perspective, the mani-festation of psychological morbidity is not the result of individual weakness but an increased receptiveness to the social anxiety brought about by rapid change (Boyce & Parker, 1989). This rapid change is a leap into the unknown, which preys on the human need for certainty and predictability. By their very nature new approaches have no reference points and create a large amount of uncertainty about the validity of how an individual lives their life.

The sociocultural model is derived from a mix of feminist, social psycho-logical, cultural and ethical perspectives, brought together to help understand the wider context of eating disorders. Feminists advocate equality and the end of persecution of women in a male-dominated society. This has led some researchers to suggest that it is not the feminine or masculine nature of the individual that is responsible for the onset of an eating disorder, but an aware-ness of the conflict that exists between the sexes. Awareness of this conflict has led some women to believe that they cannot meet the ambiguous societal demands of being a woman in the modern environment, thus increasing their anxiety. It has also been suggested that a more traditional lifestyle might lower the prevalence of eating disorders. For example, women who have a more traditional feminine role within society appear to be better protected from bulimia (Silverstein et al., 1986). Thus feminist thinking and gender equality combined with the traditional caregiving role might be responsible for the increased prevalence of eating disorders. Others argue that increased aware-ness has meant a wider choice for women, leading to role ambiguity within society. This carries weight, since a woman who has 'superwoman syndrome'[5] will be more likely to develop an eating disorder (Thornton et al., 1991).

There is much cultural evidence for the explosion of eating disorders in developed countries. Both foreign nationals living in the USA (Stark-Wroblewski et al., 2005) and inhabitants of regions that receive media from

[5] This is not a real syndrome but is used to explain the propensity of some women to try to conform to both traditional and modern female roles, whereby they must be the primary caregiver, housekeeper and equal economic provider for the family.

the developed world (Unikel et al., 2005) suddenly develop eating disorders despite no previous evidence for them. It is believed that this is manifested through the exposure to the Western view of 'thinness equalling attractiveness' (Stice, 2002), an exposure that has an irreversible impact on what it is to be a woman and have a female identity. Changing the female identity alters the decision-making process, resulting in conflict between what a woman *wants* to do versus what she thinks she *should* do. An individual's first significant life choices are made around late childhood and early adulthood. This happens to coincide with the onset of eating disorders. The mean age of onset of eating disorders is bimodally distributed[6], with two peaks – at age 14 and age 18. At age 14 in the UK, youngsters make their first choices regarding school subjects and at 18 they may leave home or go to university. Pressure to make choices places pressure on a person's identity – they question what it is they want to do, as well as who they are as an individual. The dual role highlighted by 'superwoman syndrome' means that women in modern society are pressurized by a shortened time frame (if they want children they have to do so while they are fertile). A crisis of identity leads to feelings of loss of control and anxiety, as well as having failed at one's first attempt to be independent. According to the sociocultural perspective, this leads to a loss of self-confidence, self-esteem and self-worth in one's ability to make decisions and therefore reverting to a child-like behavioural state provides respite from those important decisions. Men, in contrast, are not exposed to such pressures and suffer less from eating disorders.

The sociocultural model offers an explanation for many of the observed characteristics of the non-organic causes of anorexia nervosa and bulimia nervosa. The theory suggests that women are more susceptible to eating disorders than men and that exposure to a 'thin ideal' will result in dissatisfaction with body image and inappropriate or extreme attempts to control weight status. Individuals with increased social anxiety will internalize and try to adhere to what it is they think it is to be female, leading to increased anxiety around key life choices. Socially receptive people will try to adhere both to the 'thin ideal' perception of beauty and 'superwoman syndrome'. Perceived failure to adequately adhere to all of these pressures will result in withdrawal from society in an attempt to seek refuge in childhood. This then develops into both inappropriate means of achieving the female ideal of beauty and the rejection of female adult identity. The only real weakness of this perspective is that the theory cannot explain why some individuals go on to develop an eating disorder and others do not. Therefore, we need the psychodynamic and cognitive behavioural approaches to 'fill in' the gaps. Thus the real strength of

---

[6] This means that is has two peaks rather than just one, as observed with a normal bell-shaped distribution.

the sociocultural model is its use alongside other approaches rather than as a theory that stands alone.

The final non-organic approach is *significant events theory*. This theory states that a significant event, usually but not always sexual, precedes the eating disorder. When patients do not report sexual abuse, it is suggested that actual or perceptual loss of a parent during childhood is the cause. Around 30 per cent of patients with an eating disorder reveal childhood sexual abuse during therapy (Conners & Morse, 1993), suggesting that a minority of individuals who develop an eating disorder will have suffered sexual abuse and not all individuals who have suffered sexual abuse go on to develop an eating disorder (Everill & Waller, 1995). This has led some authors to question whether some aspect of the abuse itself caused the disorder (e.g. duration of abuse, number of incidents, relationship with perpetrator, age of child, level of aggression) (Lange et al., 1999), although recent research indicates that this is not the case, especially for bulimia nervosa (Anderson et al., 2000). There is also limited support for the belief that the death of a parent can result in a child becoming eating-disordered (Fernández et al., 2007). Thus, like the sexual abuse significant event, parental loss is not well supported as a cause for an eating disorder. When examined empirically, significant events theory has been found to be weak at predicting eating disorders. Apart from sexual abuse and parental loss, no other significant life event has been offered for scientific scrutiny. Although sexual abuse could provide a psychodynamic explanation of eating disorders, it is unable to suggest why eating disorders develop instead of any other psychiatric illness. Significant events should only be considered as an additional risk factor and not the cause of or a theoretical underpinning to the development of eating disorders. Table 9.8 provides a summary.

Many potential explanations have been offered for eating disorders. Both organic and non-organic theories and models have increased our knowledge of how an eating disorder develops but none of them can offer a full

Table 9.8   Summary of the sociocultural and significant life events theories

---

Sociocultural cues in eating disorders
- Socially hypersensitive
- Culture or country going through rapid change
- Ambiguous gender identity (especially for females)
- A wish to adhere to societal views of femininity irrespective of whether they are achievable or not
- Perceived media representations of beauty through unattainable levels of 'thinness'

Significant events that trigger eating disorders
- Sexual abuse
- Perceived (being sent away or absence of parent) or actual (death) parental loss

---

explanation. It is thus likely that a combination of factors is involved. The eating-disordered patient is likely to have minute biological differences that predispose them to different organic controls of appetite regulation. Alongside this biological infirmity, cultural or significant events occur that alter decision-making and problem-solving cues, which leads to pathological thoughts and fixation on food, eating, fat, and weight gain. These factors combined then create the right milieu for eating disorders to manifest. Finally, an interaction between personality, coping mechanisms and social support will help differentiate those who will develop a disorder and those who will not. This complex arrangement could explain why so few people do indeed develop an eating disorder and why such disorders cannot be explained from one theoretical perspective alone.

Consequences of eating disorders

The consequences of eating disorders are wide-ranging. Both anorexics and bulimics often present with medical complications resulting from the behaviours that characterize the disorder. Figure 9.1 shows the various complications associated with anorexia nervosa and bulimia nervosa. Most anorexic patients remain so for more than 6 years and around a third will never fully recover (Treasure, 2004). Up to 10 per cent of patients will die within 10 years and another 10 per cent will die within 20 years as a direct result of the condition (Costin, 1997), making anorexia nervosa the most dangerous of all of the psychological disorders (Sullivan, 2002). Most deaths result from successful suicide attempts, with anorexia increasing the likelihood of suicide 23-fold (Harris & Barraclough, 1997). Another 20 per cent will suffer from long-term consistent relapse whereby they will be in and out of treatment programmes. The remaining 30–40 per cent of anorexics, thankfully, recover within 10 years of receiving treatment. This improved prognosis is the result of better diagnoses and treatment strategies in recent years. The prognosis for bulimics appears to be a lot better than that for anorexics. Death from bulimia nervosa is very unlikely and most of those affected make a full recovery, although relapse rates are quite high.

Are all eating disorders similar?

The unsuccessful explanation of the causes and consequences of eating disorders may not be due simply to their complex aetiology. Risk of psychological disturbance is rarely specific to one disorder and is equally unlikely to present without a diagnosis of another psychological disorder or at least significant factors associated with another disorder. The presence of other psychological

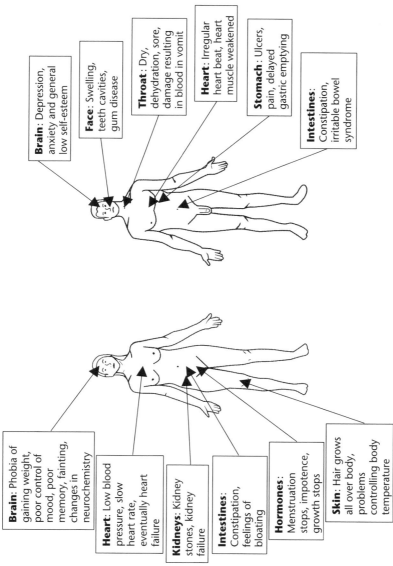

Anorexia Nervosa

Brain: Phobia of gaining weight, poor control of mood, poor memory, fainting, changes in neurochemistry

Heart: Low blood pressure, slow heart rate, eventually heart failure

Kidneys: Kidney stones, kidney failure

Intestines: Constipation, feelings of bloating

Hormones: Menstruation stops, impotence, growth stops

Skin: Hair grows all over body, problems controlling body temperature

Bulimia Nervosa

Brain: Depression, anxiety and general low self-esteem

Face: Swelling, teeth cavities, gum disease

Throat: Dry, dehydration, sore, damage resulting in blood in vomit

Heart: Irregular heart beat, heart muscle weakened

Stomach: Ulcers, pain, delayed gastric emptying

Intestines: Constipation, irritable bowel syndrome

Figure 9.1 Repercussions of having anorexia nervosa or bulimia nervosa.

disorders is termed a co-morbidity, whereby treatment will require active intervention for more than one disorder. The most common co-morbidities with eating disorders are depression, general and specific anxiety disorder, binge eating disorder, obsessive-compulsive disorder, conduct disorders, personality disorders and body dysmorphic disorder. Indeed, sometimes the absence or presence of a specific set of co-morbidities can lead to a diagnosis for a sub-type of an eating disorder.

The most common co-morbidity associated with eating disorders is *depression*. Between 25 and 80 per cent of eating-disordered patients will also be diagnosed with some form of depression at the same time as being diagnosed with an eating disorder (Herzog et al., 1992; Lynskey, 1998). Over the course of their treatment and recovery, up to 96 per cent of patients will exhibit signs of depression. The most comprehensive systematic review of the literature suggests that the prevalence of depression is different for anorexics and bulimics. Although both anorexics and bulimics report more depression than the general population, it tends to be related to bingeing behaviours. Around 60 per cent of binge-eating anorexics also display depression, whereas only 40 per cent of restrictive anorexics do (Godart et al., 2007). Furthermore, hyper self-critical thoughts associated with maintaining the depressive disorder are more common in bulimics than anorexics (Speranza et al., 2003). In short, a large proportion of patients with eating disorders are likely also to have depressive symptoms that will affect treatment programmes and successful intervention. In fact, the prevalence of depression among the eating-disordered is so great it warrants separate assessment and structured intervention upon restoration of weight status and the removal of imminent risk to health caused by low weight.

General and specific anxiety disorder is defined as clinical levels of anxiety and worry on more days than not over a six-month period. Although the prevalence of this disorder is less than that of depression, it is significantly higher in eating-disordered people than in the community at large (Garfinkel et al., 1995). Interestingly, Godart et al. (2002) suggested that general and specific anxiety disorder is more likely in restrictive-type (31 per cent) than binge-type eating disorders (13 per cent). However, in a later study the same authors (Godart et al., 2003) suggested that the prevalence of general and specific anxiety disorder is higher in both sub-types of anorexia nervosa (49–45 per cent) than bulimia nervosa (33 per cent). Thus a large proportion of anorexics and a third of bulimics present with additional anxieties beyond the simple worry surrounding weight and food.

Another disorder that is arguably a derivative of general and specific anxiety disorder and is associated with eating disorders is *obsessive-compulsive disorder*. This condition is brought on by anxiety related to performing a specific task under the misguided belief that it will help counter a specific, potentially disastrous consequence. The patient becomes obsessive about a specific situation and compulsively performs a set series of ritualistic behaviours whenever the obsessive thought surfaces. This could be as simple as turning a light switch on and off repetitively, or washing their hands over and over again. By performing the behaviour, the patient placates their increasing anxiety associated with the obsessive thoughts. Beyond preoccupations about food and weight, other obsessive-compulsive disorders are found in about 24 per cent of anorexics and 9 per cent of bulimics (Pallister & Waller, 2008). This difference is similar to that seen in general and specific anxiety disorder and reflects the fact that anxiety disorders are more closely related to restrictive practices than to bingeing.

Most anorexics and bulimics have body shape psychopathologies. They believe that a very thin body is attractive and may aspire to achieve ever-decreasing, impossibly low, body weights. In association with this distorted view of body image, they will also be fat phobic – that is, they will have a phobia towards fat and foods containing perceived high levels of fat. As a group, they also have misperceptions regarding their own body size and might fixate on a specific body part. Such obsessive thoughts about any part of the body could be considered a body dysmorphic disorder. It is true that both anorexic and bulimic patients have issues with their bodies to the point where they would be considered obsessive. *Body dysmorphic disorder* has been the source of much debate regarding whether it is a separate disorder or a subtype of obsessive-compulsive disorder. Either way, body dysmorphic disorder is associated with anxiety and inappropriate preoccupations with imagined imperfections. Early indications suggest that the disorder is specific to anorexia and not bulimia. About 25 per cent of anorexic patients present with body dysmorphic disorder (Jolanta & Tomasz, 2000).

Binge eating disorder, as the name would suggest, is seen in all bulimics; however, it is also evident in around 50 per cent of anorexics. Binge eating entails consuming a large number of calories (the daily recommended intake or more) over a very short period of time. To be defined as binge eating disorder, the behaviour must be cyclical and have occurred a minimum of twenty-four times (twice a week for three months). The prevalence of binge eating within anorexic patients is unclear, especially the numbers of binge/purging-type and restrictive-type anorexics. It is currently known that anorexic patients who do binge eat are also likely to suffer from a range of additional personality disorders. Suffering from a personality disorder alongside an eating disorder is somewhat contentious and rates have been reported to vary from 27 to 93 per cent (Vitousel & Manke, 1994).

Of all of the different sub-types of personality disorders, borderline personality disorder appears to be most associated with binge-eating symptoms. *Borderline personality disorder* is defined as having unpredictable moods, a poor or unstable self-image and problems controlling one's impulsive nature. The behaviour of individuals with borderline personality disorder is often aggressive and hostile to those around them, resulting in violence (Lish et al., 1996).

The aggressive overtones combined with the unstable self-image often lead to such individuals engaging in self-harm or drug abuse. Another component to this disorder is the need for intensity in all of their relationships, resulting in significant others withdrawing because of the unpredictable nature of the patient. This intensity within their relationships derives from an intense fear of isolation and being alone. Patients with eating disorders, irrespective of the type, also tend to have avoidant and dependant personality disorders. About 30 per cent of eating-disordered individuals also meet a diagnosis of avoidant and dependent personality disorders (Bornstein, 2001). Both of these types of personality disorder are related to anxiety. The criteria for *avoidant personality disorder* are being extremely sensitive to negative feedback and completely inhibited in social contexts because of feelings of inadequacy. *Dependent personality disorder* is associated with such behaviours as being clingy, very submissive and having an intense fear of being separated from the person one is dependent on. Although slightly different, both of these personality disorders share a similar trait of being hypersensitive to social criticism and sufferers will do anything to avoid or appease those that they perceive to be rejecting them. This makes it hard for therapists to engage with these individuals and it is difficult to get them to attend treatment sessions regularly. Among anorexic and bulimic patients, it is important to be mindful of the presence of personality disorders as well as the more obvious eating disorder. Hypersensitivity to negative comments or responses can exacerbate the problem. The presence of a personality disorder is likely to have large effect on treatment regimes and how the therapist interacts with the patient.

The co-morbidities discussed here are the more common ones, and many others will be observed in a population of eating-disordered patients (Cassin & von Ranson, 2005). The link between eating disorders and other psychological problems makes each case highly individual. Not all eating disorders are the same. Indeed, because there are so many links with other disorders it is likely that eating-disordered individuals show large variations in symptoms, making them very different from one another and thus making them hard to treat as a single group with a specific treatment regime. The presence or absence of specific combinations of co-morbidities leads to an unofficial sub-categorization of eating disorders. These classifications are gaining acceptance and many of the terms are frequently used in diagnosis.

(Sub-)types of eating disorders: anorexia nervosa and under-consumption

Restrictive type and binge/purging type

Both of these sub-types of anorexia are official categorizations found within the DSM-IV-TR. The distinction between the two sub-types is whether or not the patient engages in binging and/or purging behaviour. Not all binge/purging anorexic patients actually binge; however, they use vomiting and other inappropriate purging mechanisms and behaviours. Both binge/purging anorexia and purging anorexia form the same sub-type as they share many characteristics. Binge/purging anorexics are often considered alongside bulimics, as they share a similar personality and prevalence of co-morbidities. Although the distinction between the two diagnoses is often related to weight status, there is an element of overlap whereby the bulimic may become a binge/purging anorexic and vice versa. One distinction other than weight status lies in how quickly after binging that the inappropriate mechanisms and/or behaviours are used to purge. Immediate initiation of purge will prohibit any absorption of food and will mean that the individual will not actually have eaten anything. These time frame differences may differentiate those who will develop binge/purging anorexia within the coming months and those who will not. Patients with restrictive types of anorexia will lose weight through pure starvation rather than through employing any additional method to lose weight.

Atypical anorexia nervosa

This sub-type is a way of characterizing any individual who presents with all but one of the crucial symptoms of anorexia nervosa. These symptoms include amenorrhoea and significant weight loss (Fairburn & Walsh, 2002). Recently, another form of atypical anorexia has been proposed. This form meets all of the criteria for a DSM-IV-TR diagnosis, but the patient does not have the drive for thinness or inappropriate perceptions of their own weight status. They know they are seriously underweight and do not have any body dysmorphic-like distortions (Ramaciotti et al., 2002). Anorexic patients without a drive for thinness tend to be a little older, a little heavier and have an older age of onset as well as a better prognosis than those with other sub-types of anorexia (Abbate-Daga et al., 2007).

Anorexia athletica

Sport has long been associated with pathological views and behaviours around food. Elite athletes are at increased risk of developing eating disorders, with a rate in this group of around 13.5 per cent (Sundgot-Borgen & Torstveit, 2004). This form of anorexia is different from the other, more typical types seen across the diagnostic spectrum. Rather than having any body dysmorphic-related issues, these individuals lose weight in an attempt to improve performance or as a result of a direct comparison with others who are perceived to be more successful. Lean muscle mass is usually preserved so the individual can still engage in sport or exercise at the highest level, whereas typical anorexics tend to lose both lean and adipose tissue. Individuals with anorexia athletica are likely to lose weight through extreme exercise regimes rather than food restriction, although most anorexics use physical activity as an additional means to losing weight. The final difference between anorexia athletica and anorexia nervosa is that the reinforcer for the disorder is the sport itself. Removal of the sport from the athlete's life is also likely to see the disorder disappear (Sudi et al., 2004). People with anorexia athletica are fanatical about weight and diet and tend to exercise repeatedly beyond the requirements of good health. Compared with their unaffected peers, they may exercise to the point of collapse; this can easily occur, especially if they are limiting their energy intake. They do not find physical activity fun and will treat a training session like a competitive performance. Furthermore, they may not see their achievements as being anything special, and may base their self-worth on their short-term performance, which must improve progressively each time they train. Athletes with the disorder have also been known to train even when carrying a serious injury. Compared with other forms of anorexia, anorexia athletica also shows a gender bias, with twice as many female sufferers (up to 20 per cent) than male sufferers (8 per cent).

Cachexia or cancer-related anorexia

Cachexia refers to the rapid weight loss associated with the final stages of cancer. This is the point at which the patient begins to lose their appetite and 'waste away'. Hypothalamic cancer can lead to excessive eating usually through an insatiable appetite in its initial stages; however, this will inevitably lead to cachexia and then death. It has been documented on several occasions that an astrocytoma (brain tumour) can lead to anorexia nervosa. This suggests that on some level anorexia is controlled by a neurological circuit. Which circuit is still open to debate, although it does appear that many eating disorders have roots within some form of serotonin or dopamine dysfunction.

Child-onset and adult-onset anorexia

It was mentioned earlier in this chapter that the mean age of onset of eating disorders is bimodally distributed, with two peaks – one at age 14 and another at age 18. This bimodal distribution suggests that there may be two separate age-dependent types of anorexia nervosa, which can be loosely separated into child-onset and adult-onset anorexia nervosa. There is evidence of anorexia in children as young as 7 years (Nielsen et al., 1997). However, the diagnostic criteria state that anorexia occurs only in menorrhoeal (normal flow of the menses) females. Although this actively discriminates against diagnosis of the disorder in males, it does so also in children. Children may also meet atypical characteristics of anorexia in terms of body dissatisfaction and extremely low weight status. Children diagnosed with anorexia are almost always restrictive types and are less likely to present with depression (Peebles et al., 2006). With a lower likelihood for additional co-morbidities and perceptual distortions, the recovery rate in younger anorexic patients is higher, making early recognition and intervention important before the disorder develops into adulthood.

Orthorexia nervosa

This type of restrictive eating is relatively new to the eating disorder literature. It is not an official disorder and has received very limited attention from academics and practitioners alike. It can be described roughly as the obsessive preoccupation of eating healthy, nutritious and perceptually nutritious foods (Evillly, 2001). The obsession around superior foods means sufferers may inappropriately label entire food groups as unhealthy, leading to an unbalanced diet and weight loss. Refusal to eat any perceptually 'poor' foods can lead to social isolation via avoidance of communal or social situations where food is integral. It has been reported that the prevalence of orthorexia nervosa may be as high as 7 per cent, although this is likely to be biased towards testing people with high social economic status (Donini et al., 2004; Bosi et al., 2007). Many authors on this emerging disorder believe that it is closely associated with obsessive-compulsive disorder and may be a derivative of this anxiety disorder.

(Sub-)types of eating disorders: bulimia nervosa and over-consumption

Purging type and non-purging type

These two sub-types are both officially recognized by the DSM-IV-TR criteria for bulimia nervosa. The criteria for whether a patient is a purging type or a non-purging type bulimic is whether they use vomiting or pharmacological agents to purge their stomachs of food, or whether they habitually use extreme physical activity or extreme dieting practices to lose/maintain weight. It should be noted that it is integral to this disorder that the individual does employ inappropriate compensatory responses, otherwise they would be diagnosed with binge eating disorder. The vast majority of bulimics fall into the purging sub-type, although exact proportions are unknown. What confounds the issue further is that many purging sub-type bulimics also employ non-purging techniques to control weight (Grave et al., 2008).

Night-eating syndrome

Night-eating syndrome is defined as extremely restricted eating followed by overeating, and in some individuals binge eating, at night accompanied with long periods of insomnia-type sleep disorders (Stunkard, 2002). The syndrome appears to have roots in both anxiety and disturbance of circadian rhythms (Stunkard et al., 2005). Sufferers of this problem put on weight and become obese. It is at this point that they are diagnosed. There are also non-obese night-eaters within the wider population, but these individuals do not appear to over-consume in terms of calories during the night and therefore are not susceptible to gaining weight. Night-eating syndrome appears to respond very well to pharmacological treatments. In nearly all cases, the prescription of selective serotonin re-uptake inhibitors will eliminate the dysfunctional eating (Miyaoka et al., 2003).

Sleep-related eating disorder

Sleep-related eating disorder is, as it sounds, a sleep disorder. However, sufferers binge-eat while asleep in a similar fashion to sleepwalkers. They awake in the morning and do not remember anything. This differs from night-eating syndrome where the patient is fully aware that they are eating. This disorder is so extreme that sufferers can become paranoid that someone is playing tricks on them in their sleep. Interestingly, during an episode they eat foods that they deny themselves while awake. Furthermore, this disorder is related to dieting, alcoholism, drug abuse and, in most cases, runs in the family.

Treating eating disorders

The treatment of eating disorders is often highly complex due to their aetiology. Success rates and treatment strategies vary significantly between disorders and depending on the individual's co-morbidities. Further differences depend on local funding and the expertise and theoretical adherence of local practitioners. Broadly speaking, most interventions fall into one of four types: interpersonal psychotherapy, cognitive behavioural therapy, family therapy and pharmacotherapy. In extreme cases where risk to life is a factor, patients may require hospitalization for an extended period. An inpatient treatment regime is different from outpatient therapy, as the inpatient's disorder will be more pronounced. In addition, frequently observed co-morbidities are more severe among inpatients, requiring a stricter treatment regime and round-the-clock observation and care. In this section, the therapeutic approaches will be outlined and their effectiveness evaluated.

Interpersonal psychotherapy

This approach to treating eating disorders has received comparatively little research attention despite being one of the preferred treatment strategies.

Interpersonal psychotherapy tries to pigeon-hole the themes within the individual's eating disorder into four distinct areas: grief (abnormally strong reaction to loss), interpersonal role disputes (inability to resolve minor differences with others), role transitions (problems with natural developmental changes within life) and interpersonal deficits (perceptually poor satisfaction brought about by having too high standards and an inability to fulfil the role wanted of them by others) (Fairburn, 2002b). Following characterization of the themes within the individual's experience of the disorder, the therapeutic intervention moves to the treatment phase with weekly sessions where the therapist attempts to get the patient to come up with and implement solutions to their problems.

Interpersonal psychotherapy tends to be used within outpatient programmes, as outpatients have the ability to independently implement their solutions and judge them for efficacy. Efficacy rates of interpersonal psychotherapy in bulimia nervosa (Fairburn et al., 1993, 2003) and binge eating disorder (Hilbert et al., 2007) are similar to those of other psychological interventions. The rate of success of interpersonal psychotherapy is around 40 per cent. There are several reasons why relatively few people make a recovery after receiving interpersonal psychotherapy. The first is the need for the therapist and patient to form a close relationship rooted in feelings of trust. Trusting an individual who is effectively removing the patient's primary means of coping can be perceived as an attack rather than an intervention. Moreover, if the patient also exhibits signs of personality disorders, specifically borderline or dependency disorders, the intervention may only work as long as the therapy sessions last. The patient may also become overly reliant on the relationship with the therapist and the inevitable withdrawal will lead to a re-emergence of the disordered patterns of eating.

Cognitive behavioural therapy

This is the most common form of therapy used to provide psychological support to patients attending eating disorder clinics. The technique can be quite arduous to implement and requires rather extensive training and careful assessment of the holistic experience of the eating disorders clinic before use. A comprehensive guide to using cognitive-behavioural therapy with eating-disordered individuals is offered by Waller et al (2007). Waller et al. offer a guide to the stages of this intervention under the headings shown in Table 9.9. Of these stages, the most important are the assessment, case formulation, psycho-education, addressing central targets of the eating disorder (i.e. the eating, weight and body image pathologies), preventing relapse and ending the relationship. The theoretical underpinning of cognitive behavioural therapy is to break the previous behavioural cycles and thought patterns that

Table 9.9 Overview of the broad stages when offering cognitive behavioural therapy

---

Broad stages within implementing cognitive behavioural therapy

- *Engagement of the patient (and significant others)*: initiating contact with the patient and determining whether there are any significant individuals in their life that can aid in the recovery process
- *Assessment*: medical, psychological, psychosocial and capability risk assessment
- *Explanation of treatment and therapist/patient boundaries*: setting out how the process will work
- *Comprehensive case formulation*: creating a picture of the entire morbidity within the patient
- *Planning of treatment regime (with patient involvement)*: creating a plan for the therapy
- *Motivational enhancement*: understanding the strength of the patient's desire to change and formulating a relationship
- *Psycho-education*: empowering the patient with the ability to evaluate and change their relationship with eating
- *Introducing mealtime structure*: ensuring that the patient sets up a strictly controlled routine to eating and mealtimes – this includes meal duration, meal timing and inter-meal intervals
- *Addressing central targets*: targeted discussion about the central themes of the patient's disorder, including a focus on thoughts and anxieties about eating, weight status and body shape
- *Monitoring weight gain*: constantly ensuring that the patient is gaining weight; if this is not the case, it may be time to resort to compulsory treatments
- *Working on co-morbidities*: any additional disorders identified in the assessment phase need to be worked on after sufficient weight gain and progress with the eating disorder
- *Relapse prevention*: providing the patient with strategies to ensure they do not re-initiate their old eating patterns
- *Ending the therapist–patient relationship*: allowing the patient to stand alone by slowly withdrawing support – this may continue for a long time, as the patient will require follow-up assessments

---

constitute the disorder. The main aim of this approach is to empower the individual with the skills to cope with their disorder and co-morbidities. It tries to show them the thought patterns that lead to the abnormal eating behaviours and get them to come up with alternative solutions. This approach targets the triggers to behaviour rather than trying to alter the behaviour itself. In principle, if the triggers are identified and either removed or coped with, the eating disorder cannot be manifested. Cognitive behavioural therapy requires more active participation by the therapist than interpersonal psychotherapy. In neither of these therapeutic interventions, however, is the therapist the expert. Cognitive behavioural therapy interventions view the therapist as a guide for the patient, while interpersonal psychotherapists play a more reflective role, bouncing back questions to the patient to help them to come up with solutions. Some people refer to this intervention as the 'patient-as-scientist', exploring and finding logical and critical evidence for the assumptions they make. During the therapeutic sessions, the patient can explore their disorder and try to understand the inappropriate assumptions they are making. Once identified, the patient is encouraged to empathize with others and may engage in role reversals.

Cognitive behavioural therapy is completely effective in about 40 per cent of bulimics, and at least 80 per cent will see a dramatic reduction in symptoms (Fairburn, 2002a). For anorexics the story is a little different, with serious methodological issues and high rates of refusal to engage with cognitive behavioural therapy. Of 5512 studies identified to have used cognitive behavioural therapy, only six stand up to scientific rigour and of those only two showed any positive effect in anorexia nervosa (Zandian et al., 2007). However, it is well known that the short- and medium-term prognosis for anorexia nervosa is poor and that most treatment strategies will fail. Therefore, any strategy that is able to maintain the involvement of anorexic patients in treatment will improve their long-term prospects.

Family therapy

Family therapy, as the name suggests, draws upon the family to help explain an eating disorder and try to nullify those factors that have led to its manifestation. By employing this approach, several assumptions are made. First, the family contributes significantly not only to the cause of the disorder but also to the deterioration of the patient. Second, the family is emotionally important to the patient. Third, the family is used as a source of advice and coping by the patient. Fourth, family members are close enough to want to be involved in the treatment of the patient. And fifth, family members have the physical, intellectual and time investment capabilities to deal with the eating disorder and provide adequate support for the patient. Only if these conditions are satisfied can family therapy be beneficial as an intervention. If these conditions are met, therapy usually takes the form of empowering the members of the family to become involved in tackling the overt behaviours of the disorder, thus breaking the sense of control the patient draws from the abnormal behaviours, changing current familial dynamics and interactions. These interactions culminate in better communication pathways within the family so that each member can express valid grievances or emotions, as well as setting rigid boundaries between the roles individuals have within the family unit.

Based on these limitations, it might be expected that this form of intervention is only appropriate for patients who are young and yet to leave home, or those that indicate at the assessment stage that the family is a source of anxiety or is a trigger to abnormal eating patterns. Research indicates that this is the case, as family therapy appears to work better for the adolescent and child-onset forms (Russel et al., 1987) than for the adult forms and that the severity of the disorder also appears to have an effect on the outcome (Dare & Eisler, 2002). The efficacy of family-based therapy, however, is unclear. Its practice is widespread but always offered alongside other therapies. This undermines our understanding of the intervention. Further research is required of patients other than adolescent anorexics before conclusions can be made about the use of family therapy.

Pharmacotherapy

Pharmacological treatments for eating disorders are widespread. Most patients diagnosed with an eating disorder will be offered prescription drugs. The majority of drugs offered target the serotonin neuro pathway indirectly through selective serotonin re-uptake inhibitors (SSRIs). Treatment with such inhibitors appears to be beneficial for bulimics, since serotonin within the brain both acts as as a defence against depression and helps the patient to feel more satiated. Unfortunately, however, SSRIs do not appear to work for anorexic patients (Pederson et al., 2003) and may actually reinforce their propensity to lose weight (Bergh et al., 1996). Attempts at treatment with SSRIs in anorexics has met with limited success, having none to relatively minor effects on weight status. Furthermore, manipulating biochemistry in individuals that are underweight is especially difficult. Doses that would be harmless to individuals of normal weight can produce dramatic side-effects in malnourished, very underweight individuals. These side-effects lead patients to refuse to take the drug, thus undermining any potential benefits this therapeutic intervention might have. Moreover, drug treatments are never prescribed without psychological interventions and so it is impossible to measure their effectiveness. Some researchers believe that SSRIs negate the symptoms of obsessive-compulsive disorder and 'open the mind' of the patient to psychological treatments; however, there seems to be little support for this in anorexia nervosa (Södersten et al., 2003). For bulimics, however, SSRIs appear to be fairly effective, but they should be administered alongside psychological interventions to provide a combined therapy for them.

Full-time inpatient clinics

Full-time care in the form of inpatient clinics may be needed for the more severe forms of anorexia nervosa. On the other hand, bulimia nervosa and other eating disorders rarely require full-time support due to the very low likelihood that the disorder will result in death. If there is a direct threat to the life of an anorexic patient, an inpatient programme may be necessary. Medical irregularities such as heart complaints, unresponsiveness to outpatient treatment, extremely fast weight loss or very low weight status are all grounds for admitting an anorexic patient to an inpatient clinic. Some patients realize the severity of their illness and voluntarily admit themselves to an inpatient unit. As a last resort, they can be sectioned under the Mental Health Act. The 24-hour care provided by the clinic ensures that the patient cannot lose further weight and that they turn up to therapy sessions. To ensure that the patient cannot lose weight, the various professionals within the clinic are able to employ measures not possible with other treatment regimes[7]. These come under the relatively benign title of 'compulsory interventions'. This may include force feeding (often termed a re-feeding strategy), forced therapeutic sessions and forced psychopharmacological compliance. Depending on available resources, the patient may be placed on a psychiatric ward alongside people with other psychological disorders, which can be an additional source of anxiety. For long-term efficacy, it is important where possible for specialist clinics to be used instead of general psychiatric units (Wolfe & Grimby, 2003). In the case of forced admissions, the patient is unlikely to be compliant and the intervention could in fact have a negative short-term effect on any potential recovery. Therefore, forced intervention is used as a last resort (Woodside, 2002) and it must not become a battle for power or control between the patient and the clinician (Treasure, 2002).

Inpatient clinics are about 50 per cent effective in terms of treatment and relapse (McKenzie & Joyce, 1992). Compared with other therapeutic interventions, the inpatient approach is the most expensive and time-consuming. However, it does allow concentrated intervention and provides the patient with a 'sterile' environment in which to explore their disorder and, hopefully, overcome it.

Each of the above treatment regimes is embedded within theoretical explanations of eating disorders. Some, such as interpersonal psychotherapy and cognitive behavioural therapy, could be considered to offer similar interventions. To be most effective, a combined strategy should be used, with a team of experts offering all sorts of therapeutic intervention. However, even the efficacy of such a combined approach to 'curing' eating disorders is poor and relapse rates are high. This is especially true of anorexia nervosa. To help reduce relapse, the best way forward is to empower patients to manage their own disorder effectively. Recognition of and targeted intervention on the triggers for the abnormal eating behaviour will also aid patients in controlling their disorder. Furthermore, effective treatment of the individual co-morbidities that accompany eating disorders help to reduce relapse rates. Until such time as more effective treatment regimes become available, these are the best strategies.

[7] Practitioners do not tend to adopt these practices in the modern therapeutic setting. However, they do still have the ability to do so if they feel it is appropriate.

Summary

Eating disorders are very hard to define and conceptualize. Within individual-istic cultures where societal values are focused on each individual's uniqueness and their right to express that uniqueness, defining anyone as 'abnormal' is especially difficult. In such cases, psychologists draw on the DSM-IV-TR criteria for psychological disorders. In this way, the experienced practitioner is able to offer potential interventions that will enable the patient to recover from their dysfunctional perceptions of the world and/or of themself. Contrary to most people's perceptions, eating disorders are relatively rare, with only about 2 per cent of the general population being affected; more women than men are affected.

The aetiology of eating disorders is extremely complex and there are both biological and psychological explanations for the disorder. The main biologi-cal explanations are based within the serotonergic neurotransmitter pathway in the brain and within the receptor known as 5-HT$_{2A}$ in particular. The psy-chological explanations focus on many different aspects of life, including childhood, thought processes and family environment. Support for either type of explanation on its own is relatively weak, with many conflicting reports within the published literature. Perhaps a combination of biological predis-position and cognitive thought patterns is the best way of addressing how eating disorders manifest. Explaining the causes of eating disorders is very difficult, as they have a highly individual element to them and rarely present without other psychological disturbance. Moreover, there are several officially and unofficially recognized sub-types and variants of both anorexia nervosa and bulimia nervosa. This further compounds our ability to characterize and treat eating disorders effectively.

Just as the aetiology of eating disorders is complex, so are the potential approaches to treating them. Different practitioners favour different means of intervening in the process and development of eating disorders. Relapse rates are high and the efficacy of treatment regimes is relatively low. Eating dis-orders are dangerous, distressing and dysfunctional for both the patient and their significant others. More research is required and the hope for eating dis-orders researchers is that they can devise more effective treatments for patients with anorexia nervosa. Treatments for people with other eating disorders appear to be much more successful.

10 Tying up loose ends
Towards a combined theory of eating behaviour

What we have covered in this book

The study of eating behaviour is extremely diverse and draws on the experience of professionals in many different fields. Academics from the more bio-logical end of the spectrum offer insight into the mechanisms of appetite regulation and control, which feeds into pharmacology research culminating in specific and targeted drug treatments for aiding weight loss or weight gain. Psychologists from four main perspectives – developmental, cognitive, social and individual differences – also offer unique field-specific insights that offer explanations about almost all aspects of eating behaviour. Social psychologists provide characterizations of environmental influences on eating behaviour and describe the pressures to eat (or not) from a cultural and social perspective. Although these different areas, taken at face value, appear to be independent of each other, it is possible to bring them together, albeit in a particularly complex model, to explain human eating behaviour. Stand-alone, discipline-specific explanations have been found to be poor predictors of an individual's eating behaviour. Eating, like all other aspects of human behaviour, is a complex process and needs to be seen from multiple perspectives. Based on the information presented here, this final chapter draws together the various threads to offer an overall model of eating behaviour.

The main objective of this book is to provide a concise explanation of human eating behaviour. It offers a grounding in all aspects of eating behaviour from the biological to the psychological to the abnormal. Chapter 2 details the neurotransmitters and regions within the brain that control eating behaviour and provide the impetus and drive to search for and consume food. Without the brain's involvement in appetite regulation, a person would not know that they were hungry, whether they liked a particular food, or have the motiv-ation to continue to eat. The release of key neurotransmitters from neurons in the hypothalamus is responsible for these behaviours. Neuropeptide-Y (hunger), orexin A and dopamine (motivation and wanting), opioids (liking), cocaine and amphetamine regulated transcript, serotonin, and corticotropin releasing factor (fullness) are the main neurotransmitters concerned with eating behaviour and provide the targets for most appetite-related drugs. Chapter 3 builds on the central mechanisms of appetite regulation by considering the repercussions of consuming food for the periphery and particularly for the digestive system. The chapter looks at the role of the stomach, intestines and adipose tissue in communicating to the brain about current energy storage and digestion. Hormones released from the periphery that are important to appetite regulation include ghrelin (hunger), cholecystokinin (upper digestive tract), peptide YY (lower digestive tract), insulin (control of glucose in the blood) and leptin (signal for how much fat tissue is currently stored). Together, Chapters 2 and 3 offer an overview of the biological controls involved in appetite regulation and which provide a physical domain for the psychological concepts to operate in.

Chapter 4 considers the developmental aspects of eating behaviour. The important childhood variables are discussed and a rough guide given to the ages at which they occur. The importance of learning within habitual diet formation is addressed, culminating in an exploration of the concepts of food neophobia and picky/fussy eating. Food neophobia is described as a reluctance to try, or avoidance of, new foods. It is a natural progression with a peak between the ages of 2 and 6 years. Although an evolutionarily desirable trait, it may develop into a more problematic behaviour known as picky/fussy eating, which results in a poor diet in adolescence and adulthood. Picky/fussy children come to rely increasingly on energy-dense, highly hedonic foodstuffs, resulting in a diet of poor nutritional quality. This inevitably leads to weight gain and obesity as the child ages, as well as creating a habitual diet that can lead potentially to ill-health.

Habits and behaviours learned in childhood form the basic assumptions about what constitutes potential food sources and acceptable meals, both in terms of healthy diets and food preferences. These assumptions manifest in cognitive schemata or 'scripts' that the individual uses when making food choices. Although bound to some degree within energy cost–benefit analysis, food choices in humans are firmly controlled by expectations around both the taste and energy value of a food. It is this expectancy that predicts which foods people choose to eat, as well as provides an explanation of why it is so hard to alter an individual's diet. In addition to the concepts that underlie food choice, there are other important factors that prohibit certain foods or eating practices. For cultural or religious reasons, some foods cannot be eaten without serious social repercussions. Thus food choice is based not only on factors that make us approach foods but also on factors that make us avoid them.

The social and environmental features of eating behaviour addressed in Chapter 6 are complex and wide ranging. Irrespective of an individual's food choice and habitual diet, anyone can, and will, alter their behaviour within a group context. Strength of attitude towards foods and eating predicts the type of behaviour expressed in the group setting. The theory of reasoned action, theory of planned behaviour and theory of trying all offer insight into changes to an individual's habitual diet in the public arena and suggest that the perceptions of social stereotypes and perceived behavioural control of the situation will all come together to further predict human food choice. Furthermore, the presence or absence of others also affects how much is eaten in terms of portion size. Eating in groups invariably means that individuals eat more than they normally would, as the social situation distracts attentional resources from monitoring the amount of food eaten. Specific members of the group may also have differing impacts on an individual's eating behaviour. If a person wishes to endear themself to another person in the group, they might attempt to model another's eating behaviour or in some way try to impress others through their food choices and/or amount consumed. Females in particular may try to portray a feminine ideal through food to avoid negative social judgements from the male members of the group. This impression is borne out of perceptions about personal body image and potential attractiveness, which are heavily influenced by media representations of the 'thin ideal'. This perception of body image and its role within food choice and impression management may be attenuated by cultural or religious beliefs. Despite the power of the media, both cultural and religious beliefs may allow the individual to view their body image based on its functional capacity rather than aesthetics.

The information provided in the first six chapters is generic in nature and cannot explain the variance seen in people's eating behaviour. Individuality in eating behaviour is explained in Chapter 7 primarily through the roles of cognitive restraint, emotional eating and disinhibition. Cognitive restraint is a concept whereby an individual attempts to control their intake through psychological means rather than relying on their biological digestive feedback (i.e. satiation and satiety). Emotional eaters are people who consume food when they are down or in an attempt to avoid focusing on especially strong or distressing emotions. Disinhibition is the inability to maintain attention on food intake in the presence of other distracting information. This last component combines well with the environmental ideas and theories around eating behaviour to explain why people eat in the presence of food cues even if they are not hungry, a process known as external eating. These individual components can combine to create a unique set of eating behaviours that provide a strong framework to predict how specific individuals interact and react to food.

Chapters 8 and 9 explore what happens when eating behaviour goes wrong. Chapter 8 explores the causes, consequences and treatment regimes for overweight and obesity. We find that it is not so easy to define obesity and that treatment regimes are fairly ineffective. Surgical interventions aside, dieting and pharmacological treatments in obesity are relatively weak in terms of their efficacy and appear to rely heavily on personal motivation to lose weight. For obesity, we discover that prevention is better than a cure, although even this appears to be faltering in the current obesogenic environment. Chapter 9 explores what happens to people who develop an eating disorder. Although the main focus is on anorexia nervosa and bulimia nervosa, other eating disorders are discussed and the traditional eating disorders are characterized into sub-types. Unlike obesity, defining eating disorders is relatively straightforward if reliant on a mixture of diagnostic criteria, potential for harm and a well-trained and experienced practitioner. Further differences from obesity are observed in the comparative complexity of the aetiology of eating disorders. Many potential causes of eating disorders have been offered from both a biological and a psychological perspective. However, evidence for and against each perspective suggests marked inter-individual differences and the presence or absence of other psychological disorders concurrent with the eating disorder. Finally, the relative success of treatment regimes for eating disorders is also shown to vary. In particular, treatment for anorexia nervosa is not that successful, whereas interventions for other eating disorders enjoy much higher rates of success.

Towards a combined model of eating behaviour

For some time the various sub-fields of eating behaviour have struggled alone. We have finally reached the stage where all the various components of eating behaviour can be brought together and the relative merits and impacts of each evaluated. Figure 10.1 offers a schematic representation of how the various aspects of eating behaviour and disorders interact and develop. The emphasis is on the development of food choice and the various factors that impact on it. In essence, at any stage from childhood to adulthood something can go wrong and an eating disorder develop.

It should now be evident to the reader that eating behaviour is not a simple process of putting hand to mouth. Eating behaviour is subject to the complex interplay of many factors. However, even the most bizarre behaviours and disorders associated with eating can be explained. For example, anorexia nervosa could be considered a very extreme version of restrained eating, while bulimia nervosa has its roots in emotional eating. And there are indications of similar behaviours, if less extreme in nature, in the general population, most of whom will never develop an eating disorder.

Two spheres of influence affect all human behaviour, including eating behaviour. The age-old argument between nature and nurture is just as important to the eating behaviourist as to any other scientist. A complex interaction between genes and environment provides the setting for eating behaviours to develop both throughout childhood and through the rest of life. We never stop trying new foods and are continuously exposed to pressures that impinge

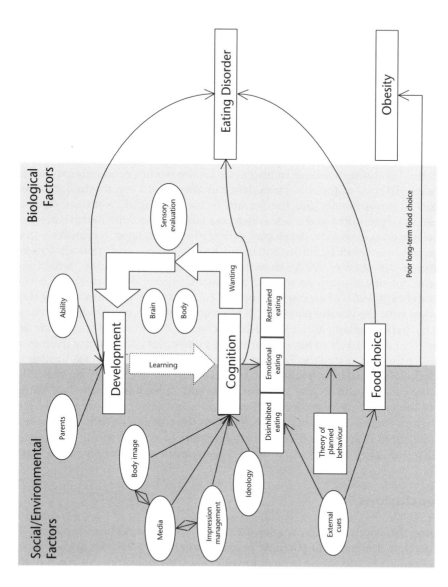

Figure 10.1 A combined model of eating behaviour and eating disorders.

on all aspects of our lives. The relatively individual experiences within the developmental process lead to a strong set of cognitive schemata around food. What is acceptable, and what is not, is bound up in the learned processes of food preferences. Social pressures can come together to create a unique and individual perspective on food and eating through altering cognitive decision-making processes.

Poor long-term food choices, probably the result of poor recovery from food neophobia in childhood and the propensity to disinhibit or eat in the absence of hunger, have led to the rapid rise in obesity. Obesity is becoming the 'normal' nutritional status of people worldwide. Something must be done to rectify the current obesogenic environment where highly hedonic energy-dense foodstuffs are readily available for minimal investment of time and effort. If the current phenomenon continues to its logical conclusion, the financial and health service implications for the world's economies are set to worsen. To combat the rising prevalence in obesity will require the combined effort of governments and the private sector. Successful treatment regimes need to be identified and made widely available, and comprehensive prevention strategies need to be developed, delivered and evaluated. It is unlikely that the same processes for other successful health intervention policies will be effective for obesity. Unlike smoking and alcohol consumption, which are borne out of addiction to specific substances, obesity develops through the natural expression of an essential need – eating. It may be that the only way to deal with the obesity pandemic is to create an environment where it 'pays' to be hyper-vigilant about every food choice. However, creating such an environment is likely to have the unwanted side-effect of increasing the prevalence of eating disorders. Few targeted obesity interventions are available, especially for children. Those that are available rely exclusively on the individual's motivation to lose or maintain weight. If we have learned anything over the last thirty years, motivation alone is not enough to prevent weight gain and eventual onset of obesity. Without the creation of dedicated professional services specialized in the intervention of obesity at all levels, it is unlikely that any strategy will work. Increasing awareness is simply not enough.

Conclusions

Eating behaviour is both complex and elegant at the same time. Advances in research techniques and scientific investigation have blown the field of appetite regulation and eating behaviour wide open. We now know so much more about the subject than we did even ten years ago. There really is a renaissance in the subject and it is an interesting time to be a researcher of eating behaviour in humans. Every year there is a revolutionary discovery within the field. Irrespective of your specific interest, eating behaviour has many frontiers to explore. Our obsession with food and eating is boundless. It permeates our thoughts and takes up a lot of our life. We do not appear to be bored with endless television programming and even whole channels dedicated to the production, collection, preparation and consumption of food. So there is only one thing really left to say and that is, long may it continue!

Appendix 1
The neurochemistry of appetite regulation

Neuropeptide Y

Neuropeptide Y (NPY) producing neurons are structurally connected to the lateral hypothalamic area (Tritos et al., 1998) and paraventricular nucleus (Blundell, 1991). High densities of NPY have also been observed in the locus ceruleus and brainstem (Hillebrand et al., 2002). This widespread distribution is mirrored by the equally widespread occurrence of the NPY receptors, Y_1 and Y_5, which have been strongly linked with the initiation of feeding behaviours (Kalra et al., 1999). NPY neurons gradually increase production and release of neurotransmitters over time until a threshold is reached and a meal is started. Therefore, unlike all other appetite-related biochemicals, NPY is controlled predominantly by the time of day and is not dependent on any other appetite-related neurotransmitter. This characteristic defines NPY as the first episodic biochemical that initiates eating behaviour. Although time is the pertinent factor for NPY release, its strength is attenuated by other signals, especially the longer-lasting tonic signals that adjust the episodic system based on current energy stores. Neuropeptide Y does not act alone; it is 'helped' by agouti-related protein.

Agouti-related protein

Agouti-related protein (AGRP) was first discovered in the cells of the skin, where it causes a yellow pigmentation (Bultman et al., 1992). It was related to eating because animals that have too much AGRP are usually obese. This led to the discovery of a similar neurotransmitter in the arcuate nucleus of humans (Ollmann et al., 1997). AGRP is released with NPY, and together they create a powerful orexigenic response (Hahn et al., 1998). How AGRP acts in the brain is still a matter of rigorous debate. Research currently suggests that AGRP not only increases food intake but may also control an individual's macronutrient selection (Wirth & Giraudo, 2000). Alterations in macronutrient intake as a result of increased AGRP in the hypothalamus appear to be specific to fat intake. Preferentially eating foods high in fat leads to weight gain and obesity. Furthermore, minor mutations in the human AGRP gene have been linked to anorexia and obesity (Hillebrand et al., 2002). Essentially, AGRP combines with NPY to create a physiological state that readies an individual to consume food. Together, NPY and AGRP make us 'think' we are hungry and that it is time to eat a meal.

Cocaine and amphetamine regulated transcript

Cocaine and amphetamine regulated transcript (CART) was first identified in the regions of the brain that are active when an individual takes psycho-active drugs (Douglass et al., 1995). Both cocaine and amphetamine work through binding with naturally occurring CART receptors in the brain. More recently, this peptide has been found in larger quantities in the hypo-thalamus, specifically in the nuclei related to feeding (Gautvik et al., 1996). When injected into the brain, CART inhibits eating behaviour in animals that have been put on a 24-hour fast, leading some researchers to believe that CART is the most powerful anorexigenic neurotransmitter known (Kalra et al., 1999). Evidence for this view comes from experimental work that has shown a strong mutual suppressive interaction between CART and NPY. Other researchers are more cautious, citing that CART knockout mice[1] have a normal body weight and food intake (Bannon et al., 2000). Until a spe-cific receptor is identified (Vicentic et al., 2006), the role of CART in appetite regulation will remain unclear. However, we do know that CART is invol-ved in appetite regulation and attenuates the control of NPY within the arcuate nucleus.

Pro-opiomelanocortin

A small group of neurons that produce pro-opiomelanocortin (POMC) exist in the arcuate nucleus (Carr, 2002). POMC neurons innervate key feeding-related areas such as the paraventricular nucleus. Interestingly, POMC neurons create several different neurotransmitters involved in appetite regulation and they are co-released alongside CART. Essentially, they play a similar role with CART to that played by AGRP with NPY. Chief among the neurotransmitters of POMC neurons is alpha melanocyte-stimulating hormone (αMSH). Central infusion of αMSH decreases food intake and increases energy expenditure in rodents (Forbes et al., 2001), which can be reversed by administration of

---

[1] These are mice that cannot naturally create CART in their brain because of a genetic mutation.

a melanocortin-receptor 3/4 antagonist[2] (Adage et al., 2001). Humans (Vaisse et al., 1998) and animals (Huszer et al., 1997) that lack melanocortin-receptor 4 are obese and overeat. αMSH does not affect energy intake in the short term, as stopping αMSH from working does not affect the quantity of food eaten (Schioth et al., 1998). A long-term infusion of αMSH antagonist does, however, lead to obesity. This suggests that αMSH may be a target for more long-term (tonic) manipulations of episodic appetite regulation or ensures the suppression of behaviours related to appetite regulation.

Melanin-concentrating hormone

It is generally accepted that melanin-concentrating hormone (MCH) is downstream[3] of NPY, as it has both structural links with the arcuate nucleus and administration of NPY increases MCH (Hillebrand et al., 2002). Moreover, compared with NPY, MCH has a shorter stimulation effect on the duration of eating. Currently, two receptors have been found for MCH, with MCH-R2 being more important than MCH-R1 in appetite regulation. Without MCH, animals will not eat, and production and release of this neurotransmitter is found during fasting (Ahima & Osei, 2001). Moreover, over-expression of MCH results in obesity (Ludwig et al., 2001). Genetic models of the increase of MCH production show spontaneous obesity even in mice on a low-fat diet (Bergen et al., 1999); however, there is conflicting evidence, as MCH at low doses decreases food intake (Presse et al., 1996). Altogether, this would suggest that MCH is reliant on another neurotransmitter responsible for eating or is a 'link in the chain' rather than naturally initiating feeding on its own. Its exact behavioural role is ambiguous, but it is definitely involved in initiating a meal.

Orexin A and orexin B

Orexin A and orexin B are neurotransmitters within the hypocretin family that are important to eating behaviour. Orexins A and B were first discovered in 1999 in the lateral hypothalamic area and perifornical area of the rat brain. Both orexins have been associated with feeding behaviour (Ahima & Osei, 2001), with orexin A being a more potent appetite stimulator than orexin B (Sakurai et al., 1998). Like NPY and MCH, orexins (especially orexin A) are found in high concentrations during fasting. Most authors agree that orexins

---

[2] These are drugs that block the receptors and stop them from working.

[3] This means it requires a signal from another neurotransmitter to release its own neurotransmitter. Unlike NPY, which releases its neurotransmitters dependent on the time of day, it will do nothing until NPY binds to its receptors and causes it to release MCH.

are controlled by NPY, as orexins are less effective at stimulating feeding and have receptors and structural links with NPY/AGRP neurons. Structurally, orexin neurons also provide a feedback loop to the arcuate nucleus (Sakurai et al., 1998), inhibiting POMC cells and increasing the release of NPY. The involvement of orexins in appetite regulation is unquestionable; however, evidence for their exact role is limited, especially in terms of receptor sub-types. To date, two receptors for orexin have been isolated (Al-Barazanji et al., 2001) and different preferences for receptors A and B have been reported (Smart et al., 1999). Although these receptors are found throughout the brain, the sub-types have different distributions (Al-Barazanji et al., 2001). Orexin 1 receptor (O1R) is expressed in the lateral hypothalamic area, whereas orexin 2 receptor (O2R) is found in the paraventricular nucleus (Cutler et al., 1999). The two orexins have an equal ability to bind with O2R, but orexin A has a ten-fold preference for O1R compared with orexin B. Also, infusions of orexin A into the lateral hypothalamic area and paraventricular nucleus result in initiation of eating, suggesting an important role for O2R (Kalra et al., 1999). However, it is unclear why orexin A and orexin B have the same affinity for O2R but differing effects on feeding. One possible explanation could be the multi-functional role of orexins – feeding, drinking (Kunii et al., 1999), arousal (Hagan et al., 1999) and keeping us awake (Piper et al., 2000). The most likely explanation, however, is that O1R is the more important receptor for meal initiation (Rodgers et al., 2002). Moreover, the inhibition of O1R causes the loss of orexin A-induced overeating (Rodgers et al., 2001). This would explain the different appetite-related effects of the orexins based on receptor affinity[4]. The available evidence would suggest that, overall, the orexins are involved in cognitions and awareness (Voisin et al., 2003) around searching for food rather than direct episodic meal initiation, which is more likely to be controlled by the arcuate nucleus and its related neurotransmitters.

Corticotropin releasing factor

Corticotropin releasing factor (CRF) is widely accepted as the hypothalamic factor that terminates eating. There are two known receptors for CRF; however, it is unclear which is involved in feeding behaviour. What is known is that central infusion of CRF produces anorexia in normal and fasted animals (Morley & Levine, 1982). The anorexic action of CRF is limited to the paraventricular nucleus, as only micro-injections to this region inhibit NPY-induced eating (Heinrichs et al., 1993). Another member of the CRF family that has a more potent effect on feeding behaviour has also been isolated. Urocortin

[4] The propensity for a receptor to bind with one neurotransmitter rather than another.

shares a 45 per cent homology with CRF[5]. It selectively binds to CRF-2R better than CRF and central and peripheral infusion of urocortin increases satiation, reduces meal size and increases satiety (Pan & Kastin, 2008). This suggests that urocortin has both episodic and tonic roles (Spina et al., 1996). Finally, there are two other types of urocortin (Uro II and Uro III), although their physiological functions and effects have yet to be elucidated.

Serotonin

For the last 25 years, serotonin (5-hydroxytryptamine or 5-HT) has been linked with satiation and satiety (Blundell, 1977) more than any other monoamine (Halford et al., 2004a), including dopamine, noradrenaline and histamine. Increasing 5-HT by direct infusion into the brain decreases meal size and eating rate, causing early termination of a meal. Furthermore, no compensatory effect has been observed in animals or humans through increasing the number of meals eaten or by decreasing satiety, which suggests that 5-HT also has affects on satiety (Halford et al., 2003). Serotonin production is dependent on tryptophan, which is absorbed in our diets through carbohydrate intake (Blundell et al., 1995). Guy et al. (1988) described structural connections between 5-HT terminals and NPY-producing neurons' dendrites in the arcuate nucleus. This shows that the serotonin system directly inhibits the production and release of NPY (Dube et al., 1992). The importance of serotonin in appetite regulation is reflected in its being the neurotransmitter most often targeted in pharmacological treatments for obesity. The receptors for serotonin that have been consistently shown to be involved in appetite regulation are 5-HT$_{2C}$, 5-HT$_{1A}$ and 5-HT$_{1B}$. The most important of these receptors is 5-HT$_{2C}$, which has been shown to inhibit food intake. If 5-HT$_{2C}$ is removed through genetic manipulation, the animal will quickly become obese through overeating.

Dopamine and noradrenaline

Dopamine and noradrenaline are important neurotransmitters in the control of food intake. Animals that do not have the ability to create the dopamine neurotransmitter cannot initiate a meal (Meister, 2007). Furthermore, dopamine is associated with meal duration and also appears to be associated with meal frequency (Meguid et al., 2000). Research into the exact effects of dopamine is ongoing. However, dopamine is a strong orexigenic signal that interacts with the other large amine pathways to control meal size and

[5] This means that CRF shares 45 per cent of the same chain of amino acids – the building blocks of proteins and therefore most biological structures and chemicals – as urocortin.

energy intake throughout the day. Dopamine is also important in the reward pathways, or, more specifically, in the motivations associated with eating. Noradrenaline appears to be heavily involved in satiety. Destruction of noradrenaline neurons results in overeating and obesity and direct infusion into the brain causes under-consumption. Taken together, these two amines are implicated in eating behaviour and appear to have distinct and highly specialized roles in appetite regulation.

Appendix 2
Hormonal control of appetite regulation

Ghrelin

Ghrelin is the first episodic orexigenic signal to be discovered outside of the central nervous system (Inui, 2001). It is created by specialist cells in the stomach (Wren et al., 2001) and is released into the circulatory system (Date et al., 2000). Ghrelin promotes feeding and is attenuated by tonic signals released from fat tissue (namely leptin). Episodic ghrelin concentrations fluctuate throughout the day with three distinct peaks just before mealtimes. Ghrelin concentrations in the blood are lower in people with a high percentage of body fat and high fasting concentrations of insulin and leptin. It has also been shown to be significantly lower in obese people compared with lean controls (Tschöp et al., 2001). Ghrelin can block NPY receptors (NPY-R1) (Lawrence et al., 2002) and a single peripheral injection causes activation of NPY-releasing neurons (Wang et al., 2002). This suggests that ghrelin acts through NPY in the arcuate nucleus causing meal initiation (Cummings et al., 2002). Due to its unique nature, the attention given to ghrelin was intense for a few years, but has since begun to wane. The advances in our understanding of all aspects of appetite regulation over the last few years can be attributed to the discovery and isolation of ghrelin. To say that the brain may be subservient to the body in some specific circumstances would have been unheard of ten years ago. Today, scientists have a greater understanding of the gut–brain interaction and a more accurate, if a little more complex, model to work with.

Insulin and glucagon

Insulin is integral to glucose utilization in the body. Most cells cannot take glucose directly from the blood without the metabolic consequences of insulin. Therefore, without the release of insulin from the pancreas, glucose will remain in the blood and the cells of the body will begin to starve. The absence or unresponsiveness of insulin is known as diabetes. Diabetes has two known sub-types: type-I and type-II. Type-I diabetes is an autoimmune disorder that results in the immune system inappropriately identifying the pancreas as a foreign body and destroying the insulin-creating beta cells within it. Type-II diabetes used to be known as adult-onset diabetes, as it was usually associated with excessive weight that causes insensitivity to insulin through continuously high concentrations of glucose in the blood. The current obesogenic environment and high prevalence of childhood obesity across the world has meant that this disorder has had to be renamed.

The main function of insulin is to alter the metabolism of adipose, liver and bone cells to start absorbing glucose from the blood for storage. In addition to this role, insulin receptors are also found throughout the hypothalamus and specifically NPY/AGRP and POMC neurons (Wanting Xu et al., 2005). When insulin is injected directly into the brain it reduces eating behaviour (Vettor et al., 2002), suggesting that it has properties that make it an episodic anorexigenic appetite-related hormone.

Pancreatic glucagon opposes the action of insulin by increasing the amount of glucose in circulation. The target for glucagon is the liver, where it causes the metabolism of glycogen stores into glucose. It does not have the same far-reaching effects as insulin and does not appear to have much of an effect on appetite. As such, it has received little attention within the appetite literature. Other members of the same hormonal family as glucagon – glucagon-like peptide 1 (GLP-1) peptide 2 (GLP-2) – are released further down in the digestive system and appear to have greater ramifications for appetite regulation.

Cholecystokinin

Cholecystokinin (CCK) plays a role as a signalling molecule both centrally and peripherally and is found throughout the gastrointestinal tract but predominantly in the duodenum and jejunum (Moran, 2000). The ability of CCK to inhibit food intake episodically has been known since 1973 (Gibbs et al., 1973). CCK was found to reduce meal size and duration without causing harm. Furthermore, the injection of CCK had no effect on water intake and the behavioural responses were consistent with satiation and satiety. Since this original study, much research has focused on the role of CCK in feeding. It is now known that endogenous CCK is released in response to nutrients in the blood, specifically fat and protein (Halford et al., 2003), and results in elevated subjective feelings of fullness (Burton-Freeman et al., 2002). CCK has two known receptors: CCK_A and CCK_B. It is the CCK_A sub-type that is most important in feeding behaviours (Lieverse et al., 1994). CCK_A receptors are found throughout the gut and related organs, as well as the vagal nerve and a number of key brain structures. In contrast, the CCK_B receptor sub-type is more prominent centrally and is widely distributed throughout the brain (Moran, 2000).

Taken together, all this information suggests that CCK is a potent satiety-inducing hormone that monitors fatty acid or lipid concentrations in the circulatory system, and energy regulation is controlled by CCK_A receptors (Halford et al., 2003).

Glucagon-like peptide 1 and peptide 2

Glucagon-like peptide 1 (GLP-1) targets the stomach and appetite-related regions in the brain. It increases gastric emptying time and therefore controls the release of chyme from the stomach. Thus, GLP-1 informs the stomach whether there is room in the intestine for more food to be processed (digestion, absorption or excretion) (Nauck et al., 1997). Another consequence of GLP-1 is that the release of digestive juices from the pancreas and stomach are stopped. Here, GLP-1 informs the rest of the digestive system that the food is now lower down and the enzymes are no longer required. Centrally, GLP-1 appears to have strong episodic effects but they last for only a short time (Deacon et al., 1998). This means that GLP-1 needs to be maintained at a high concentration in the circulatory system to have any effect on appetite regulation. Unlike CCK, GLP-1 does not have to target the vagal nerve and the brainstem to alter eating behaviour. Receptors for GLP-1 are found in both the arcuate nucleus and paraventricular nucleus, which suggests that GLP-1 manipulates NPY/AGRP, CART/POMC and CRF interactions. The message that it sends to the brain is 'do not worry, we have food in the system and we are working on it, do not eat anything else until I stop telling you that'.

GLP-2 may share structural similarities with GLP-1 but it appears to have very different effects. Injections of GLP-2 do not seem to affect eating behaviour or food intake and do not affect gastric emptying (Schmidt et al., 2003). It would appear that GLP-2 is involved more in the mechanics of moving the food through the small and large intestines rather than on the content or appetite regulation of food.

Peptide YY

Peptide YY (PYY) is a member of the pancreatic polypeptide family and is released from the ileum in response to food (Adrian et al., 1985). It competes for the same receptors as NPY and effectively blocks NPY's communication within the brain. Due to its structural similarities with NPY, some researchers (Morley et al., 1985) have suggested that PYY is a potent orexigenic peptide; however, injecting PYY into the arcuate nucleus has shown it to have an anorexigenic effect (Kelner & Helmuth, 2003). What is now known is that PYY inhibits food intake and reduces appetite (Batterham et al., 2002). The concentration of PYY is also lower in the blood of obese individuals (Batterham et al., 2003) and may become unresponsive to food intake in some types of obesity (Daousi et al., 2005; English et al., 2006). This suggests that PYY is a potent satiety factor in humans and is likely to work via active competition with NPY (Kelner & Helmuth, 2003).

Leptin

Leptin is a tonic signal that is released by adipose tissue to signify current levels of stored energy (in the form of fat) in the body (Maffei et al., 1995). Leptin was found to be absent in a small group of rodents that suffered from severe early-onset morbid obesity caused by extreme overeating (Pelleymounter et al., 1995). Its absence was due to a genetic mutation that meant the rodents could not create leptin. When leptin was injected into the animals, all the observed effects were lost and the animals quickly lost weight (Pelleymounter et al., 1997). Although hailed as the cure for obesity in the mid-1990s, it was soon found that most obese animals and humans have higher, not lower, concentrations of natural leptin than lean individuals. Following extensive screening, only one family living in rural Pakistan has been identified as being obese due to leptin abnormalities. This does not rule out a role for leptin in the pathogenesis of obesity entirely, as long-term obesity may result in insensitivity to leptin in the same way as diabetics become insensitive to insulin. Thus they may not respond to high levels of leptin in the same way as other people. Either way, insensitivity to leptin would be a consequence rather than a cause of obesity. When leptin is injected into the brain, or the blood, it causes a dramatic reduction in food intake. It targets all aspects of appetite regulation and specifically decreases the activity of NPY/AGRP, orexin-A and ghrelin, and increases the CART, CRF and CCK signals.

Adiponectin

Adiponectin is one of the most abundant tonic signals released from the adipose tissue (Vendrell et al., 2004). Recent evidence points to adiponectin having a role in improving insulin sensitivity to glucose (Scherer et al., 1995) and preventing liver damage (Masaki et al., 2004). Adiponectin concentrations in the blood are much higher than those of any other hormone, but are lower in obese individuals and increase with moderate weight loss (Ouchi et al., 1999). Preliminary evidence suggested that adiponectin increases after a meal in obese participants (English et al., 2003). However, this finding has yet to be replicated (Karlsson et al., 2004). It is likely that the results obtained by English et al. (2003) are an anomaly; indeed, the authors themselves believe this to be the case (English et al., 2004). Adiponectin appears to alter food intake in a similar way to leptin, but more data are required before we have an accurate picture of how adiponectin interacts with the appetite system. Therefore, it is concluded that adiponectin has a tonic and indirect role in appetite regulation through interactions with insulin (and possibly leptin) rather than directly affecting eating behaviour.

Further reading

Central and peripheral mechanisms of appetite regulation

Berridge, K. C. (2004). Motivational concepts in behavioural neuroscience. *Physiology and Behavior*, *81*(2), 179–209.

Halford, J. C. G., Cooper, G. D., & Dovey, T. M. (2004a). The pharmacology of human appetite expression. *Current Drug Targets*, *5*(3), 1–20.

Hetherington, M. M., Bell, A., & Rolls, B. J. (2000). Effects of repeat consumption on pleasantness, preference and intake. *British Food Journal*, *102*, 507–521.

Kalra, S. P., Dube, M. G., Pu, S., Xu, B., Horvath, T. L., & Kalra, P. S. (1999). Interacting appetite-regulating pathways in the hypothalamic regulation of body weight. *Endocrine Reviews*, *20*(1), 68–100.

Valassi, E., Scacchi, M., & Cavagnini, F. (2008). Neuroendocrine control of food intake. *Nutrition, Metabolism and Cardiovascular Diseases*, *18*, 158–168.

Developmental aspects of eating behaviour

Birch, L. L. (1999). Development of food preferences. *Annual Review of Nutrition*, *19*, 41–62.

Dovey, T. M., Farrow, C. V., Martin, C. I., Isherwood, E., & Halford, J. C. G. (2009). When does food refusal require professional intervention? *Current Nutrition and Food Science*, *5*(3), 160–171.

Ross, B. H., & Murphy, G. L. (1999). Food for thought: Cross-classification and category organization in a complex real-world domain. *Cognitive Psychology*, *38*, 495–553.

Cognitive aspects of eating behaviour

Blake, C. E., Bisogni, C. A., Sobal, J., Jastran, M., & Devine, C. M. (2008). How adults construct evening meals: Scripts for food choice. *Appetite*, *51*, 654–662.

Higgs, S. (2008). Cognitive influences on food intake: The effects of manipulating memory for recent eating. *Physiology and Behavior*, *94*, 734–739.

Lieberman, L. S. (2006). Evolutionary and anthropological perspectives on optimal foraging in obesogenic environments. *Appetite*, *47*, 3–9.

Social aspects of eating behaviour

Conner, M., & Armitage, C. J. (2002). *The social psychology of food*. Buckingham: Open University Press.

Grogen, S. (1999). *Body image: Understanding body dissatisfaction in men, women and children*. London: Routledge.

Hesse-Biber, S., Leavy, P., Quinn, C. E., & Zoino, J. (2006). The mass marketing of disordered eating and eating disorders: The social psychology of women, thinness and culture. *Women's Studies International Forum, 29*, 208–224.

Vartanian, L. R., Herman, C. P., & Polivy, J. (2007). Consumption stereotypes and impression management: How you are what you eat. *Appetite, 48*, 265–277.

Combined aspects of eating behaviour

Heatherton, T. F., & Baumeister, R. F. (1991). Binge eating as escape from self-awareness. *Psychological Bulletin, 110*, 86–108.

Lowe, M. R., van Steenburgh, J., Ochner, C., & Coletta, M. (2009). Neural correlates of individual differences related to appetite. *Physiology and Behavior, 97*, 561–571.

Macht, M. (2008). How emotions affect eating: A five-way model. *Appetite, 50*, 1–11.

Obesity

Finer, N. (2006). Medical consequences of obesity. *Medicine, 34*, 510–514.

Ford, E. S., Giles, W. H., & Dietz, W. H. (2002). Prevalence of the metabolic syndrome among US adults: Findings from the third National Health and Nutrition Examination Survey. *Journal of the American Medical Association, 287*, 356–359.

Hubert, H., Guinhouya, C. B., Allard, L., & Durocher, A. (2008). Comparison of the diagnostic quality of body mass index, waist circumference and waist-to-height ratio in screening skinfold-determined obesity among children. *Journal of Science and Medicine in Sports, 12*, 449–451.

Wisniewski, A. B., & Chernausek, S. D. (2009). Gender in childhood obesity: Family environment, hormones and genes. *Gender Medicine, 6*(1), 76–85.

Eating disorders

Cooper, M. J. (2005). Cognitive theory in anorexia nervosa and bulimia nervosa: Progress, development and future directions. *Clinical Psychology Review, 25*, 511–531.

Dovey, T. M., Farrow, C. V., Martin, C. I., Isherwood, E., & Halford, J. C. G. (2009). When does food refusal require professional intervention? *Current Nutrition and Food Science*, 5(3), 160–171.

Fairburn, C. G., & Brownell, K. D. (Eds.) (2002). *Eating disorders and obesity: A comprehensive handbook*. London: Guilford Press.

References

Abbate-Daga, G., Pierò, A., Gramaglia, C., Gandione, M., & Fassino, S. (2007). An attempt to understand the paradox of anorexia nervosa without drive for thinness. *Psychiatry Research, 149*, 215–221.

Abrams, K. K., Allen, L. R., & Gray, J. J. (1993). Disordered eating attitudes and behaviors, psychological adjustment, and ethnic identity: A comparison of black and white female college students. *International Journal of Eating Disorders, 14*, 49–57.

Adage, T., Scheurink, A. J., de Boer, S. F., de Vries, K., Konsman, J. P., & Kuipers, F. (2001). Hypothalamic, metabolic, and behavioural responses to pharmacological inhibition of CNS melanocortin signalling in rats. *Journal of Neuroscience, 21*, 3639–3645.

Adrian, T. E., Ferri, G. L., Bacarese-Hamilton, A. J., Fuessi, H. S., Polak, J. M., & Bloom, S. R. (1985). Human distribution and release of a putative new gut hormone, peptide YY. *Gastroenterology, 89*, 1070–1077.

Ahima, R. S., & Osei, S. Y. (2001). Molecular regulation of eating behaviour: New insights and prospects for therapeutic strategies. *Trends in Molecular Medicine, 7*(5), 205–213.

Ajzen, I., & Fishbein, M. (2000). Attitudes and the attitude–behaviour relation: Reasoned and automatic processes. *European Journal of Social Psychology, 11*, 1–33.

Al-Barazanji, K. A., Wilson, S., Baker, J., Jessop, D. S., & Harbuz, M. S. (2001). Central orexin-A activates hypothalamic–pituitary–adrenal axis and stimulates hypothalamic corticotropin releasing factor and arginine vasopressin neurones in conscious rats. *Journal of Neuroendocrinology, 13*(5), 421–424.

American College of Sports Medicine (1995). *ACSM's guidelines for exercise testing and prescription*. Baltimore, MD: Williams & Wilkins.

American Psychiatric Association (2000). *Diagnostic and statistical manual of mental disorders-IV-TR*. Arlington, VA: American Psychiatric Association.

Anand, B. K., & Brobeck, J. R. (1951). Hypothalamic control of food intake in rats and cats. *Yale Journal of Biological Medicine, 24*, 123–140.

Anderson, A. S., & Sheppard, R. (1989). Beliefs and attitudes towards 'healthier eating' among women attending maternity hospital. *Journal of Nutrition Education, 21*, 208–213.

Anderson, K. P., LaPorte, D. J., & Crawford, S. (2000). Child sexual abuse and bulimic symptomatology: Relevance of specific abuse variables. *Child Abuse and Neglect, 24*, 1495–1502.

Armitage, C. J., & Conner, M. (2001). Efficacy of the theory of planned behaviour: A meta-analytic review. *British Journal of Social Psychology*, *40*, 471–499.

Arterburn, D. E., Crane, P. K., & Veenstra, D. L. (2004). The efficacy and safety of sibutramine for weight loss: A systematic review. *Archives of Internal Medicine*, *164*, 994–1003.

Auvray, M., & Spence, C. (2008). The multisensory perception of flavour. *Consciousness and Cognition*, *17*, 1016–1031.

Bäckström, A., Pirttilä-Backman, A.-M., & Tuofila, H. (2004). Willingness to try new foods as predicted by social representations and attitude and trait scales. *Appetite*, *43*, 75–83.

Baer, R. A., Fischer, S., & Huss, D. B. (2005). Mindfulness-based cognitive therapy to binge eating: A case study. *Cognitive and Behavioral Practice*, *12*, 351–358.

Bagozzi, R. P. (1992). The self-regulation of attitudes, intentions and behaviour. *Social Psychology Quarterly*, *55*, 178–204.

Bagozzi, R. P., & Edwards, E. A. (2000). Goal-striving and the implementation of goal intentions in the regulation of body weight. *Psychology and Health*, *15*, 255–271.

Bagozzi, R. P., Wong, N., Abe, S., & Bergami, M. (2000). Cultural and situational contingencies and the theory of reasoned action: Application to fast food restaurant consumption. *Journal of Consumer Psychology*, *9*(2), 97–106.

Baicy, K. (2005). Can food be addictive? Insights on obesity from neuroimaging and substance abuse treatment and research. *Nutrition Noteworthy*, *7*, 1–7.

Bailer, U. F., Price, J. C., Meltzer, C. C., Mathis, C. A., Frank, G. K., Weissfeld, L., McConaha, C. W., Henry, S. E., Brooks-Achenbach, S., Barbarich, N. C., & Kaye, W. H. (2004). Altered 5-HT2A receptor binding after recovery from bulimia-type anorexia nervosa: Relationships to harm avoidance and drive for thinness. *Neuropsychopharmacology*, *29*, 1143–1155.

Baker, T. B., Morse, E., & Sherman, J. E. (1986). The motivation to use drugs: A psychobiological analysis of urges. In P. C. Rivers (Ed.), *The Nebraska symposium on motivation: Alcohol use and abuse* (pp. 257–323). Lincoln, NB: University of Nebraska Press.

Bandura, A. (1977). *Social learning theory*. Englewood Cliffs, NJ: Prentice-Hall.

Bannon, A. W., Seda, J., Carmouche, M., Richards, W. G., Fan, W., Jarosinski, M., McKinzie, A. A., & Douglass, J. (2000). Biological functions of cocaine- and amphetamine-regulated transcript (CART): Data with CART peptides and CART knockout mice. *Society of Neuroscience Abstracts*, *26*, 2041.

Barker, M. E., Tandy, M., & Stookey, J. D. (1999). How are consumers of low-fat and high-fat diets perceived by those with lower and higher fat intake? *Appetite*, *33*, 309–317.

Basow, S. A., & Kobrynowicz, D. (1993). What is she eating? The effects of meal size on impressions of a female eater. *Sex Roles*, *28*, 335–344.

Battersham, R. L., Cowley, M. A., Small, C. J., Herzog, H., Cohen, M. A., Dakin, C. L., Wren, A. M., Cone, R. D., & Bloom, S. R. (2002). Gut hormone PYY physiologically inhibits food intake. *Nature*, *418*, 650–654.

Batterham, R. L., Le Roux, C. R., Ellis, S. M., Cohen, M. A., Park, A. J., Patterson, M., Frost, G. S., Ghatei, M., & Bloom, S. R. (2003). Pancreatic polypeptide reduces appetite and food intake in humans. *Journal of Clinical Endocrinology and Metabolism*, *88*, 3989–3992.

Baum, J. G., Clark, H. B., & Sandler, J. (1991). Preventing relapse in obesity through posttreatment maintenance systems: Comparing the relative efficacy of two levels of therapist support. *Journal of Behavioral Medicine*, *14*, 287–302.

Baumrind, D. (1966). Effects of authoritative parental control on child behavior. *Child Development*, *37*, 887–907.

Bellisle, F., Dalix, A.-M., & de Castro, J. M. (1999). Eating patterns in French subjects studied by the 'weekly food diary' method. *Appetite*, *32*, 46–52.

Benton, D. (2001). Micro-nutrient supplementation and intelligence of children. *Neuroscience and Biobehavioral Reviews*, *25*, 297–309.

Bergen, H. T., Mizuno, T., Taylor, J., & Mobbs, C. V. (1999). Resistance to diet-induced obesity is associated with increased proopiomelanocortin mRNA and decreased neuropeptide Y mRNA in the hypothalamus. *Brain Research*, *851*(1/2), 198–203.

Bergh, C., Eriksson, M., Lindberg, G., & Södersten, P. (1996). Selective serotonin reuptake inhibitors in anorexia. *Lancet*, *348*, 1459–1460.

Berridge, K. C. (2004). Motivational concepts in behavioural neuroscience. *Physiology and Behavior*, *81*(2), 179–209.

Bertorelli, R., Ferri, N., Adami, M., & Ongini, E. (1996). Effects of selective agonists and antagonists for A1 or A(2A) adenosine receptors on sleep–waking patterns in rats. *Drug Development and Research*, *37*, 65–72.

Bigler-Doughten, S., & Jenkins R. M. (1987). Adolescent snacks: Nutrient density and nutritional contribution to total intake. *Journal of the American Dietetics Association*, *87*, 1678–1679.

Bindra, D. (1978). How adaptive behaviour is produced: A perceptual-motivational alternative to response reinforcement. *Behavioural and Brain Sciences*, *1*, 41–91.

Birch, L. L. (1980). Effects of peer models' food choices and eating behaviours on preschoolers' food preferences. *Child Development*, *51*, 489–496.

Birch, L. L. (1999). Development of food preferences. *Annual Review of Nutrition*, *19*, 41–62.

Birch, L. L., & Fisher, J. O. (1998). Development of eating behaviors among children and adolescents. *Pediatrics*, *101*, 539–549.

Birch, L. L., Fisher, J. O., Grimm-Thomas, K., Markey, C. N., Sawyer, R., & Johnson, S. L. (2001). Confirmatory factor analysis of the Child Feeding Questionnaire: A measure of parental attitudes, beliefs and practices about child feeding and obesity proneness. *Appetite*, *36*, 201–210.

Birch, L. L., Gunder, L., Grimm-Thomas, K., & Laing, D. G. (1998). Infants' consumption of a new food enhances acceptance of similar foods. *Appetite*, *30*, 283–295.

Birch, L. L., Marlin, D. W., & Rotter, J. (1984). Eating as the 'means' activity in a contingency: Effects on young children's food preference. *Child Development*, *55*, 432–439.

Birch, L. L., McPhee, L., Shoba, B. C., Pirok, E., & Steinberg, L. (1987). What kind of exposure reduces children's food neophobia? Looking vs. tasting. *Appetite, 9,* 171–178.

Bisogni, C. A., Conners, M., Devine, C. M., & Sobal, J. (2002). Who we are and how we eat: A qualitative study of identities in food choice. *Journal of Nutrition Education and Behavior, 34,* 128–139.

Black, A. E., Bingham, S. A., Johansson, G., & Coward, W. A. (1997). Validation of dietary intakes of protein and energy against 24 hour urinary N and DLW energy expenditure in middle-aged women, retired men and post-obese subjects: Comparisons with validation against presumed energy requirements. *European Journal of Clinical Nutrition, 51,* 405–413.

Blake, A. J., Guthrie, H. A., & Smiciklas-Wright, J. (1989). Accuracy of food portion estimation by overweight and normal-weight subjects. *Journal of the American Dietetic Association, 89,* 962–964.

Blake, C. E. (2008). Individual differences in the conceptualization of food across eating contexts. *Food Quality and Preference, 19,* 62–70.

Blake, C. E., Bisogni, J. S., Devine, C. M., & Jastran, M. (2007). Classifying foods in contexts: How adults categorize foods for different eating settings. *Appetite, 49,* 500–510.

Blake, C. E., Bisogni, C. A., Sobal, J., Jastran, M., & Devine, C. M. (2008). How adults construct evening meals: Scripts for food choice. *Appetite, 51,* 654–662.

Blomqvist, A. G., & Herzog, H. (1997). Y-receptor subtypes – how many more? *Trends in Neuroscience, 20*(7), 294–298.

Blundell, J. E. (1977). Is there a role for serotonin (5-hydroxy-tryptamine) in feeding? *International Journal of Obesity, 1,* 15–42.

Blundell, J. (1991). Pharmacological approaches to appetite suppression. *Trends in Pharmacological Sciences, 12*(4), 147–157.

Blundell, J. E., & Finlayson, G. (2004). Is susceptibility to weight gain characterized by homeostatic or hedonic risk factors for overconsumption? *Physiology and Behavior, 82,* 21–25.

Blundell, J. E., & Hill, A. J. (1988). Descriptive and operational study of eating in humans. In B. J. Blinder, B. F. Chaitin & R. Goldstein (Eds.), *The eating disorders* (pp. 65–85). New York: PMA Publishing.

Blundell, J. E., Lawton, C. L., & Halford, J. C. G. (1995). Serotonin, eating behaviour, and fat intake. *Obesity Research, 3,* 471–476.

Blundell, J. E., & Rodgers, P. J. (1991). Hunger, hedonics and the control of satiation and satiety. In M. I. Friedman, M. G. Tordoff & M. R. Kane (Eds.), *Chemical senses, Vol. 4: Appetite and nutrition* (pp. 127–148). New York: Marcel Dekker.

Bolles, R. C. (1972). Reinforcement, expectancy and learning. *Psychological Reviews, 79,* 394–409.

Borg, P., Kukkonen-Harjula, K., Fogelholm, M., & Pasanen, M. (2002). Effects of walking or resistance training on weight loss maintenance in obese, middle-aged men: A randomized trail. *International Journal of Obesity and Related Metabolic Disorders, 26*, 676–683.

Bornstein, R. F. (2001). A meta-analysis of the dependency–eating-disorders relationship: Strength, specificity, and temporal stability. *Journal of Psychopathology and Behavioral Assessment, 23*, 151–162.

Bosaeus, I. (2004). Fibre effects on intestinal functions (diarrhoea, constipation and irritable bowel syndrome). *Clinical Nutrition Supplements, 1*(2), 33–38.

Bosi, A. T. B., Çamur, D., & Güler, C. (2007). Prevalence of orthorexia nervosa in resident medical doctors in the Faculty of Medicine (Ankara, Turkey). *Appetite, 49*, 661–666

Bouwman, L. I., Molder, H. T., Koelen, M. M., & van Woerkum, C. M. J. (2009). I eat healthfully but I am not a freak: Consumers' everyday life perspective on healthful eating. *Appetite, 53*, 390–398.

Boyce, P., & Parker, G. (1989). Development of a scale to measure interpersonal sensitivity. *Australian and New Zealand Journal of Psychiatry, 23*, 341–351.

Boynton-Jarrett, R., Thomas, T. N., Peterson, K. E., Wiecha, J., Sobol, A. M., & Gortmarker, S. L. (2003). Impact of television viewing on fruit and vegetable intake consumption among adolescents. *Pediatrics, 112*, 1321–1326.

Braet, C., & Van Strien, T. (1997). Assessment of emotional, externally induced and restrained eating behaviour in nine- to twelve-year-old obese and non-obese children. *Behaviour Research and Therapy, 35*, 863–873.

Brobeck, J. R., Tepperman, J., & Long, C. N. H. (1943). Experimental hypothalamic hyperphagia in the albino rat. *Yale Journal of Biological Medicine, 15*, 831–853.

Brownell, K. D. (1991). Dieting and the search for the perfect body: Where physiology and culture collide. *Behavior Therapy, 22*, 1–12.

Brunier, G., & Graydon, J. (1996). A comparison of two methods of measuring fatigue in patients on chronic haemodialysis: Visual analogue vs. Likert scale. *International Journal of Nursing Studies, 33*, 338–348.

Brunstrom, J. M. (2007). Associative learning and the control of human dietary behaviour. *Appetite, 49*, 268–271.

Bulik, C. M., Devlin, B., Bacanu, S. A., Thornton, L., & Klump, K. L. (2003). Significant linkage on chromosome 10p in families with bulimia nervosa. *American Journal of Human Genetics, 72*, 200–207.

Bultman, S. J., Michaud, E. J., & Woychik, R. P. (1992). Molecular characterization of the mouse agouti locus. *Cell, 72*, 1195–1204.

Burger, K. S., Kern, M., & Coleman, K. J. (2007). Characteristics of self-selected portion size in young adults. *Journal of the American Dietetic Association, 107*, 611–618.

Burton, G. W., & Traber, M. G. (1990). Vitamin E: Antioxidant activity, biokinetics, and bioavailability. *Annual Review of Nutrition, 10*, 357–382.

Burton-Freeman, B., Davis, P. A., & Schneeman, B. O. (2002). Plasma cholecystokinin is associated with subjective measures of satiety in women. *American Journal of Nutrition, 76*, 659–667.

Byrne, S. M. (2002). Psychological aspects of weight maintenance and relapse in obesity. *Journal of Psychosomatic Research, 53*, 1029–1036.

Cabanac, M. (1992). Pleasure: The common currency. *Journal of Theoretical Biology, 155*, 173–200.

Calderon, L. L., Yu, C. K., & Jambazian, P. (2004). Dieting practices in high school students. *Journal of the American Dietetic Association, 104*, 1369–1374.

Cannon, B., & Washburn, A. L. (1912). An explanation of hunger. *American Journal of Physiology, 12*, 441–454.

Carlsson, A. M. (1983). Assessment of chronic pain. I. Aspects of the reliability and validity of the visual analogue scale. *Pain, 16*, 87–101.

Carr, J. A. (2002). Stress, neuropeptides, and feeding behavior: A comparative perspective. *Integrative and Comparative Biology, 42*, 582–590.

Carruth, B. R., & Skinner, J. D. (2000). Revisiting the 'picky/fussy' eater phenomenon: Neophobic behaviours of young children. *Journal of the American College of Nutrition, 19*, 771–780.

Carruth, B. R., Ziegler, P. J., Gordon, A., & Barr, S. I. (2004). Prevalence of 'picky/fussy' eaters among infants and toddlers and their caregivers' decision about offering new food. *Journal of the American Dietetic Association, 104*, S57–S64.

Cashdan, E. (1998). Adaptiveness of food learning and food aversions in children. *Social Science Information, 37*, 613–632.

Cassin, S. E., & von Ranson, K. M. (2005). Personality and eating disorders: A decade in review. *Clinical Psychology Review, 25*, 895–916.

Chaiken, S., & Pliner, P. (1987). Women, but not men, are what they eat: The effect of meal size and gender on perceived femininity and masculinity. *Personality and Social Psychology Bulletin, 13*, 166–176.

Chatoor, I., & Ganiban, J. (2003). Food refusal by infants and young children: Diagnosis and treatment. *Cognitive and Behavioral Practice, 10*, 138–146.

Cohen, R. J., Rivera, L. L., Canahuati, J., Brown, K. H., & Dewey, K. H. (1995). Delaying the introduction of a complementary food until 6 months does not affect appetite or mother's report of food acceptance of breast fed infants from 6–12 months in a low income, Honduran population. *Journal of Nutrition, 125*(11), 2787–2792.

Conger, J. C., Conger, A. J., Costanzo, P. R., Wright, K. L., & Matter, L. A. (1980). The effect of social cues on the eating behaviour of obese and normal subjects. *Journal of Personality, 48*, 258–271.

Conner, M. (2000). Meta-analysis of the attitude–behaviour relationship in food choice. Cited in Conner, M., & Armitage, C. J. (2002). *The social psychology of food*. Buckingham: Open University Press.

Conner, M., Norman, P., & Bell, R. (2002). The theory of planned behaviour and healthy eating. *Health Psychology, 21*, 194–201.

Conners, M. E., & Morse, W. (1993). Sexual abuse and eating disorders: A review. *International Journal of Eating Disorders, 13*, 1–11.

Contento, I. R., Basch, C., & Zybert, P. (2003). Body image, weight and food choices of Latina women and their young children. *Journal of Nutrition Education and Behaviour*, *35*, 236–248.

Cooke, L., Wardle, J., & Gibson, E. L. (2003). Relationship between parental report of food neophobia and everyday food consumption in 2–6-year-old children. *Appetite*, *41*, 205–206.

Cooke, L., Wardle, J., Gibson, E. L., Sapochnik, M., Sheiham, A., & Lawson, M. (2004). Demographic, familial and trait predictors of fruit and vegetable consumption by pre-school children. *Public Health Nutrition*, *7*(2), 295–302.

Cools, J., Schotte, D. E., & McNally, R. J. (1992). Emotional arousal and overeating in restrained eaters. *Journal of Abnormal Psychology*, *101*(2), 348–351.

Coon, K. A., & Tucker, K. L. (2002). Television and children's consumption patterns: A review of the literature. *Minerva Pediatrica*, *54*, 423–436.

Cooper, M. J. (2005). Cognitive theory in anorexia nervosa and bulimia nervosa: Progress, development and future directions. *Clinical Psychology Review*, *25*, 511–531.

Cooper, Z., & Fairburn, C. G. (2001). A new cognitive behavioural approach to the treatment of obesity. *Behaviour Research and Therapy*, *39*, 499–511.

Corcos, M., & Jeammet, P. (2001). Eating disorders: Psychodynamic approach and practice. *Biomedical Pharmacotherapy*, *55*, 479–488.

Cossrow, N. H., Jeffrey, R. W., & McGuire, M. T. (2001). Weight stigmatization: A focus group study. *Journal of Nutrition Education*, *33*, 208–214.

Costin, C. (1997). *The eating disorder sourcebook: A comprehensive guide to the causes, treatments, and preventions of eating disorders*. Los Angeles, CA: Lowell House.

Coulthard, H., & Harris, G. (2003). Early food refusal: The role of maternal mood. *Journal of Reproductive and Infant Psychology*, *21*, 335–345.

Crisp, A. H. (1967). Anorexia nervosa. *Hospital Medicine*, *1*, 713–718.

Crisp, A. H. (1980). *Anorexia nervosa: Let me be*. London: Academic Press.

Cullen, K. W., Baranowski, T., Rittenberry, L., Cosart, C., Hebert, D., & de Moor, C. (2001). Child reported family and peer influences on fruit juice and vegetable consumption: Reliability and validity of measures. *Health Education Research*, *16*, 187–200.

Cummings, D. E., Clement, K., Purnell, J. Q., Vaisse, C., Foster, K. E., Frayo, R S., Schwartz, M. W., Basdevant, A., & Weigle, D. S. (2002). Elevated plasma ghrelin levels in Prader-Willi syndrome. *Nature Medicine*, *8*(7), 643–644.

Cummings, S., Apovian, C. M., & Khaodhiar, L. (2008). Obesity surgery: Evidence for diabetes prevention/management. *Journal of the American Dietetic Association*, *108*, S40–S44.

Cupples, W. A. (2002). Integrating the regulation of food intake. *American Journal of Physiology: Regulatory, Integrative and Comparative Physiology*, *283*, R356–R357.

Curioni, C. C., & Lourenço, P. M. (2005). Long-term weight loss after diet and exercise: A systematic review. *International Journal of Obesity and Related Metabolic Disorders*, *29*, 1168–1174.

Currie, P. J., Coscina, D. V., Bishop, C., Coiro, C. D., Koob, G. F., Rivier, J., & Vale, W.

(2001). Hypothalamic paraventricular nucleus injections of urocortin alter food intake and respiratory quotient. *Brain Research, 916*, 222–228.

Cusatis, D. C., & Shannon, B. M. (1996). Influences on adolescent eating behavior. *Journal of Adolescent Health, 18*, 27–34.

Cusumano, D. L., & Thompson, K. J. (1997). Body image and body shape ideals in magazines: Exposure, awareness and internalization. *Sex Roles, 37*, 701–721.

Cutler, D. J., Morris, R., Sheridhar, V., Wattam, T. A. K., Holmes, S., Patel, S., Arch, J. R. S., Wilson, S., Buckingham, R. E., Evans, M. L., Leslie, R. A., & Williams, G. (1999). Differential distribution of orexin-A and orexin-B immunoreactivity in the rat brain and spinal cord. *Peptides, 20*, 1455–1470.

Dahl, M., & Sundelin, C. (1986). Early feeding problems in an affluent society – I. Categories and clinical signs. *Acta Paediatricia Scandinavica, 75*, 370–379.

Daousi, C., MacFarlane, I. A., English, P. J., Wilding, J. P. H., Patterson, M., Dovey, T. M., Halford, J. C. G., Ghatei, M. A., & Pinkney, J. H. (2005). Is there a role for ghrelin and peptide-YY in the pathogenesis of obesity in adults with acquired structural hypothalamic damage? *Journal of Clinical Endocrinology and Metabolism, 90*, 5025–5030.

Dare, C., & Eisler, I. (2002). Family therapy and eating disorders. In C. G. Fairburn & K. D. Brownell (Eds.), *Eating disorders and obesity: A comprehensive handbook* (pp. 314–319). London: Guilford Press.

Dare, C., Eisler, I., Russel, G., Treasure, J., & Dodge, L. (2001). Psychological therapies for adults with anorexia nervosa. *British Journal of Psychiatry, 178*, 216–221.

Date, Y., Kojima, M., Hosoda, H., Sawaguchi, A., Mondal, M. S., Suganuma, T., Matsukura, S., Kangawa, K., & Nakazato, M. (2000). Ghrelin, a novel growth hormone-releasing acylated peptide, is synthesized in a distinct endocrine cell type in the gastrointestinal tracts of rats and humans. *Endocrinology, 141*, 4255–4261.

Davis, C., Patte, K., Levitan, R., Reid, C., Tweed, S., & Curtis, C. (2007). From motivation to behaviour: A model of reward sensitivity, overeating, and food preferences in the risk profile for obesity. *Appetite, 48*, 12–19.

de Castro, J. M. (1990). Social facilitation of duration and size but not rate of the spontaneous meal intake of humans. *Physiology and Behavior, 47*, 1129–1135.

de Castro, J. M. (1991). Social facilitation of the spontaneous meal size of humans occurs on both weekdays and weekends. *Physiology and Behavior, 49*, 1289–1291.

de Castro, J. M. (1994). Family and friends produce greater social facilitation of food intake than other companions. *Physiology and Behavior, 56*, 445–455.

de Castro, J. M., Brewer, E. M., Elmore, D. K., & Orozco, S. (1990). Social facilitation of spontaneous meal size of humans occurs regardless of time, place, alcohol or snacks. *Appetite, 15*, 89–101.

Deacon, C. F., Hughes, T. E., & Holst, J. J. (1998). Dipeptidyl IV inhibition potentiates the insulinotropic effect of glucagon-like peptide I in the anesthetized pig. *Diabetes, 47*, 764–769.

Despres, J. P., Lemieux, I., & Prud'homme D. (2001). Treatment of obesity: Need to focus on high risk abdominally obese patients. *British Medical Journal, 322,* 716–720.

Dewberry, C., & Ussher, J. M. (1994). Restraint and perception of body weight among British adults. *Journal of Social Psychology, 134,* 609–619.

Dixon, J. B., Dixon, M. E., & O'Brian, P. E. (2001). Quality of life after lap-band placement: Influence of time, weight loss, and co-morbidities. *Obesity Research, 9,* 713–721.

Donini, L. M., Marsili, D., Gaziani, M. P., Imbriale, M., & Cannella, C. (2004). Orthorexia nervosa: A preliminary study with a proposal for diagnosis and an attempt to measure the dimension of the phenomenon. *Eating and Weight Disorders, 9,* 151–157.

Douglass, J., McKinzie, A. A., & Couceyro, P. (1995). PCR differential display identifies a rat brain mRNA that is transcriptionally regulated by cocaine and amphetamine. *Journal of Neuroscience, 15,* 2471–2481.

Dovey, T. M., Clark-Carter, D., Boyland, E. J., & Halford, J. C. G. (2009a). A guide to analysing Universal Eating Monitor data: Assessing the impact of different analysis techniques. *Physiology and Behavior, 96,* 78–84.

Dovey, T. M., Farrow, C. V., Martin, C. I., Isherwood, E., & Halford, J. C. G. (2009b). When does food refusal require professional intervention? *Current Nutrition and Food Science, 5*(3), 160–171.

Dovey, T. M., Staples, P. A., Gibson, E. L., & Halford, J. C. G. (2008). Food neophobia and picky/fussy eating: A review. *Appetite, 50*(2/3), 181–193.

Drewnowski, A., & Spector, S. E. (2004). Poverty and obesity: The role of energy density and energy costs. *American Journal of Clinical Nutrition, 79,* 6–16.

Dube, M. G., Sahu, A., Phelps, C. P., Kalra, P. S., & Kalra, S. P. (1992). Effect of D-fenfluramine on neuropeptide Y concentration and release in the paraventricular nucleus of food-deprived rats. *Brain Research Bulletin, 29,* 865–869.

Eccles, J. S., & Wigfield, A. (2002). Motivational beliefs, values, and goals. *Annual Reviews in Psychology, 53,* 109–132.

Eghbal-Ahmadi, M., Avishai-Eliner, S., Hatalski, C. G., & Baram, T. Z. (1999). Differential regulation of the expression of corticotropin-releasing factor receptor type 2 (CRF2) in the hypothalamus and amygdala of the immature rat by sensory input and food intake. *Journal of Neuroscience, 19*(10), 3982–3991.

English, P. J., Coughlin, S. R., Hayden, K., Malik, I. A., & Wilding, J. P. (2003). Plasma adiponectin increases postprandially in obese, but not in lean, subjects. *Obesity Research, 11,* 839–844.

English, P. J., Coughlin, S. R., Hayden, K., Malik, I. A., & Wilding, J. P. (2004). Response: Postprandial adiponectin revisited. *Obesity Research, 12*(6), 1032–1034.

English, P. J., Gillett, A., Patterson, M., Dovey, T. M., Halford, J. C. G., Harrison, J., Eccelstone, D., Bloom, S. R., Ghatei, M. A., & Wilding, J. P. H. (2006). Fasting plasma PYY$_{3-36}$ concentrations are elevated but do not rise post-prandially in type 2 diabetes: Evidence for PYY$_{3-36}$ resistance in type 2 diabetes. *Diabetologica, 49*(9), 2219–2221.

Everill, J., & Waller, G. (1995). Reported sexual abuse and eating psychopathology: A review of evidence for a causal link. *International Journal of Eating Disorders, 18*, 1–11.

Evilly, C. M. (2001). The price of perfection. *Nutrition Bulletin, 26*, 275–276.

Fairburn, C. G. (2002a). Cognitive-behavioural therapy for bulimia nervosa. In C. G. Fairburn & K. D. Brownell (Eds.), *Eating disorders and obesity: A comprehensive handbook* (pp. 298–307). London: Guilford Press.

Fairburn, C. G. (2002b). Interpersonal psychotherapy for eating disorders. In C. G. Fairburn & K. D. Brownell (Eds.), *Eating disorders and obesity: A comprehensive handbook* (pp. 320–324). London: Guilford Press.

Fairburn, C. G., & Brownell, K. D. (Eds.) (2002). *Eating disorders and obesity: A comprehensive handbook*. London: Guilford Press.

Fairburn, C. G., Cooper, Z., & Shafran, R. (2003). Cognitive behaviour therapy for eating disorders: A 'transdiagnostic' theory and treatment. *Behaviour Research and Therapy, 41*, 509–528.

Fairburn, C. G., & Harrison, P. J. (2003). Eating disorders. *Lancet, 361*, 407–416.

Fairburn, C. G., Jones, R., Peveler, R. C., Hope, R. A., & O'Conner, M. (1993). Psychotherapy and bulimia nervosa: The long-term effects of interpersonal psychotherapy, behaviour therapy and cognitive behaviour therapy. *Archives of General Psychiatry, 50*, 419–428.

Fairburn, C. G., & Walsh, B. T. (2002). Atypical anorexia nervosa. In C. G. Fairburn & K. D. Brownell (Eds.), *Eating disorders and obesity: A comprehensive handbook* (pp. 298–307). London: Guilford Press.

Fairburn, C. G., Welch, S. L., Doll, H. A., Davies, B. A., & O'Conner, M. E. (1997). Risk factors for bulimia nervosa: A community-based case-control study. *Archives of General Psychiatry, 54*, 509–517.

Felitti, V. J. (1993). Childhood sexual abuse, depression and family dysfunction in adult obese patients. *Southern Medical Journal, 86*, 732–735.

Felitti, V. J., Anda, R. F., Nordenberg, D., Williamson, D. F., Spitz, A. M., Edwards, V., Koss, M. P., & Marks, J. S. (1998). Relationship of childhood abuse and household dysfunction to many of the leading causes of death in adults: The Adverse Childhood Experiences (ACE) study. *American Journal of Preventive Medicine, 14*, 245–258.

Fernández, M. A. P., Labrador, F. J., & Raich, R. M. (2007). Prevalence of eating disorders among an adolescent and young adult scholastic population in the region of Madrid (Spain). *Journal of Psychosomatic Research, 62*, 681–690.

Field, A. E., Colditz, G. A., & Peterson, K. E. (1997). Racial/ethnic and gender differences in concern with weight and in bulimic behaviors among adolescents. *Obesity Research, 5*, 447–454.

Finer, N. (2006). Medical consequences of obesity. *Medicine, 34*, 510–514.

Fonagy, P., Roth, A., & Higgett, A. (2005). The outcome of psychodynamic psychotherapy for psychological disorders. *Clinical Neuroscience Research, 4,* 367–377.

Forbes, S., Bui, S., Robinson, B. R., Hochgeschwender, U., & Brennan, M. B. (2001). Integrated control of appetite and fat metabolism by the leptin–proopiomelanocortin pathway. *Proceedings of the National Academy of Sciences USA, 98,* 4233–4237.

Ford, E. S., Giles, W. H., & Dietz, W. H. (2002). Prevalence of the metabolic syndrome among US adults: Findings from the third National Health and Nutrition Examination Survey. *Journal of the American Medical Association, 287,* 356–359.

Frank, G. K., Bailer, U. F., Henry, S. E., Drevets, W., Meltzer, C. C., Price, J. C., Mathis, C. A., Wagner, A., Hoge, J., Ziolko, S., Barbarich-Marsteller, N., Weissfeld, L., & Kaye, W. H. (2005). Increased dopamine D2/D3 receptor binding after recovery from anorexia nervosa measured by positron emission tomography and [11C]raclopride. *Biological Psychiatry, 58,* 908–912.

Frank, G. K., Kaye, W. H., Meltzer, C. C., Price, J. C., Greer, P., McConaha, C., & Skovira, K. (2002). Reduced 5-HT2A receptor binding after recovery from bulimia-type anorexia nervosa. *Biological Psychiatry, 52,* 896–906.

Franken, I. H. A., & Muris, P. (2005). Individual differences in reward sensitivity are related to food craving and relative body weight in healthy women. *Appetite, 45,* 198–201.

Frost, G. S., Brynes, A. E., Dhillo, W. S., Bloom, S. R., & McBurney, M. I. (2003). The effects of fiber enrichment of pasta and fat content on gastric emptying, GLP-1, glucose, and insulin responses to a meal. *European Journal of Clinical Nutrition, 57,* 293–298.

Gadoth, N. (2008). On fish oil and omega-3 supplementation in children: The role of such supplementation on attention and cognitive dysfunction. *Brain and Development, 30,* 309–312.

Gallistel, C. R., Mark, T. A., King, A., & Latham, P. (2002). A test of Gibbon's feedforward model of matching. *Learning and Motivation, 33,* 46–62.

Galloway, A. T., Fiorito, L., Lee, Y., & Birch, L. L. (2005). Parental pressure, dietary patterns and weight status among girls who are 'picky/fussy' eaters. *Journal of the American Dietetic Association, 105,* 541–548.

Galloway, A. T., Lee, Y., & Birch, L. L. (2003). Predictors and consequences of food neophobia and pickiness in children. *Journal of the American Dietetic Association, 103,* 692–698.

Garfinkel, P. E., Lin, E., Goering, P., Speg, C., Goldbloom, D. S., Kennedy, S., Kaplan, A. S., & Woodside, D. B. (1995). Bulimia nervosa in a Canadian community sample: Prevalence and comparison of subgroups. *American Journal of Psychiatry, 152,* 1052–1058.

Garner, D. M., Olmstead, M. P., & Polivy, J. (1983). Development and validation of a multidimensional eating disorder inventory for anorexia nervosa and bulimia. *International Journal of Eating Disorders, 2,* 15–34.

Garrow, J. S. (1987). Energy expenditure in man – an overview. *American Journal of Clinical Nutrition, 45*, 1114–1119.

Gautvik, K. M., de Lecea, L., Gautvik, V. T., Danielson, P. E., Tranque, P., & Dopazo, A. (1996). Overview of the most prevalent hypothalamus-specific mRNAs, as identified by directional tag PCR subtraction. *Proceedings of the National Academy of Sciences USA, 93*, 8733–8738.

Gendall, K. A., Joyce, P. R., Sullivan, P. F., & Bulik, C. M. (1998). Personality and dimensions of dietary restraint. *International Journal of Eating Disorders, 24*, 371–379.

Gerrish, C. J., & Mennella, J. A. (2001). Flavor variety enhances food acceptance in formula-fed infants. *American Journal of Clinical Nutrition, 73*, 1080–1085.

Geschwind, N., Roefs, A., Lattimore, P., Fett, A.-K., & Jansen, A. (2008). Dietary restraint moderates the effects of food exposure on women's body and weight satisfaction. *Appetite, 51*, 735–738.

Ghaderi, A., & Scott, B. (2001). Prevalence, incidence and prospective risk factors for eating disorders. *Acta Psychiatrica Scandinavica, 104*, 122–130.

Gibbon, J. (1995). Dynamics of time matching: Arousal makes better seem worse. *Psychonomic Bulletin and Review, 2*, 208–215.

Gibbs, J., Young, R. C., & Smith, G. P. (1973). Cholecystokinin decreases food intake in rats. *Journal of Comparative Physiology and Psychology, 84*, 488–497.

Gillman, M. W., Rifas-Shiman, S. L., Frazier, A. L., Rockett, H. R. H., Camargo, C. A., Field, A. E., Berkey, C. S., & Colditz, G. A. (2000). Family dinner and the diet quality among older children and adolescents. *Archives of Family Medicine, 9*, 235–240.

Godart, N. T., Flament, M. F., Curt, F., Perdereau, F., Lang, F., Venisee, J. L., Halfon, O., Bizouard, P., Loas, G., Corcos, M., Jeammet, P., & Fermanian, J. (2003). Anxiety disorders in subjects seeking treatment for eating disorders: A DSM-IV controlled study. *Psychiatry Research, 117*, 245–258.

Godart, N. T., Flament, M. F., Perdereau, F., & Jeammet, P. (2002). Comorbidity between eating disorders and anxiety disorders: A review. *International Journal of Eating Disorders, 23*, 253–270.

Godart, N. T., Perdereau, F., Rein, Z., Bertoz, S., Wallier, J., Jeammet, P., & Flament, M. F. (2007). Comorbidity studies of eating disorders and mood disorders: Critical review of the literature. *Journal of Affective Disorders, 97*, 37–49.

Goethals, I., Vervaet, M., Audenaert, K., Jacobs, F., Ham, H., & Van Heeringen, C. (2007). Does regional brain perfusion correlate with eating disorder symptoms in anorexia and bulimia nervosa patients? *Journal of Psychiatric Research, 41*, 1005–1011.

Goldman, S. J., Herman, C. P., & Polivy, J. (1991). Is the effect of a social model on eating attenuated by hunger? *Appetite, 17*, 129–140.

Gormally, J., Black, S., Daston, S., & Rardin, D. (1982). The assessment of binge eating severity among obese persons. *Addictive Behaviours, 7*, 47–55.

Gough, B., & Conner, M. T. (2006). Barriers to healthy eating amongst men: A qualitative analysis. *Social Science and Medicine, 62*, 387–395.

Grave, R. D., Calugi, S., & Marchesini, G. (2008). Compulsive exercise to control shape or weight in eating disorders: Prevalence, associated features, and treatment outcome. *Comprehensive Psychiatry, 49*, 346–352.

Grice, D., Halmi, K., Fichter, M., Strober, M., Woodside, D., Treasure, J., Kaplan, A., Magistretti, P., Goldman, D., & Bulik, C. (2002). Evidence for a susceptibility gene for anorexia nervosa on chromosome 1. *American Journal of Human Genetics, 70*, 787–792.

Grogen, S. (1999). *Body image: Understanding body dissatisfaction in men, women and children*. London: Routledge.

Grogen, S. C., Bell, R., & Conner, M. (1998). Eating sweet snacks: Gender differences in attitudes and behaviour. *Appetite, 28*, 19–31.

Guy, J., Pelletier, G., & Bosler, O. (1988). Serotonin innervation of neuropeptide Y-containing neurons in the rat arcuate nucleus. *Neuroscience Letters, 85*, 9–13.

Guyatt, G. H., Townsend, M., Berman, L. B., & Keller, J. L. (1987). A comparison of Likert and visual analogue scales for measuring change in function. *Journal of Chronic Disease, 40*, 1129–1133.

Hagan, J. J., Leslie, R. A., Patel, S., Evans, M. L., Wattam, T. A. K., Holmes, S., Benham, C. D., Taylor, S. G., Routledge, C., Hemmati, P., Munton, R. P., Ashmeade, T. E., Shah, A. S., Hatcher, J. P., Hatcher, P. D., Jones, D. N. C., Smith, M. I., Piper, D. C., Hunter, A. J., Porter, R. A., & Upton, N. (1999). Orexin A activates locus coeruleus cell firing and increases arousal in the rat. *Proceedings of the National Academy of Sciences USA, 96*, 10911–10916.

Hahn, T. M., Breininger, J. F., Baskin, D. G., & Schwartz, M. W. (1998). Coexpression of Agrp and NPY in fasting-activated hypothalamic neurons. *Nature Neuroscience, 1*, 271–272.

Halford, J. C. G., Boyland, E. J., Cooper, S. J., Dovey, T. M., Huda, M. S. B., Dourish, C. T., Dawson, G. R., & Wilding, J. P. H. (2008a). The effects of sibutramine on the microstructure of eating behaviour and energy expenditure in obese women. *Journal of Psychopharmacology* (DOI: 10.1177/0269881108095195).

Halford, J. C. G., Boyland, E. J., Cooper, G. D., Dovey, T. M., Smith, C. J., Williams, N., Lawton, C. L., & Blundell, J. E. (2008b). Children's preferences for branded and non-branded foods: Effects of weight status and television food advertisements (commercials). *International Journal of Paediatric Obesity, 3*, 31–38.

Halford, J. C. G., Boyland, E., Hughes, G., & Dovey, T. M. (2008c). Beyond-brand effect of television (TV) food advertisements on food choice in children: The effects of weight status. *Public Health Nutrition, 11*(9), 897–904.

Halford, J. C. G., Boyland, E., Hughes, G., Oliveira, L. P., & Dovey, T. M. (2007). Beyond-brand effect of television (TV) food advertisements/commercials on caloric intake and food choice of 5 to 7 years old children. *Appetite, 49*, 263–267.

Halford, J. C. G., Cooper, G. D., & Dovey, T. M. (2004a). The pharmacology of human appetite expression. *Current Drug Targets, 5*(3), 1–20.

Halford, J. C. G., Cooper, G. D., Dovey, T. M., Iishi, Y., Rodgers, J., & Blundell, J. E. (2003). The psychopharmacology of appetite: Targets for potential anti-obesity agents. *Current Medicinal Chemistry: Central Nervous System Agents*, *3*, 283–310.

Halford, J. C. G., Gillespie, J., Brown, V., Pontin, E. E., & Dovey, T. M. (2004b). Effect of television advertisements for foods on food consumption in children. *Appetite*, *42*(2), 221–225.

Harkin, T. (2007). Preventing childhood obesity: The power of policy and political will. *American Journal of Preventive Medicine*, *33*(suppl. 1), S165–S166.

Harper, L. V., & Sanders, K. M. (1975). The effect of adults' eating on young children's acceptance of unfamiliar foods. *Journal of Experimental Child Psychology*, *20*, 206–214.

Harris, E. C., & Barraclough, B. (1997). Suicide as an outcome for mental disorders. *British Journal of Psychiatry*, *170*, 205–228.

Harris, G. (1993). Introducing the infant's first solid food. *British Food Journal*, *95*(9), 7–10.

Hauptman, J. B., Jeunet, F. S., & Hartmann, D. (1992). Initial studies in humans with the novel gastrointestinal lipase inhibitor Ro18.0467 (tetrahydrolipastatin). *American Journal of Clinical Nutrition*, *55*, 309S–313S.

Hauser, G. J., Chitayat, D., Berns, L., Braver, D., & Muhlbauer, B. (1985). Peculiar odours in newborns and maternal pre-natal ingestion of spicy foods. *European Journal of Pediatrics*, *144*(4), 403.

Haynes, C., Lee, M. D., & Yeomans, M. R. (2003). Interactive effects of stress, dietary restraint, and disinhibition on appetite. *Eating Behaviors*, *4*, 369–383.

Heatherton, T. F., & Baumeister, R. F. (1991). Binge eating as escape from self-awareness. *Psychological Bulletin*, *110*, 86–108.

Heaven, P. C. L., Mulligan, K., Merrilees, R., Woods, T., & Fairooz, Y. (2001). Neuroticism and conscientiousness as predictors of emotional, external, and retrained eating behaviors. *International Journal of Eating Disorders*, *30*(2), 161–166.

Hebben, N., Corkin, S., Eichenbaum, H., & Shedlack, K. (1985). Diminished ability to interpret and report internal states after bilateral medial temporal resection – case HM. *Behavioural Neuroscience*, *99*, 1031–1039.

Hébert, J. R., Peterson, K. E., Hurley, T. G., Stoddard, A. M., Cohen, N., Field, A. E., & Sorensen, G. (2001). The effect of social desirability trait on self-reported dietary measures among multi-ethnic female health center employees. *Annals of Epidemiology*, *11*, 417–427.

Hebl, M. R., & Mannix, L. M. (2003). The weight of obesity in evaluating others: A mere proximity effect. *Personality and Social Psychology Bulletin*, *29*, 28–38.

Hegele, R. A., Harris, S. B., Hanley, A. J., Sadikian, S., Connelly, P. W., & Zinman, B. (1996). Genetic variation of intestinal fatty acid-binding protein associated with variation in body mass in aboriginal Canadians. *Journal of Clinical Endocrinology and Metabolism*, *81*, 4334–4337.

Heinrichs, S. C., Menzaghi, F., Pich, E. M., Hauger, R. L., & Koob, G. F. (1993).

Corticotropin-releasing factor in the paraventricular nucleus modulates feeding induced by neuropeptide Y. *Brain Research, 611,* 18–24.

Hemilä, H. (2003). Vitamin C, respiratory infections and the immune system. *Trends in Immunology, 24*(11), 579–580.

Henderson, M., & Freeman, C. P. (1987). A self-rating scale for bulimia: The 'BITE'. *British Journal of Psychiatry, 150,* 18–24.

Herman, C. P., & Mack, D. (1975). Restrained and unrestrained eating. *Journal of Personality, 43,* 646–660.

Herman, C. P., Olmsted, M. P., & Polivy, J. (1983). Obesity, externality, and susceptibility to social-influence: An integrated analysis. *Journal of Personality and Social Psychology, 45*(4), 926–934.

Herman, C. P., & Polivy, J. (1980). Restrained eating. In A. J. Stunkard (Ed.), *Obesity* (pp. 208–225). Philadelphia, PA: Saunders.

Herman, C. P., & Polivy, J. (1984). A boundary model for the regulation of eating. In A. B. Stunkard & E. Stellar (Eds.), *Eating and its disorders* (pp. 141–156). New York: Raven Press.

Herman, C. P., & Polivy, J. (2008). External cues in the control of food intake in humans: The sensory–normative distinction. *Physiology and Behaviour, 94,* 722–728.

Herman, C. P., Polivy, J., Pliner, P., Threlkeld, J., & Munic, D. (1978). Distractibility in dieters and non-dieters: An alternative view of externality. *Journal of Personality and Social Psychology, 36,* 536–548.

Herman, C. P., Roth, D. A., & Polivy, J. (2003). Effects of the presence of others on food intake: A normative interpretation. *Psychological Bulletin, 129*(6), 873–886.

Hermans, R. C. J., Larsen, J. K., Herman, C. P., & Engels, R. C. M. E. (2008). Modeling of palatable food intake in female young adults: Effects of perceived body size. *Appetite, 51,* 512–518.

Herrnstein, R. J., & Prelec, D. (1991). Melioration: A theory of distributed choice. *Journal of Economic Perspectives, 5,* 137–156.

Herzog, D. B., Keller, M. B., Sacks, N. R., Yeh, C. J., & Lavori, P. W. (1992). Psychiatric morbidity in treatment-seeking anorexics and bulimics. *Journal of the American Academy of Child and Adolescent Psychiatry, 31,* 810–818.

Hesse-Biber, S., Leavy, P., Quinn, C. E., & Zoino, J. (2006). The mass marketing of disordered eating and eating disorders: The social psychology of women, thinness and culture. *Women's Studies International Forum, 29,* 208–224.

Hetherington, A. W., & Ranson, S. W. (1940). Hypothalamic lesions and adiposity in the rat. *Anatomy Records, 78,* 149–172.

Hetherington, M. M., Anderson, A. S., Norton, G. N. M., & Newson, L. (2006). Situational effects on meal intake: A comparison of eating alone and eating with others. *Physiology and Behavior, 88,* 498–505.

Hetherington, M. M., Bell, A., & Rolls, B. J. (2000). Effects of repeat consumption on pleasantness, preference and intake. *British Food Journal, 102,* 507–521.

Hetherington, M. M., Rolls, B. J., & Burley, V. J. (1989). The time course of sensory-specific satiety. *Appetite, 12*, 57–68.

Higgs, S. (2002). Memory for recent eating and its influence on subsequent food intake. *Appetite, 39*, 159–166.

Higgs, S. (2008). Cognitive influences on food intake: The effects of manipulating memory for recent eating. *Physiology and Behavior, 94*, 734–739.

Hilbert, A., Saelens, B. E., Stein, R. I., Mockus, D. S., Welch, R. R., Matt, G. E., & Wilfley, D. E. (2007). Pretreatment and process predictors of outcome in interpersonal and cognitive behavioral psychotherapy for binge eating disorder. *Journal of Consulting and Clinical Psychology, 75*, 645–651.

Hill, A., & Pallin, V. (1998). Dieting awareness and low self-worth: Related issues in 8-year-old girls. *International Journal of Eating Disorders, 24*, 405–414.

Hill, J., & Peters, J. (1998). Environmental contributors to the obesity epidemic. *Science, 280*, 1371–1374.

Hillebrand, J. J. G., de Wied, D., & Adan, R. A. H. (2002). Neuropeptides, food intake and body weight regulation: A hypothalamic focus. *Peptides, 6539*, 1–24.

Hoek, H. W. (2002). Distribution of eating disorders. In C. G. Fairburn & K. D. Brownell (Eds.), *Eating disorders and obesity: A comprehensive handbook* (pp. 233–237). London: Guilford Press.

Horie, L. M., Barbosa-Silva, M. C. G., Torrinhas, R. S., de Mello, M. T., Cecconello, I., & Waitzberg, D. L. (2008). New body fat prediction equations for severely obese patients. *Clinical Nutrition, 27*, 350–356.

House of Commons Select Committee (2004) *Obesity: Third Report of Session 2003/04*. London: The Stationery Office.

Huang, Q., Rivest, R., & Richard, D. (1998). Effects of leptin on CRF synthesis and CRF neuron activation in the paraventricular hypothalamic nucleus of obese (ob/ob) mice. *Endocrinology, 139*(4), 1524–1532.

Hubbs-Tait, L., Kennedy, T. S., Page, M. C., Topham, G. L., & Harrist, A. W. (2008). Parental feeding practices predict authoritative, authoritarian, and permissive parenting styles. *Journal of the American Dietetic Association, 108*, 1154–1161.

Hubert, H., Guinhouya, C. B., Allard, L., & Durocher, A. (2008). Comparison of the diagnostic quality of body mass index, waist circumference and waist-to-height ratio in screening skinfold-determined obesity among children. *Journal of Science and Medicine in Sports, 12*, 449–451.

Hudson, J. I., Lalonde, J. K., Berry, J. M., Pindyck, L. J., Bulik, C. M., Crow, S. J., McElroy, S. L., Laird, N. M., Tsuang, M. T., Walsh, B. T., Rosenthal, N. R., & Pope, H. G., Jr. (2006). Binge-eating disorder as a distinct familial phenotype in obese individuals. *Archives of General Psychiatry, 63*, 313–319.

Humphrey, L. L. (1986). Family relations in bulimic-anorexic and nondistressed families. *International Journal of Eating Disorders, 5*, 223–232.

Huon, G. F., Qian, M., Oliver, K., & Xiao, G. L. (2002). A large-scale survey of eating disorder symptomatology among female adolescents in the People's Republic of China. *International Journal of Eating Disorders, 32*, 192–205.

Huszer, D., Lynch, C. A., Fairchild-Huntress, V., Dunmore, J. H., Fang, Q., & Berkemeier, L. R. (1997). Targeted disruption of the melanocortin-4 receptor results in obesity in mice. *Cell*, *88*, 131–141.

Hutchinson, D. M., & Rapee, R. M. (2007). Do friends share similar body image and eating problems? The role of social networks and peer influences in early adolescence. *Behaviour Research and Therapy*, *45*, 1557–1577.

Illius, A. W., Tikamp, B. J., & Yearsley, J. (2002). The evolution of the control of food intakes. *Proceedings of the Nutrition Society*, *61*, 465–472.

Inui, A. (2001). Ghrelin: An orexigenic and somatotrophic signal from the stomach. *Nature Reviews Neuroscience*, *2*, 551–560.

Jebb, S. (2004). Obesity: Causes and consequences. *Women's Health Medicine*, *1*, 38–41.

Jeffery, R. W., Bjornson-Benson, W. M., Rosenthal, B. S., Lindquist, R. A., Kurth, C. L., & Johnson, S. L. (1984). Correlates of weight loss and its maintenance over two years of follow-up among middle-aged men. *Preventative Medicine*, *13*, 155–168.

Jeffery, R. W., Hellerstedt, W. L., French, S. A., & Baxter, J. E. (1995). A randomised evaluation of a low fat *ad libitum* carbohydrate diet for weight reduction. *International Journal of Obesity*, *17*, 623–629.

Jekanowski, M. (2001). Convenience, accessibility and demand for fast food. *Journal of Agricultural and Resource Economics*, *26*, 58–74.

Johnson, D. B., Gerstein, D. E., Evens, A. E., & Woodward-Lopez, G. (2006). Preventing obesity: A life-cycle perspective. *Journal of the American Dietetic Association*, *106*, 97–102.

Jolanta, J. R.-J., & Tomasz, M. S. (2000). The links between body dysmorphic disorder and eating disorders. *European Psychiatry*, *15*, 302–305.

Joyce, C. R. B., Zutshi, D. W., Hrubes, V., & Mason, R. M. (1975). Comparison of fixed interval and visual analogue scales for rating chronic pain. *European Journal of Clinical Pharmacology*, *8*, 415–429.

Kalra, S. P., Dube, M. G., Pu, S., Xu, B., Horvath, T. L., & Kalra, P. S. (1999). Interacting appetite-regulating pathways in the hypothalamic regulation of body weight. *Endocrine Reviews*, *20*(1), 68–100.

Kaplan, H. I., & Kaplan, H. S. (1957). The psychosomatic concept of obesity. *Journal of Nervous and Mental Disorders*, *125*, 181–201.

Karlsson, F. A., Engstrom, B. E., Lind, L., & Ohrvall, M. (2004). No postprandial increase of plasma adiponectin in obese subjects. *Obesity Research*, *12*(6), 1031–1032.

Kauer, J., Rozin, P., & Pelchat, M. L. (2002). *Adult picky eating*. Paper presented to the Annual Meeting of the Society for the Study of Ingestive Behavior, Santa Cruz, CA.

Kelner, K., & Helmuth, L. (2003). Obesity: What is to be done? *Science*, *299*, 845–849.

Kemm, J. (1987). Eating patterns in childhood and adult health. *Nutrition and Health*, *4*, 205–215.

Kennedy, G. C. (1953). The role of depot fat in the hypothalamic control of food intake in the rat. *Proceedings of the Royal Society of London B, 140*, 578–592.

Kim, K. H. (2006). Religion, body dissatisfaction and dieting. *Appetite, 46*, 285–296.

Kim, K. H. (2007). Religion, weight perception and weight controlling behaviour. *Eating Behavior, 8*, 121–131.

Kim, K. H., Sobal, J., & Wethington, E. (2003). Religion and body weight. *International Journal of Obesity, 27*, 469–477.

Kluck, A. S. (2008). Family factors in the development of disordered eating: Integrating dynamic and behavioral explanations. *Eating Behaviours, 9*, 471–483.

Koivisto-Hursti, U.-K., & Sjöden, P. (1997). Food and general neophobia and their relationship with self-reported food choice: Familial resemblance in Swedish families with children of ages 7–17 years. *Appetite, 29*, 89–103.

Koizumi, M., & Kimura, S. (2002). Enterostatin increases extra cellular seroton in and dopamine in the lateral hypothalamic area in rats measured by *in vivo* microdialysis. *Neuroscience Letters, 329*, 96–98.

Kojima, M., Hosoda, H., Date, Y., Nakazato, M., Matsuo, H., & Kangawa, K. (1999). Ghrelin is a growth-hormone-releasing acylated peptide from the stomach. *Nature, 402*, 656–660.

Kong, M.-F., Chapman, I., Goble, A., Wishart, J., Wittert, G., Morris, H., & Horowitz, M. (1999). Effects of oral fructose and glucose on plasma GLP-1 and appetite in normal subjects. *Peptides, 20*, 545–551.

Kral, T. V. E. (2006). Effects of hunger and satiety, perceived portion size and pleasantness of taste of varying the portion size of foods: A brief review of selected studies. *Appetite, 46*, 103–105.

Kral, T. V. E., Meeng, J. S., Wall, D. E., Roe, L. S., & Rolls, B. J. (2004). Combined effects of energy density and portion size on energy intake in women. *American Journal of Clinical Nutrition, 79*, 962–968.

Krall, J. S., & Lohse, B. (2009). Interviews with low-income Pennsylvanians verify a need to enhance eating competence. *Journal of the American Dietetic Association, 109*, 468–473.

Kubik, M. Y., Lytle, L., & Fulkerson, J. A. (2005). Fruits, vegetables, and football: Findings from focus groups with alternative high school students regarding eating and physical activity. *Journal of Adolescent Health, 36*, 494–500.

Kunii, K., Yamanaka, A., Nambu, T., Matsuzaki, I., Goto, K., & Sakurai, T. (1999). Orexins/hypocretins regulate drinking behaviour. *Brain Research, 842*, 256–261.

Kyle, U. G., Bosaeus, I., De Lorenzo, A. D., Deurenberg, P., Elia, M., Gómez, J. M., Heitmann, B. L., Kent-Smith, L., Melchior, J.-C., Pirlich, M., Scharfetter, H., Schols, A. M. W. J., & Pichard, C. (2004). Bioelectrical impedance analysis – part II: Utilization in clinical practice. *Clinical Nutrition, 23*, 1430–1453.

Laflamme, D. P. (2006). Understanding and managing obesity in dogs and cats. *Veterinary Clinics of North America: Small Animal Practice, 36*, 1283–1295.

Lange, A., De Beurs, E., Dolan, C., Lachnit, T., Sjollema, S., & Hanewald, G. (1999). Long-term effects of childhood sexual abuse: Objective and subjective characteristics of the abuse and psychopathology in later life. *Journal of Nervous and Mental Disease, 187*, 150–158.

Lavin, J. H., Wittert, G. A., Andrews, J., Yeap, B., Wishart, J. M., Morris, H. A., Morley, J. E., Horowitz, M., & Read, N. W. (1998). Interaction of insulin, glucagon-like peptide 1, gastric inhibitory polypeptide, and appetite in response to intraduodenal carbohydrate. *American Journal of Clinical Nutrition, 68*, 591–598.

Lawrence, C. B., Snape, A. C., Baudoin F. M. H., & Luckman, S. M. (2002). Acute central ghrelin and GH secretagogues induce feeding and activate brain appetite centers. *Endocrinology, 143*, 155–162.

Lazarus, R. S., & Launier, R. (1978). Stress-related transactions between person and environment. In L. A. Pervin & M. Lewis (Eds.), *Perspectives in interactional psychology* (pp. 287–327). New York: Plenum Press.

Lean, M. E. J., Han, T. S., & Seidall, J. C. (1998). Impairment of health and quality of life in people with large waist circumference. *Lancet, 351*, 853–856.

Lee, S. (1993). How abnormal is the desire for slimness? A survey of eating attitudes and behaviour among Chinese undergraduates in Hong Kong. *Psychological Medicine, 23*, 437–451.

Levitsky, D. A. (2002). Putting behavior back into feeding behavior: A tribute to George Collier. *Appetite, 38*, 143–148.

Lieberman, L. S. (2006). Evolutionary and anthropological perspectives on optimal foraging in obesogenic environments. *Appetite, 47*, 3–9.

Lieverse, R. J., Jansen, J. B. M. J., Masclee, A. A. M., Rovati, L. C., & Lamers, C. B. H. W. (1994). Effect of a low dose of intraduodenal fat on satiety in humans: Studies using the type A cholecystokinin receptor antagonist loxiglumide. *Gut, 35*, 501–505.

Lilenfeld, L. R. R., Ringham, R., Kalarchian, M. A., & Marcus, M. D. (2008). A family history study of binge-eating disorder. *Comprehensive Psychiatry, 49*, 247–254.

Lin, L., & York, D. A. (1997). Comparisons of the effects of enterostatin on food intake and gastric emptying in rats. *Brain Research, 745*, 205–209.

Lindeman, M., & Sirelius, M. (2001). Food choice ideologies: The modern manifestations of normative and humanist views of the world. *Appetite, 37*, 175–184.

Lish, J. D., Kavoussi, R. J., & Coccaro, E. F. (1996). Aggressiveness. In G. C. Costello (Ed.), *Personality characteristics of the personality disorder* (pp. 24–27). New York: Wiley.

Lockwood, G. B. (2007). The hype surrounding nutraceutical supplements: Do consumers get what they deserve? *Nutrition, 23*, 771–772.

López, L. B., Langini, S. H., & Pita de Portela, M. L. (2007). Maternal iron status and neonatal outcomes in women with pica during pregnancy. *International Journal of Gynecology and Obstetrics, 98*, 151–152.

Lowe, M. R., & Eldredge, K. L. (1993). The role of impulsiveness in normal and disordered eating. In W. G. McCown, J. L. Johnson & M. B. Shure (Eds.), *The impulsive client: Theory, research and treatment* (pp. 185–224). Washington, DC: American Psychological Association.

Lowe, M. R., & Fisher, E. B. (1983). Emotional reactivity, emotional eating, and obesity: A naturalistic review. *Journal of Behavioral Medicine, 6*, 135–149.

Ludwig, D. S., Peterson, K. E., & Gortmaker, S. L. (2001). Relation between consumption of sugar-sweetened drinks and childhood obesity: A prospective, observational analysis. *Lancet, 357*, 505–508.

Ludwig, D. S., Tritos, N. A., Mastaitis, J. W., Kulkarni, R., Kokkotou, E., Elmquist, J., Lowell, B., Flier, J. S., & Maratos-Flier, E. (2001). Melanin-concentrating hormone over expression in transgenic mice leads to obesity and insulin resistance. *Journal of Clinical Investigation, 107*, 379–386.

Lui, M., Doi, T., Shen, L., Woods, S. W., Seeley, R. J., Zheng, S., Jackman, A., & Tso, P. (2001). Intestinal satiety protein apolipoprotein AIV is synthesized and regulated in rat hypothalamus. *American Journal of Physiology: Regulatory, Integrative and Comparative Physiology, 280*, R1382–R1387.

Lynskey, M. T. (1998). The comorbidity of alcohol dependence and affective disorders: Treatment implications. *Drug and Alcohol Dependence, 52*, 201–209.

MacArthur, R. H., & Pianka, E. R. (1966). On optimal use of a patchy environment. *American Naturalist, 100*, 603–609.

Macht, M. (2008). How emotions affect eating: A five-way model. *Appetite, 50*, 1–11.

Maffei, M., Halaas, J., Ravussin, E., Partley, R. E., Lee, G. H., Zhang, Y., Fei, H., Kim, S., Lallone, R., Ranganathan, S., Kern, P. A., & Friedman, J. M. (1995). Leptin levels in human and rodent: Measurement of plasma leptin and *ob* RNA in obese and weight-reduced subjects. *Nature Medicine, 1*, 1155–1161.

Manzoni, G. M., Pagnini, F., Gorini, A., Preziosa, A., Castelnuovo, G., Molinari, E., & Riva, G. (2009). Can relaxation training reduce emotional eating in women with obesity? An exploration study with 3 months of follow-up. *Journal of the American Dietetic Association, 109*, 1427–1432.

Marcelino, A. S., Adam, A. S., Couronne, T., Koster, E. P., & Sieffermann, J. M. (2001). Internal and external determinants of eating initiation in humans. *Appetite, 36*(1), 9–14.

Marchi, M., & Cohen, P. (1990). Early childhood eating behaviors and adolescent eating disorders. *Journal of the American Academy of Child and Adolescent Psychiatry, 29*, 112–117.

Marshall, K., Laing, D. G., Jinks, A. L., & Hutchinson, I. (2006). The capacity of humans to identify components in complex odor–taste mixtures. *Chemical Senses, 31*, 539–545.

Masaki, T., Chiba, S., Tatsukawa, H., Yasuda, T., Noguchi, H., Seike, M., & Yoshimatsu, H. (2004). Adiponectin protects LPS-induced liver injury through modulation of TNF-alpha in KK-Ay obese mice. *Hepatology, 40*(1), 177–184.

Matheson, D. M., Killen, J. D., Wany, Y., Varadt, A., & Robinson, T. (2004). Children's food consumption and television viewing. *American Journal of Clinical Nutrition, 79*, 1088–1094.

Mayer, J. (1953). Glucostatic mechanism of regulation of food intake. *New England Journal of Medicine*, *249*, 13–16.

McBurney, D. H., & Gent, J. F. (1979). On the nature of taste qualities. *Psychological Bulletin*, *86*, 151–167.

McCormack, H. M., Horne, D. J. de L., & Sheather, S. (1988). Clinical applications of visual analogue scales: A critical review. *Psychological Medicine*, *18*, 1007–1019.

McFarlane, T., & Pliner, P. (1997). Increased willingness to taste novel foods: Effects of nutrition and taste information. *Appetite*, *28*, 227–238.

McKenna, R. J. (1972). Some effects of anxiety level and food cues on the eating behavior of obese and normal subjects: A comparison of the Schachterian and psychosomatic conceptions. *Journal of Personality and Social Psychology*, *22*, 311–319.

McKenzie, J. M., & Joyce, P. R. (1992). Hospitalisation for anorexia nervosa. *International Journal of Eating Disorders*, *11*, 235–241.

McLean, J. A., & Barr, S. I. (2003). Cognitive dietary restraint is associated with eating behaviors, lifestyle practices, personality characteristics and menstrual irregularity in college women. *Appetite*, *40*(2), 185–192.

McNulty, S. J., Ur, E., & Williams, G. A. (2003). A randomized trial of sibutramine in the management of type 2 diabetic patients treated with metformin. *Diabetes Care*, *26*, 125–131.

Meguid, M. M., Fetissov, S. O., Varma, M., Sato, T., Zhang, L., Laviano, A., & Rossi-Fannelli, F. (2000). Hypothalamic dopamine and serotonin in the regulation of food intake. *Nutrition*, *16*, 843–857.

Meister, B. (2007). Neurotransmitters in key neurons of the hypothalamus that regulate feeding behaviour and body weight. *Physiology and Behavior*, *92*, 263–271.

Mela, D. J. (2001). Determinants of food choice: Relationships with obesity and weight control. *Obesity Research*, *9*, S249–S255.

Mellinkoff, S. M., Frankland, M., Boyle, D., & Greipel, M. (1956). Relationship between serum amino acid concentration and fluctuations in appetite. *Journal of Applied Physiology*, *8*, 535–538.

Mennella, J. A., & Beauchamp, G. K. (1999). Experience with flavor in mothers' milk modifies the infant's acceptance of flavored cereal. *Developmental Psychobiology*, *35*, 197–203.

Mennella, J. A., Kennedy, J. M., & Beauchamp, G. K. (2006). Vegetable acceptance by infants: Effects of formula flavors. *Early Human Development*, 82, 463–468.

Meno, C. A., Hannum, J. W., Espelage, D. E., & Low, K. S. (2008). Familial and individual variables as predictors of dieting concerns and binge eating in college females. *Eating Behaviors*, *9*, 91–101.

Meyer, J.-E., & Pudel, V. (1972). Experimental studies on food intake in obese and normal weight subjects. *Journal of Psychiatric Research*, *16*, 305–308.

Michel, S., Lutz, T., & Riediger, T. (2007). Nutrients modulate amylin's effect on c-Fos expression in the area postrema and on food intake. *Appetite*, *49*, 314.

Miller, E., Joseph, S., & Tudway, J. (2004). Assessing the component structure of four self-report measures of impulsivity. *Personality and Individual Differences,* *37,* 349–358.

Minuchin, S., Rosman, B. L., & Baker, L. (1978). *Psychosomatic families: Anorexia nervosa in Context.* Cambridge, MA: Harvard University Press.

Mitchell, S. L., & Perkins, K. A. (1998). Interaction of stress, smoking, and dietary restraint in women. *Physiology and Behavior, 64,* 103–109.

Miyaoka, T., Yasukawa, R., Tsubouchi, K., Miura, S., Shimizu, Y., & Sukegawa, T. (2003). Successful treatment of nocturnal eating/drinking syndrome with selective serotonin reuptake inhibitors. *International Clinical Psychopharmacology, 18,* 175–177.

Mondada, L. (2009). The methodical organization of talking and eating: Assessments in dinner conversations. *Food Quality and Preference, 20,* 558–571.

Mooney, K. M., & Amico, T. (2000). *Food scrutiny: We are all watching what you eat.* Poster session presented at the Annual Meeting of the American Psychological Society, Miami Beach, FL.

Moore, S., Tapper, K., & Murphy, S. (2007). Feeding strategies used by mothers of 3–5-year-old children. *Appetite, 49*(3), 704–707.

Moran, T. (2000). Cholecystokinin and satiety: Current perspectives. *Nutrition, 16,* 858–865.

Morley, J. E., Levine, A. S., Grace, M. K., & Kniep, J. (1985). Peptide YY (PYY), a potent orexigenic agent. *Brain Research, 341,* 200–203.

Murcott, A. (1982). On the social significance of the 'cooked dinner' in South Wales. *Social Science Information, 21,* 677–695.

Murray, P. (1999). Fundamental issues in questionnaire design. *Accident and Emergency Nursing, 7,* 148–153.

Nahum, J., & Kerr, B. (2008). Optimal foraging: A bird in the hand released. *Current Biology, 18*(9), R385–R386.

Näslund, E., & Hellström, P. M. (2007). Appetite signalling: From gut peptides and enteric nerves to brain. *Physiology and Behavior, 92,* 256–262.

National Audit Office (2001). *Tackling obesity in England.* Report by the Comptroller and Auditor-General, HC 220. London: The Stationery Office.

Nauck, M. A., Niedereichholz, U., Ettler, R., Holst, J. J., Ørskov, C., Ritzel, R., & Schmiegel, W. H. (1997). Glucagon-like peptide 1 inhibition of gastric emptying outweighs its insulinotropic effects in healthy humans. *American Journal of Physiology: Endocrinology and Metabolism, 273,* E981–E988.

Nehlig, A. (1999). Are we dependent upon coffee and caffeine? A review on human and animal data. *Neuroscience and Biobehavioral Reviews, 23,* 563–576.

Neumark-Sztainer, D., Story, M., Renick, M., & Casey, M. A. (1999). Factors influencing food choices of adolescents: Findings from focus-group discussions with adolescents. *Journal of the American Dietetic Association, 99*(8), 929–937.

Neumark-Sztainer, D., Wall, M., Haines, J., Story, M., & Eisenberg, M. E. (2007). Why does dieting predict weight gain in adolescents? Findings from Project

EAT-II: A 5-year longitudinal study. *Journal of the American Dietetic Association*, *107*, 448–455.

Nguyen, S. P., & Murphy, G. L. (2003). An apple is more than just a fruit: Cross-classification in children's concepts. *Child Development*, *74*(6), 1783–1806.

Nicklaus, S., Boggio, V., Chababnet, C., & Issanchou, S. (2005). Prospective study of food variety seeking in childhood, adolescence and early adult life. *Appetite*, *44*, 289–297.

Nielsen, G. B., Lausch, B., & Thomsen, P. H. (1997). Three cases of severe early-onset eating disorder: Are they cases of anorexia nervosa? *Psychopathology*, *30*, 49–52.

Nisbett, R. E., & Storms, M. D. (1974). Cognitive and social determinants of food intake. In H. London & R. E. Nisbett (Eds.), *Thought and feeling: Cognitive alterations of feeling states* (pp. 190–208). Chicago, IL: Aldine.

Nishijo, H., Uwano, T., Tamura, R., & Ono, T. (1998). Gustatory and multimodal neuronal responses in the amygdala during licking and discrimination of sensory stimuli in awake rats. *Journal of Neurophysiology*, *79*(1), 21–36.

Oates, M. E., & Slotterback, C. S. (2004). Prejudgments of those who eat a 'healthy' versus an 'unhealthy' food for breakfast. *Current Psychology*, *23*, 267–277.

Ogden, J., & Taylor, C. (2000). Body size evaluation and body dissatisfaction within couples. *International Journal of Health Psychology*, *5*, 25–32.

Ogden, J., & Wardle, J. (1990). Control of eating and attribution style. *British Journal of Clinical Psychology*, *29*, 445–446.

Ollmann, M. M., Wilson, B. D., Yang, Y. K., Kerns, J. A., Chen, Y. R., Gantz, I., & Barsh, G. S. (1997). Antagonism of central melanocortin receptors *in vitro* and *in vivo* by Agouti-related protein. *Science*, *278*, 135–138.

Ongaa, T., Zabieski, R., & Kato, S. (2002). Multiple regulation of peptide YY in the digestive tract. *Peptide*, *23*, 279–290.

Opdenacker, J., Boen, F., De Bourdeaudhuij, I., & Vanden Auweele, Y. (2008). Explaining the psychological effects of a sustainable lifestyle physical activity intervention among rural women. *Mental Health and Physical Activity*, *1*, 74–81.

Orr, J., & Davy, B. (2005). Dietary influences on peripheral hormones regulating energy intake: Potential applications for weight management. *Journal of the American Dietetic Association*, *105*, 1115–1124.

Orrell-Valente, J. K., Hill, L. G., Brechwald, W. A., Dodge, K. A., Pettit, G. S., & Bates, J. E. (2007). 'Just three more bites': An observational analysis of parents' social-ization of children's eating at mealtime. *Appetite*, *48*, 37–45.

Ouchi, N., Kihara, S., Arita, Y., Maeda, K., Kuriyama, H., Okamoto, Y., Hotta, K., Nishida, M., Takahashi, M., Nakamura, T., Yamashita, S., Funahashi, T., & Matsuzawa, Y. (1999). Novel modulator for endothelial adhesion molecules: Adipocyte-derived plasma protein adiponectin. *Circulation*, *100*(25), 2473–2476.

Page, R. M., & Brewster, A. (2009). Depiction of food as having drug-like properties in televised food advertisements directed at children: Portrayals as pleasure enhancing and addictive. *Journal of Pediatric Health Care*, *23*, 150–157.

Paisley, C. M., & Sparks, P. (1998). Expectations of reducing fat intake: The role of perceived need within the Theory of Planned Behaviour. *Psychology and Health,* *13*, 341–353.

Pallister, E., & Waller, G. (2008). Anxiety in the eating disorders: Understanding the overlap. *Clinical Psychology Review, 28*, 366–386.

Pan, W., & Kastin, A. J. (2008). Urocortin and the brain. *Progress in Neurobiology,* *84*, 148–156.

Papas, E. B., & Schultz, B. L. (1997). Repeatability and comparison of visual analogue and numerical rating scales in the assessment of visual quality. *Ophthalmic and Physiological Optics, 17*, 492–498.

Pavlou, K., Krey, S., & Steffee, W. (1989) Exercise as an adjunct to weight loss and maintenance in moderately obese subjects. *American Journal of Clinical Nutrition, 49*, 1115–1123.

Pedersen, E. R., LaBrie, J. W., & Lac, A. (2008). Assessment of perceived and actual alcohol norms in varying contexts: Exploring social impact theory among college students. *Addictive Behaviors, 33*, 552–564.

Pederson, K. J., Roerig, J. L., & Mitchel, J. E. (2003). Towards the pharmacotherapy of eating disorders. *Expert Opinions in Pharmacotherapy, 4*, 1659–1678.

Peebles, R., Wilson, J. L., & Lock, J. D. (2006). How do children with eating disorders differ from adolescents with eating disorders at initial evaluation. *Journal of Adolescent Health, 39*, 800–805.

Pelchat, M. L. (1996). Picky eater profile: What is normal? *Pediatric Basics, 75*, 8–12.

Pelchat, M. L., & Pliner, P. (1986). Antecedents and correlates of feeding problems in young children. *Journal of Nutrition Education, 18*, 23–29.

Pelleymounter, M. A., Cullen, M. J., Baker, M. B., Hecht, R., Winters, D. W., Boone, T., & Collins, F. (1995). Effects of the obese gene-product on body-weight regulation in *ob/ob* mice. *Science, 269*, 540–543.

Pelleymounter, M. A., Cullen, M. J., Baker, M. B., Hecht, R., Winters, D. W., Boone, T., & Collins, F. (1997). On raising energy expenditure in ob/ob mice: Response. *Science, 276*, 1132–1133.

Perri, M. G., McAllister, D. A., Gange, J. J., Jordan, R. C., McAdoo, W. G., & Nezu, A. M. (1988). Effects of four maintenance programs on the long-term management of obesity. *Journal of Consulting Clinical Psychology, 56*, 529–534.

Piper, D. C., Upton, N., Smith, M. I., & Hunter, A. J. (2000). The novel brain neuropeptide, orexin-A, modulates the sleep–wake cycle of rats. *European Journal of Neuroscience, 12*, 726–730.

Pliner, P., Bell, R., Hirsch, E. S., & Kinchla, M. (2006). Meal duration mediates the effect of 'social facilitation' on eating in humans. *Appetite, 46*, 189–198.

Pliner, P., & Hobden, K. (1992). Development of a scale to measure the trait of food neophobia in humans. *Appetite, 19*, 105–120.

Pliner, P., Pelchat, M., & Grabski, M. (1993). Reduction of neophobia in humans by exposure to novel foods. *Appetite, 20*, 309–314.

Pontiroli, A. E. (2008). Surgical treatment of obesity: Impact of diabetes and other comorbidities. *Nutrition, Metabolism and Cardiovascular Diseases, 18*, 1–6.

Popkin, B. M., Duffey, K., & Gordon-Larsen, P. (2005). Environmental influences on food choice, physical activity and energy balance. *Physiology and Behaviour, 86,* 603–613.

Povey, R., Conner, M., Sparks, P., James, R., & Shepherd, R. (1998). Interpretations of healthy and unhealthy eating, and implications for dietary change. *Health Education Research, 13,* 171–183.

Prentice, A. M., & Jebb, S. A. (1995). Obesity in Britain: Gluttony or sloth? *British Medical Journal, 311,* 437–439.

Prentice, A. M., & Jebb, S. A. (2003). Fast food, energy density and obesity: A possible mechanistic link. *Obesity Reviews, 4,* 187–194.

Presse, F., Sorokovsky, I., Max, J.-P., Nicolaidis, S., & Nahon, J.-L. (1996). Melanin-concentrating hormone is a potent anorectic peptide regulated by food-deprivation and glucopenia in the rat. *Neuroscience, 71*(3), 735–745.

Pudel, V., & Westenhoefer, J. (1992). Dietary and behavioural principles in the treatment of obesity. *International Monitor on Eating Patterns and Weight Control, 1,* 2–7.

Raben, A., Agerholm-Larsen, L., Flint, A., Holst, J. J., & Astrup, A. (2003). Meals with similar energy densities but rich in protein, fat, carbohydrate, or alcohol have different effects on energy expenditure and substrate metabolism but not appetite and energy intake. *American Journal of Clinical Nutrition, 77,* 91–100.

Ramaciotti, C. E., Dell'Oso, L., Paoli, R. A., Ciapparelli, A., Coli, E., Kaplan, A. S., & Garfinkel, P. (2002). Characteristics of eating disorders patients without a drive for thinness. *International Journal of Eating Disorders, 32,* 206–212.

Reid, N. W. (1992). Role of gastrointestinal factors in hunger and satiety in man. *Proceedings of the Nutrition Society, 51,* 7–11.

Reilly, S. M., Skuse, D. H., Wolke, D., & Stevenson, J. (1999). Oral–motor dysfunction of children who fail to thrive: Organic or non-organic? *Developmental Medical Child Neurology, 41,* 115–122.

Riebe, D., Blissmer, B., Greene, G., Caldwell, M., Ruggiero, L., Stillwell, K. M., & Nigg, C. R. (2005). Long-term maintenance of exercise and healthy eating behaviors in overweight adults. *Preventive Medicine, 40*(6), 769–778.

Rigal, N., Frelut, M.-L., Monneuse, M.-O., Hladik, C.-M., Simmen, B., & Pasquet, P. (2006). Food neophobia in the context of a varied diet induced by a weight reduction program in massively obese adolescents. *Appetite, 46,* 207–214.

Roberts, S. J., McGuinness, P. J., Bilton, R., & Maxwell, S. M. (1999). Dieting behaviour among 11–15-year-old girls in Merseyside and the northwest of England. *Journal of Adolescent Health, 25,* 62–67.

Robinson, C. C., Mandleco, B., Olsen, S. F., & Hart, C. H. (1995). Authoritative, authoritarian and permissive parenting practices: Development of a new measure. *Psychology Reports, 77,* 819–830.

Robinson, T. M., Gray, R. W., Yeomans, M. R., & French, S. J. (2005). Test-meal palatability alters the effects of intragastric fat but not carbohydrate preloads on intake and related appetite in healthy volunteers. *Physiology and Behavior*, *84*, 193–203.

Robinson, T. N., Killen, J. D., Litt, I. F., Hammer, L. D., Wilson, D. M., Haydel, K. F., Hayward, C., & Taylor, C. B. (1996). Ethnicity and body dissatisfaction: Are Hispanic and Asian girls at increased risk for eating disorders? *Journal of Adolescent Health*, *19*, 384–393.

Rock, C. L., & Coulston, A. M. (1988). Weight control approaches: A review by the California Dietetic Association. *Journal of the American Dietetic Association*, *88*, 44–48.

Rodgers, R. J., Halford, J. C. G., Nunes de Souza, R. L., Canto de Souza, A. L., Piper, D. C., Arch, J. R. S., & Blundell, J. E. (2001). SB-334867, a selective orexin-1 receptor antagonist, enhances behavioural satiety and blocks the hyperphagic effect of orexin-A in rats. *European Journal of Neuroscience*, *13*, 1444–1452.

Rodgers, R. J., Ishii, Y., Halford, J. C., & Blundell, J. E. (2002). Orexins and appetite regulation. *Neuropeptides*, *36*(5), 303–325.

Rodin, J. (1981). Current status of the internal–external hypothesis for obesity: What went wrong? *American Psychologist*, *36*, 361–372.

Roemmich, J. N., Wright, S. N., & Epstein, L. H. (2002). Dietary restraint and stress-induced snacking in youth. *Obesity Research*, *10*, 1120–1126.

Rohan, M. J. (2000). A rose by any other name? The values construct. *Personality and Social Psychology Review*, *4*, 255–277.

Rolls, B. J., Hetherington, M., & Burley, V. J. (1988). The specificity of satiety: The influence of foods of different macronutrient content on the development of satiety. *Physiology and Behavior*, *43*, 145–153.

Rolls, B. J., Morris, E. L., & Roe, L. S. (2002). Portion size of food affects energy intake in normal-weight and overweight men and women. *American Journal of Clinical Nutrition*, *76*, 1207–1213.

Rolls, B. J., Roe, L. S., Kral, T. V. E., Meengs, J. S., & Wall, D. E. (2004). Increasing portion size of a packaged snack increases energy intake in men and women. *Appetite*, *42*, 63–69.

Ross, B. H., & Murphy, G. L. (1999). Food for thought: Cross-classification and category organization in a complex real-world domain. *Cognitive Psychology*, *38*, 495–553.

Roth, D. A., Herman, C. P., Polivy, J., & Pliner, P. (2001). Self-presentational conflict in social eating situations: A normative perspective. *Appetite*, *36*, 165–171.

Royack, G. A., Nguyen, M. P., Tong, D. C., Poot, M., & Oda, D. (2000). Response of human oral epithelial cells to oxidative damage and the effect of vitamin E. *Oral Oncology*, *36*, 37–41.

Royal College of Physicians of London (1998). *Clinical management of overweight and obese patients with particular reference to the use of drugs*. A Report of the Royal College of Physicians. London: Publications Department.

Rozin, P. (1979). Preference and affect in food selection. In J. H. A. Kroeze (Ed.),

Preference, behaviour and chemoreception (pp. 289–297). London: Information Retrieval Limited.

Rozin, P. (1982). 'Taste–smell confusions' and duality of the olfactory sense. *Perception and Psychophysics, 31*, 397–401.

Rozin, P., & Schiller, D. (1980). The nature and acquisition of a preference for chilli pepper by humans. *Motivation and Emotion, 4*, 77–101.

Rudolf, M. C. J., Sahoto, P., Barth, J. H., & Walker, J. (2001). Increasing prevalence of obesity in primary school children: Cohort study. *British Medical Journal, 322*, 1094–1095.

Russel, G. F. M., Szmukler, G. I., Dare, C., & Eisler, I. (1987). An evaluation of family therapy in anorexia nervosa and bulimia nervosa. *Archives of General Psychiatry, 44*, 1047–1056.

Sakurai, T., Amemiya, A., Ishii, M., Matsuzaki, I., Chemelli, R. M., Tanaka, H., Clay Williams, S., Richardson, J. A., Kozlowski, G. P., Wilson, S., Arch, J. R. S., Buckingham, R. E., Haynes, A. C., Carr, S. C., Annan, R. S., McNulty, D. E., Liu, W.-S., Terrett, J. A., Elshourbagy, N. A., Bergsma, D. J., & Yanagisawa, M. (1998). Orexins and orexin receptors, a family of hypothalamic neuropeptides and G protein-coupled receptors that regulate feeding behavior. *Cell, 92*, 573–585.

Salvy, S.-J., Jarrin, D., Paluch, R., Irfan, N., & Pliner, P. (2007). Effects of social influence on eating in couples, friends and strangers. *Appetite, 49*, 92–99.

Salvy, S.-J., Vartanian, L. R., Coelho, J. S., Jarrin, D., & Pliner, P. P. (2008). The role of familiarity on modeling of eating and food consumption in children. *Appetite, 50*, 514–518.

Saunders, R. P., & Rahilly, S. A. (1990). Influences on intention to reduce dietary intake of fat and sugar. *Journal of Nutrition Education, 22*, 169–176.

Schachter, S. (1968). Obesity and eating. *Science, 16*, 751–756.

Schachter, S., Goldman, R., & Gordon, A. (1968). Effects of fear, food deprivation and obesity on eating. *Journal of Personality and Social Psychology, 92*, 210–215.

Scherer, P. E., Williams, S., Fogliano, M., Baldini, G., & Lodis, H. F. (1995). A novel protein similar to Clq, produced exclusively in adipocytes. *Journal of Biological Chemistry, 270*, 26746–26749.

Schioth, H. B., Mutulis, F., Muceniece, R., Prusis, P., & Wikberg, J. E. (1998). Discovery of novel melanocortin 4 receptor selective MSH analogues. *British Journal of Pharmacology, 124*, 75–82.

Schmidt, P. T., Näslund, E., Grybäck, P., Jacobsson, H., Hartmann, B., Holst, J. J., & Hellström, P. M. (2003). Peripheral administration of GLP-2 to humans has no effect on gastric emptying or satiety. *Regulatory Peptides, 116*, 21–25.

Schmidt, U. (2005). Epidemiology and aetiology of eating disorders. *Psychiatry, 4*, 5–9.

Scott, J., & Huskisson, E. C. (1976). Graphic representation of pain. *Pain, 2*, 175–184.

Seymour, R. A., Simpson, J. M., Charlton, J. E., & Phillips, M. E. (1985). An evaluation of the length and endphase of visual analogue scales in dental pain. *Pain, 21*, 177–185.

Shenkin, A. (2006). The key role of micronutrients. *Clinical Nutrition, 25*, 1–13.

Sheppard, B. H., Hartwick, J., & Warshaw, P. R. (1988). The theory of reasoned action: A meta-analysis of past research with recommendations for modifications and future research. *Journal of Consumer Research, 15*, 325–343.

Silverstein, B., Perdue, L., Peterson, B., & Kelly, E. (1986). The role of the mass media in promoting a thin standard of bodily attractiveness for women. *Sex Roles, 14*, 519–532.

Sjostedt, J. P., Schumaker, J. F., & Nathawat, S. S. (1998). Eating disorders among Indian and Australian university students. *Journal of Social Psychology, 138*, 351–357.

Smart, D., Jerman, J. C., Brough, S. J., Rushton, S. L., Murdock, P. R., Jewitt, F., Elshourbagy, N. A., Ellis, C. E., Meddlemiss, D. N., & Brown, F. (1999). Characterization of recombinant human orexin receptor pharmacology in a Chinese hamster ovary cell-line using FLIPR. *British Journal of Pharmacology, 128*, 1–3.

Smith, A. M., Roux, S., Naidoo, N. T. R., & Venter, D. J. L. (2005). Food choices of tactile defensive children. *Nutrition, 21*, 14–19.

Smith, C. F., Williamson, D. A., Bray, G. A., & Ryan, D. H. (1999). Flexible vs. rigid dieting strategies: Relationship with adverse behavioral outcomes. *Appetite, 32*, 295–305.

Smith, J. (2009). Judging research quality: From certainty to contingency. *Qualitative Research in Sport and Exercise, 1*, 91–100.

Smith, M. H., Richards, P. S., & Maglio, C. J. (2004). Examining the relationship between religious orientation and eating disturbances. *Eating Behavior, 5*, 171–180.

Södersten, P., Bergh, C., & Ammar, A. (2003). Anorexia nervosa: Towards a neurobiological based therapy. *European Journal of Pharmacology, 480*, 67–74.

Sørensen, L. B., Møller, P., Flint, A., Martens, M., & Raben, A. (2003). Effect of sensory perception of foods on appetite and food intake: A review of studies on humans. *International Journal of Obesity, 27*, 1152–1166.

Speranza, M., Atger, F., Corcos, M., Loas, G., Guilbaud, O., Stéphan, P., Perez-Diaz, F., Halfon, O., LucVenisse, J., Bizouard, P., Lang, F., Flament, M., & Jeammet, P. (2003). Depressive psychopathology and adverse childhood experiences in eating disorders. *European Psychiatry, 18*, 377–383.

Spina, M., Merlo-Pich, E., Chan, R. K., Basso, A. M., Rivier, J., & Vale, W. (1996). Appetite-suppressing effects of urocortin, a CRF-related neuropeptide. *Science, 273*, 1561–1564.

Stark-Wroblewski, K., Yanico, B. J., & Lupe, S. (2005). Acculturation, internalization of western appearance norms, and eating pathology among Japanese and Chinese international student women. *Psychology of Women Quarterly, 29*, 38–46.

Stein, L. J., Nagai, H., Nakagawa, M., & Beauchamp, G. K. (2003). Effects of repeated exposure and health-related information on hedonic evaluation and acceptance of a bitter beverage. *Appetite*, *40*, 119–129.

Stein, R. I., & Nemeroff, C. J. (1995). Moral overtones of food: Judgements of others based on what they eat. *Personality and Social Psychology Bulletin*, *21*, 480–490.

Steiner, J. E. (1979). Human facial expressions in response to taste and smell stimulation. *Advances in Child and Developmental Behavior*, *13*, 257–295.

Stellar, E. (1954). The physiology of motivation. *Psychological Reviews*, *61*, 5–22.

Stevenson, C., Doherty, G., Barnett, J., Muldoon, O. T., & Trew, K. (2007). Adolescents' views of food and eating: Identifying barriers to healthy eating. *Journal of Adolescence*, *30*, 417–434.

Stice, E. (1998). Modeling of eating pathology and social reinforcement of the thin-ideal predict onset of bulimic symptoms. *Behaviour Research and Therapy*, *36*, 931–944.

Stice, E. (2002). Risk and maintenance factors for eating pathology: A meta-analytic review. *Psychological Bulletin*, *128*, 825–848.

Stice, E., Burton, E. M., & Shaw, H. (2004a). Prospective relations between bulimic pathology, depression, and substance abuse: Unpacking comorbidity in adolescent girls. *Journal of Consulting and Clinical Psychology*, *72*, 62–71.

Stice, E., Cameron, R. P., Killen, C. H., & Taylor, C. B. (1999). Naturalistic weight-reduction efforts prospectively predict growth in relative weight and onset of obesity among female adolescents. *Journal of Consulting and Clinical Psychology*, *67*, 967–974.

Stice, E., Fisher, M., & Lowe, M. R. (2004b). Are dietary restraint scales valid measures of acute dietary restriction? Unobtrusive observational data suggest not. *Psychological Assessment*, *16*, 51–59.

Stuart, G. W., Laraia, M. T., Ballenger, J. C., & Lydiard, R. B. (1990). Early family experiences of women with bulimia and depression. *Archives of Psychiatric Nursing*, *4*, 43–52.

Stunkard, A. J. (2002). Night eating syndrome. In C. G. Fairburn & K. D. Brownell (Eds.), *Eating disorders and obesity: A comprehensive handbook* (pp. 183–187). London: Guilford Press.

Stunkard, A. J., Allison, K. C., & O'Reardon, J. P. (2005). The night eating syndrome: A progress report. *Appetite*, *45*, 182–186.

Stunkard, A. J., & Messick, S. (1985). The Three Factor Eating Questionnaire to measure dietary restraint and hunger. *Journal of Psychosomatic Research*, *29*, 71–83.

Sturm, R. (2008). Stemming the global obesity epidemic: What can we learn from data about social and economic trends? *Public Health*, *122*, 739–746.

Sudi, K., Öttl, K., Payerl, D., Baumgartl, P., Tauschmann, K., & Müller, W. (2004). Anorexia athletica. *Nutrition*, *20*, 657–661.

Sullivan, P. F. (2002). Course and outcome of anorexia nervosa and bulimia nervosa. In C. G. Fairburn & K. D. Brownell (Eds.), *Eating disorders and obesity: A comprehensive handbook* (pp. 226–230). London: Guilford Press.

Sundgot-Borgen, J., & Torstveit, M. K. (2004). Prevalence of eating disorders in elite athletes is higher than in the general population. *Clinical Journal of Sport Medicine*, *14*, 25–32.

Symon, G., & Cassell, C. (1998). Reflections on the use of qualitative methods. In G. Symon & C. Cassell (Eds.), *Qualitative methods and analysis in organizational research: A practical guide* (pp. 1–9). London: Sage.

Takakura, Y., Yoshioka, K., Umekawa, T., Kogure, A., Toda, H., Yoshikawa, T., & Yoshida, T. (2005). Thr54 allele of the FABP2 gene affects resting metabolic rate and visceral obesity. *Diabetes Research and Clinical Practice*, *67*, 36–42.

Tepper, B. J. (1999). Does genetic taste sensitivity to PROP influence food preferences and body weight? *Appetite*, *32*, 442.

Thelen, M. H., Farmer, J., Wonderlich, S., & Smith, M. (1991). A revision of the Bulimia Test: The BULIT-R. *Psychological Assessment: A Journal of Consulting and Clinical Psychology*, *3*, 119–124.

Thomsen, C., Storm, H., Holst, J. J., & Hermansen, K. (2003). Differential effects of saturated and monounsaturated fats on postprandial lipemia and glucagon-like peptide 1 responses in patients with type 2 diabetes. *American Journal of Clinical Nutrition*, *77*, 605–611.

Thorndike, E. L. (1911). *Animal intelligence*. New York: Macmillan.

Thornton, B., Leo, R., & Albert, K. (1991). Gender role typing, the superwoman ideal and the potential for eating disorders. *Sex Roles*, *25*, 469–484.

Tiggemann, M. (1994). Dietary restraint as a predictor of reported weight loss and affect. *Psychological Reports*, *75*, 1679–1682.

Tiggemann, M., & Kemps, E. (2005). The phenomenology of food cravings: The role of mental imagery. *Appetite*, *45*, 305–313.

Toates, F. M. (1986). *Motivational systems*. Cambridge: Cambridge University Press.

Torgerson, J. S., & Sjöström, L. (2001). The Swedish Obese Subjects (SOS) study – rationale and results. *International Journal of Obesity*, *25*(suppl. 1), S2–S4.

Treasure, J. (2002). Compulsory treatment in the management of eating disorders. In C. G. Fairburn & K. D. Brownell (Eds.), *Eating disorders and obesity: A comprehensive handbook* (pp. 314–319). London: Guilford Press.

Treasure, J. (2004). Eating disorders. *Medicine*, *32*, 63–66.

Tritos, N. A., Vicent, D., Gillette, J., Ludwig, D. S., Flier, E. S., & Maratos-Flier, E. (1998). Functional interactions between melanin concentrating hormone, neuropeptide Y, and anorectic neuropeptides in the rat hypothalamus, *Diabetes*, *47*, 1687–1692.

Tschöp, M., Weyer, C., Tataranni, P. A., Devanarayan, V., Ravussin, E., & Heiman, M. L. (2001). Circulating ghrelin levels are decreased in human obesity. *Diabetes*, *50*, 707–709.

Unikel, C., Aguilar, J., & Gomez-Peresmitre, G. (2005). Predictors of eating behaviors in a sample of Mexican women. *Eating and Weight Disorders*, *10*, 33–39.

Vaisse, C., Clement, K., Guy-Grand, B., & Froguel, P. A. (1998). Frameshift mutation in human MC4R is associated with dominant form of obesity. *Nature Genetics*, *20*, 113–114.

van Aggel-Leijssen, D. P., Saris, W. H., Hul, G. B., & van Baak, M. A. (2002). Long-term effects of low-intensity exercise training on fat metabolism in weight-reduced obese men. *Metabolism*, *51*, 1003–1010.

Vansteelandt, K., Pieters, G., Vandereycken, W., Claes, L., Probst, M., & Van Mechelen, I. (2004). Hyperactivity in anorexia nervosa: A case study using experience sampling methodology. *Eating Behaviors*, *5*, 67–74.

Van Strien, T., Frijters, J. E. R., Bergers, G. P. A., & Defares, P.B. (1986). The Dutch Eating Behavior Questionnaire for assessment of restrained, emotional and external eating behaviour. *International Journal of Eating Disorders*, *5*, 295–315.

Vartanian, L. R., Herman, C. P., & Polivy, J. (2007). Consumption stereotypes and impression management: How you are what you eat. *Appetite*, *48*, 265–277.

Vendrell, J., Broch, M., Vilarrasa, N., Moltna, A., Gomez, J. M., Gutterrez, G., Simon, I., Soler, J., & Richari, C. (2004). Resistin, adiponectin, ghrelin, leptin, and proinflammatory cytokines: Relationships in obesity. *Obesity Research*, *12*(6), 962–971.

Vettor, R., Fabris, R., Pagano, C., & Federspil, G. (2002). Neuroendocrine regulation of eating behaviour. *Journal of Endocrinological Investigation*, *25*, 836–854.

Vicentic, A., Lakatos, A., & Jones, D. (2006). The CART receptors: Background and recent advances. *Peptides*, *27*, 1934–1937.

Videon, T. M., & Manning, C. K. (2003). Influences on adolescent eating patterns: The importance of family meals. *Journal of Adolescent Health*, *32*, 365–373.

Viner, R. M., & Cole, T. J. (2005). Television viewing in early childhood predicts adult body mass index. *Journal of Pediatrics*, *147*, 429–435.

Vitousel, K. M., & Manke, F. (1994). Personality variables and disorders in anorexia nervosa and bulimia nervosa. *Journal of Abnormal Psychology*, *103*, 137–147.

Voisin, T., Rouet-Benzineb, P., Reuter, N., & Laburthe, M. (2003). Orexins and their receptors, structural aspects and role in peripheral tissues. *Cellular and Molecular Life Sciences*, *60*(1), 72–87.

Volkow, N. D., Wang, G.-J., Fowler, J. S., Logan, J., Jayne, M., Francesschi, D., Wong, C., Gatley, S. J., Gifford, A. N., Ding, Y. S., & Pappas, N. (2002). 'Nonhedonic' food motivation in humans involves dopamine in the dorsal striatum and methyphenidate amplifies this effect. *Synapse*, *44*, 175–180.

Wade, T. D., Bergin, J. L., Tiggemann, M., Bulik, C. M., & Fairburn, C. G. (2006). Prevalence and long-term course of lifetime eating disorders in an adult Australian 487 twin cohort. *Australian and New Zealand Journal of Psychiatry*, *40*, 121–128.

Wade, T. J., & DiMaria, C. (2003). Weight halo effects: Individual differences in perceived life success as a function of women's race and weight. *Sex Roles*, *48*, 461–465.

Wagner, W., Duveen, G., Farr, R., Jovchelovitch, S., Lorenzo-Cioldi, F., Marková, I.,

& Rose, D. (1999). The theory and method of social representations. *Asian Journal of Social Psychology*, *2*, 95–125.

Waller, G., Cordery, H., Corstorphine, E., Hinrichsen, H., Lawson, R., Mountford, V., & Russell, K. (2007). *Cognitive behavioral therapy for eating disorders: A comprehensive treatment guide*. Cambridge: Cambridge University Press.

Wallis, D. J., & Hetherington, M. M. (2004). Stress and eating: The effects of ego-threat and cognitive demand on food intake in restrained and emotional eaters. *Appetite*, *43*, 39–46.

Wang, L. X., Saint-Pierre, D. H., & Tache, Y. (2002). Peripheral ghrelin selectively increases Fos expression in neuropeptide Y-synthesizing neurons in mouse hypothalamic arcuate nucleus. *Neuroscience Letters*, *325*, 47–51.

Wansink, B. (2004). Environmental factors that unknowingly increase a consumer's food intake and consumption volume. *Annual Reviews in Nutrition*, *24*, 455–479.

Wansink, B., Painter, J. E., & North, J. (2005). Bottomless bowls: Why visual cues of portion size may influence intake. *Obesity Research*, *13*, 93–100.

Wansink, B., & van Ittersum, K. (2007). Portion size me: Downsizing our consumption norms. *Journal of the American Dietetic Association*, *107*(7), 1103–1106.

Wanting Xu, A., Kaelin, C. B., Takeda, K., Akira, S., Schwartz, M. W., & Barsh, G. S. (2005). P13K integrates the action of insulin and leptin on hypothalamic neurons. *Journal of Clinical Investigation*, *115*, 951–958.

Wardle, J., & Beales, S. (1986). Restraint, body image, and food attitudes in children from 12 to 18 years. *Appetite*, *7*, 209–227.

Wardle, J., Brodersen, N. H., & Boniface, D. (2007). School-based physical activity and changes in adiposity. *International Journal of Obesity*, *31*, 1464–1468.

Wardle, J., Carnell, S., & Cooke L. (2005). Parental control over feeding and children's fruit and vegetable intake: How are they related? *Journal of the American Dietetic Association*, *105*, 227–232.

Wardle, J., Cooke, L. J., Gibson, E. L., Sapochnik, M., Sheiham, A., & Lawson, M. (2003a). Increasing children's acceptance of vegetables: A randomised trial of parent-led exposure. *Appetite*, *40*, 155–162.

Wardle, J., Herrera, M.-L., Cooke, L. J., & Gibson, E. L. (2003b). Modifying children's food preferences: The effects of exposure and reward on acceptance of an unfamiliar food. *European Journal of Clinical Nutrition*, *57*, 341–348.

Wardle, J., & Huon, G. (2000). An experimental investigation of the influence of health information on children's taste preferences. *Health Education Research*, *15*, 39–44.

Weinstein, S. E., Shide, D. J., & Rolls, B. J. (1997). Changes in food intake in response to stress in men and women: Psychological factors. *Appetite*, *28*, 7–18.

Westenhoefer, J. (1991). Dietary restraint and disinhibition: Is restraint a homogenous construct. *Appetite*, *16*, 45–55.

Westerterp-Plantenga, M. S., Kempen, K. P., & Saris, W. H. (1998). Determinants of weight maintenance in women after diet-induced weight reduction. *International Journal of Obesity and Related Metabolic Disorders*, *22*, 1–6.

Whitehouse, P. J., & Harris, G. (1998). The inter-generational transmission of eating disorders. *European Eating Disorders Review*, *6*, 238–254.

Williamson, D. A., Martin, C. K., & Stewart, T. (2004a). Psychological aspects of eating disorders. *Best Practice and Research: Clinical Gastroenterology*, *18*, 1073–1088.

Williamson, D. A., White, M. A., York-Crowe, E., & Stewart, T. M. (2004b). Cognitive-behavioral theories of eating disorders. *Behavioral Modification*, *28*, 711–738.

Winzelberg, A. (1997). The analysis of an electronic support group for individuals with eating disorders. *Computers in Human Behavior*, *13*, 393–407.

Wirth, M. M., & Giraudo, S. Q. (2000). Agouti-related protein in the hypothalamic paraventricular nucleus: Effect on feeding. *Peptides*, *21*, 1369–1375.

Wolfe, T. L., & Grimby, L. B. (2003). Caring for the hospitalized patient with an eating disorder. *Nursing Clinics of North America*, *38*, 75–99.

Wonderlich, S. A., Connolly, K. M., & Stice, E. (2004). Impulsivity as a risk factor for eating disorder behaviour: Assessment implications with adolescents. *International Journal of Eating Disorders*, *36*, 172–182.

Woodside, D. B. (2002). Inpatient treatment and medical management of anorexia nervosa and bulimia nervosa. In C. G. Fairburn & K. D. Brownell (Eds.), *Eating disorders and obesity: A comprehensive handbook* (pp. 335–339). London: Guilford Press.

World Health Organization (2007). *International statistical classification of diseases and related health problems* (10th edn.). Geneva: WHO.

Wren, A. M., Seal, L. J., Cohen, M. A., Brynes, A. E., Frost, G. S., Murphy, K. G., Dhillo, W. S., Ghatei, M. A., & Bloom, S. R. (2001). Ghrelin enhances appetite and increases food intake in humans. *Journal of Clinical Endocrinology and Metabolism*, *86*, 5992–5997.

Xiao, G., Qian, M., & Wang, Y. (2001). Rate of eating disorder in Beijing girls. *Chinese Mental Health Journal*, *15*, 362.

Xu, B., Li, B. H., Rowland, N. E., & Kalra, S. P. (1995). Neuropeptide Y injection into the fourth cerebroventricle stimulates c-fos expression in the paraventricular nucleus and other nuclei in the forebrain: Effects of food consumption. *Brain Research*, *698*, 227–231.

Yalug, I., Kirmizi-Alsan, E., & Tufan, A. E. (2007). Adult onset paper pica in the context of anorexia nervosa with major depressive disorder and a history of childhood geophagia: A case report. *Progress in Neuro-Psychopharmacology and Biological Psychiatry*, *31*, 1341–1342.

Yasuhara, D., Homan, N., Nagai, N., Naruo, T., Komaki, G., Nakao, K., & Nozoe, S.-I. (2002). A significant nationwide increase in the prevalence of eating disorders in Japan: 1998-year survey. *International Congress Series*, *1241*, 297–301.

Yeomans, M. R. (2000). Rating changes over the course of meals: What do they tell us about motivation to eat? *Neuroscience and Biobehavioral Reviews*, *24*, 249–259.

Yeomans, M. R., Caton, S., & Hetherington, M. M. (2003). Alcohol and food intake. *Current Opinion in Clinical Nutrition and Metabolism, 6*, 639–644.

Yeomans, M. R., & Gray, R. W. (1997). Effects of naltrexone on food intake and changes in subjective appetite during eating: Evidence for opioid involvement in the appetizer effect. *Physiology and Behavior, 62*(1), 15–21.

Young, L. R., & Nestle, M. (2002). The contribution of expanding portion sizes to the US obesity epidemic. *American Journal of Public Health, 92*, 246–249.

Zajonc, R. B. (1968). Attitudinal effects of mere exposure [monograph]. *Journal of Personality and Social Psychology, 9*(2, Part 2).

Zandian, M., Ioakimidis, I., Bergh, C., & Södersten, P. (2007). Cause and treatment of anorexia nervosa. *Physiology and Behavior, 92*, 283–290.

Zegman, M. A. (1984). Errors in food recording and calorie estimation: Clinical and theoretical implications for obesity. *Addictive Behaviors, 9*, 347–350.

Index